SOUTHERN WOMEN

SOUTHERN WOMEN

Edited by

CAROLINE MATHENY DILLMAN
Reinhardt College
Waleska, Georgia

● **HEMISPHERE PUBLISHING CORPORATION**
A member of the Taylor & Francis Group

New York   Washington   Philadelphia   London

SOUTHERN WOMEN

1 2 3 4 5 6 7 8 9 0   E B E B   8 9 8

This book was set in Times Roman by The Sheridan Press. The editor was Linda Lee Stringer.
Edwards Brothers, Inc. was printer and binder.

Library of Congress Cataloging in Publication Data

Southern women/edited by Caroline Matheny Dillman.
    p.   cm.
  Bibliography: p.
  Includes index.
  1. Women—Southern States—Social conditions. I. Dillman,
Caroline Matheny.
HQ1438.A13S62 1988
305.4'2'0975—dc19

ISBN 0-89116-668-8 (cloth)
ISBN 0-89116-838-9 (paper)

CONTENTS

v

CONTRIBUTORS

MAXINE P. ATKINSON, Associate Professor of Sociology, North Carolina State University, Raleigh

JACQUELINE BOLES, Associate Professor of Sociology, Georgia State University, Atlanta

SARAH BRABANT, Professor of Sociology, University of Southwestern Louisiana, Lafayette

ELIZABETH BROWN-GUILLORY, Assistant Professor of English, Dillard University, New Orleans, Louisiana

JAN K. BRYANT, Research Associate, Manpower Demonstration Research Corporation, New York

JULIA BURKART, Assistant Professor of Sociology, Arkansas State University, State University

DONNA KELLEHER DARDEN, Associate Professor of Sociology, University of Arkansas, Fayetteville

CAROLINE MATHENY DILLMAN, Director of Off-Campus Programs and Continuing Education and Associate Professor of Sociology, Reinhardt College, Waleska, Georgia

MARY CAROLYN ELLIS, Professor of Law, University of Mississippi Law Center, Oxford

MARY GEHMAN, Instructor of English, Loyola University and Delgado Community College, New Orleans, Louisiana

BECKY L. GLASS, Associate Professor of Sociology, State University of New York, Geneseo

JOANNE V. HAWKS, Director of the Sarah Isom Center for Women's Studies and Assistant Professor of History, University of Mississippi, Oxford

WILLIAM F. KENKEL, Professor of Sociology, University of Kentucky, Lexington

VIRGINIA KENT ANDERSON LESLIE, Decatur, Georgia

ELAINE LEVIN, Professor of Psychology, Counseling Center, Georgia State University, Atlanta

JOHN LYNXWILER, Assistant Professor of Sociology, University of Alabama at Birmingham

SUSAN MIDDLETON-KEIRN, Associate Professor of Anthropology, California State University, Stanislaus, Turlock, California

PATRICIA MORTON, Associate Professor of History, Trent University, Peterborough, Ontario, Canada

KATHRYN PALUMBO, Agency Coordinator, Atlanta Community Food Bank, Georgia

SARAH M. SHOFFNER, Assistant Professor of Child Development and Family Relations, University of North Carolina at Greensboro

LYN THAXTON, Associate Professor, Library, Georgia State University, Atlanta

SUSAN TUCKER, Fellow, Newcomb Center for Research on Women, Tulane University, New Orleans, Louisiana

CAROLYN E. WEDIN, Professor of English and Women's Studies, University of Wisconsin-Whitewater

MICHELE WILSON, Associate Professor of Sociology, University of Alabama at Birmingham

PREFACE

Southern Women is a collection of chapters about women *of* the South, that is, women who not only were born and reared in the South but more importantly have a heritage of Southern culture and generations of Southerners in their family background, both dating back to antebellum days. Gastil has written, "[N]early all Southerners trace their ancestry in this country back before 1850, and most of them before 1800."[1] The importance of differentiating between studies of women *in* the South and those *of* the South is in accord with Hill's emphasis on differentiating between studies *in* the South and those *of* the South.[2]

Most authors of books on the South, its culture, and/or Southerners state early on, usually in a footnote, that the term *Southerner* is commonly used to mean *white* Southerners, incorrect though that may be. And the writers proceed to exclude black Southerners from their works. I am happy to report that this book very much includes black Southern women. In addition, the articles span a time frame from antebellum days to contemporary times. The Southern women presented here also span a spectrum of classes, an unusual aspect of a work on Southern women since most of the body of literature on the subject centers on middle- and upper-class Southern women.

In 1970, with the emergence of the women's movement reflected in new works on women and eventually on Southern women, Scott decried the sparsity of publications on Southern women.[3] Even as late as 1983, Hawks and Skemp, speaking mainly of historians, called "the paucity of available source material" the most serious problem in studying and researching Southern women.[4] Now, several years later, works on Southern women are finally beginning to reach the public in the form of publications as well as lectures, seminars, and courses.

Early on Hawks and Skemp offered as a solution to the problem the development of "new methodologies" and reliance "on an interdisciplinary approach."[5] Recommending a similar turn in direction for the entire spectrum of social sciences to draw more heavily on the humanities, that is, to broaden their methods further than simply introducing an interdisciplinary approach, *The Chronicle of Higher Education* reported that a "growing number of scholars in anthropology, economics, history, political science, and sociology are questioning just how scientific the social sciences can and should be" and are "calling for a new mode of inquiry that draws as much from the humanities as from the natural sciences."[6]

The reporter goes on to cite sociologist Robert N. Bellah in his attack on
" 'the recent and quite arbitrary boundary between the social sciences and the
humanities' "; economist Albert O. Hirschman's warning that his discipline's
model " 'is far from covering all aspects of human and experience' "; anthropologist Clifford Geertz's identification of a " 'refiguration of social
thought,' " in which " 'many social scientists have turned away from a laws
and instances ideal of explanation toward a cases and interpretations one' ";
historian Lawrence Stone's citation of " 'widespread disillusionment' with the
new social history that has made the field of history more scientific."[7]

In summary, then, there is a current acknowledgment of a need for disciplines (e.g., sociology, anthropology, psychology) within an area (e.g., social
sciences) to become not only more interdisciplinary but also to aim for a better
balance between and a blending of the sciences and the humanities. Daniel Bell
says, " 'There is a sense that no single interpretation or explanation can be
complete.' "[8]

Taking into consideration, then, the research problems peculiar to the
study of Southern women and the paucity, until very recently, of research publications on Southern women, as editor of this book, I have joined ranks not only
with Hawks and Skemp in their insistence on the necessity of interdisciplinary
studies of Southern women but also with the aforementioned scholars from a
number of disciplines who are questioning the iron-clad scientific positivism,
are calling for new modes of inquiry, and are recommending a mix of ap-
proaches and perspectives within the social sciences as well as a blending with
those of the humanities.

It is indeed mandatory to examine the subject of Southern women through
wide-angle lenses that include a number of interdisciplinary methodologies and
analyses. The result here is that this work represents not only a number of
disciplines but also includes an eclectic mix of modes of observations and tech-
niques. The authors of these articles include not only historians, sociologists, an
anthropologist, and a psychologist but also professors of English, law, and
women's studies as well as a librarian, a director and a fellow of a women's
studies center, two Ph.D. candidates in a graduate institute for liberal arts, a
social service administrator, and a research associate. In addition to the expected quantitative approach with structured questionnaires and interview
schedules, the articles have also incorporated qualitative methodology in the use
of ethnographic and historical accounts and even an autobiographical case
study.

The first chapter, "The Sparsity of Research and Publications on Southern Women: Definitional Complexities, Methodological Problems, and Other
Impediments," is a review of the current and historical literature on Southern
women and a discussion about the lack of works on Southern women and the
underlying reasons.

The second chapter, Virginia Kent Anderson Leslie's "A Myth of the
Southern Lady: Antebellum Proslavery Rhetoric and the Proper Place of

Woman,'' sets the stage for the next five chapters about black and white Southern women in the antebellum period and Civil War times. Leslie takes us back
to the antebellum days when the special culture of the South had been entrenched for a number of decades. Her work examines the close connection
between the status of slaves and the "place of women" and demonstrates the
necessity for a myth of the Southern lady to justify chattel slavery. Rather than
compile a historical account of those women's viewpoints or present a contemporary women's scholarly interpretation, Leslie, in a clever display of the rhetoric of three prominent men of that era, lets the men of that period speak for
themselves about Southern women. Thus we have the background and foundation for the articles that follow immediately.

   '' 'My Ol' Black Mammy' in American Historiography'' by Patricia
Morton examines the Southern black woman as mammy, exemplified by the
narrow media images in particular. By reviewing the mammy in American
history, Morton attempts to ascertain how and why this figure has become a
virtual historical untouchable. Mary Gehman's "Toward an Understanding of
the Quadroon Society of New Orleans" centers on a kind of black Southern
woman about whom there are few records and little written history. The author
sorts out conjecture, rumor, and romanticism that surrounds the legacy of these
antebellum free women of color and using the scant scholarly body of literature
on the subject paints for us a picture of this unusual group of Southern women.
Elizabeth Brown-Guillory in her "Lorraine Hansberry as Visionary: Black and
White Antebellum Southern Women in Concert" uses one of Hansberry's plays
as a vehicle for analyzing the relationship between black and white Southern
women, between mistress and slave, in antebellum times. Brown-Guillory demonstrates how their lives were interwoven and dependent upon each other for
survival, how they acted "in concert."

   The next two chapters focus on Southern women in the years immediately
preceding the Civil War, the war years themselves, and a touch of the aftermath
period. Kathryn Palumbo's "Growing Up Female, White, and Southern in the
1850s and 1860s" and Carolyn E. Wedin's "The Civil War and Black Women
on the Sea Islands" contrast in two finely etched case studies, both taken from
personal documents, the lives of upper-class white Southern women with those
of black slave women, respectively.

   We move into the 20th century with Joanne V. Hawks and Mary Carolyn
Ellis's "Heirs of the Southern Progressive Tradition: Women in Southern Legislatures in the 1920s," a portrait of Southern white middle-class women fighting an uphill battle to enter politics, usually to seek "reform but not radical
change." The accomplishments of these pioneers were indeed a breakthrough,
but we are shocked back into the social reality of the times with Susan Tucker's
"The Black Domestic in the South: Her Legacy as Mother and Mother Surrogate." Here, we see the plight of the Southern black woman in domestic service
in white homes, as mother to white children as well as her own. Covering a
period from about 1880 to 1965, Tucker utilizes an interdisciplinary approach

that includes historical and literary analyses and open-ended interviews with 100 women as they enter and somehow survive life in the 20th century before the advent of the civil rights movement.

Just as Leslie's chapter prepares us for those on antebellum Southern women, Sarah Brabant's chapter, "Socialization for Change: The Cultural Heritage of the White Southern Woman," prepares us for the remaining chapters, which focus on or include contemporary white Southern women. Using a life history—her own—Brabant stunningly demonstrates the continuity of the socialization process for Southern women over many generations. In this portrait of a Southern woman, first as a child and then as a young adult, we see the continued influence of her mother and of Southern children's literature of those times that reinforced each other in the perpetuation of the cultural ideals. The expectations here, in the 1930s and 1940s, are the same ones that were requisite for Southern women in the 19th century. Brabant focuses on the strength of Southern women—though denied, unacknowledged, and/or simply ignored by males—that tragic circumstances, economic shifts, and changes have always required of Southern women. The behavior of mother and daughter chillingly echoes that of Ellen Glasgow's *Virginia* as the heroine tries in vain to summon from the depths of her being some action, something other than simply standing and facing the overwhelming traumas.[9] Glasgow's adamant statement in her own autobiography, "I will not be defeated," reflects her stand during innumerable heartbreaking crises and could have been—and probably was, in one form or another—said before her times by colonial Southern women, by antebellum Southern women, and by those Civil War unsung heroines who bore the brunt of the homefront responsibilities and terrors.[10] Now we see Brabant's mother, one of Glasgow's contemporaries, socializing Brabant and, in turn, Brabant socializing her daughter with the same coping strategies in the form of admonitions to "survive with dignity" and "accept responsibility for others." This firsthand account lends credibility and validity to the findings in the remaining chapters when they focus on contemporary white Southern women.

Beginning with the next chapter, we move into contemporary times. The first two of the remaining chapters address upper-status white Southern women. "The Code of the New Southern Belle: Generating Typifications to Structure Social Interaction" by John Lynxwiler and Michele Wilson examines how contemporary Southern white women appropriate a particular social type to structure encounters. Using two sources of information, unstructured interviews with 20 women and 10 men and participant observation, the authors focused their study on isolated features that distinguish the New Southern Belle as a social type from other cultural images of Southern women and to explain the New Southern Belle's code specific for structuring her subsequent behavior and interpretation.

Moving from the young Southern woman to an older version, Jacqueline Boles and Maxine P. Atkinson begin their chapter on contemporary Southern women, "Ladies: South by Northwest," with the image of the Southern lady as the ideal in antebellum times in the South—a continuation of Leslie's theme— and identify temperamental and behavioral traits of Southern women in that era. Next, they contrast the exemplification of this ideal among women of the Old South with the exemplification among those of the frontier West. Boles and Atkinson then use the constructed type of the lady to examine the salience of the lady image as role model for a sample of contemporary upper-status Southern women compared with a similar sample of women in the Northwest. This chapter and the preceding one by Lynxwiler and Wilson set a solid foundation for understanding the underlying direct socialization process for upper-status white Southern women as well as the indirect idealized socialization for lower-status white Southern women.

The next four chapters address black and white lower-status Southern women. The first of these, "Magnolias and Microchips: Regional Subcultural Constructions of Femininity" by Susan Middleton-Keirn, focuses on the current gender role ideology of working-class white women of the South and of a comparable sample of women in the West. In this anthropological study, she reports differences between the two groups that confirm others' works on the South as a regional subculture in general and on the distinctiveness of Southern women in particular. The image/ideal of the antebellum Southern lady, she argues, is still an influential part of the lives of contemporary Southern women from blue- and pink-collar backgrounds, who cling tenaciously to the ideal of the Southern lady.

Using data from a longitudinal study that compared the occupational and educational aspirations and expectations of young Southern children in low-income subcultures with their actual achievement, William F. Kenkel and Sarah M. Shoffner in their chapter, "And the Girls Became Women: Aspirations and Expectations versus Attainments of Low-Income Black and White Southern Females," examine the differences between the aspirations and achievement of Southern black and white females and focus on the role of race in such differences. Several hundred girls and their mothers were included in the smaller study presented here, which includes the original three waves of the research: when the children were fifth- and sixth-graders, when they were juniors or seniors in high school, and when, as young adults three to four years after they could be expected to have graduated from high school, their actual educational and occupational achievement could be measured.

Jan K. Bryant's chapter, "Southern Women and Textile Work: Job Satisfaction," focuses on lower-status white Southern women who work in a textile mill and the effect of Southern culture on their lives. Bryant's methodology includes case studies of the women and the author's firsthand experiences in the same setting. In contrast, Julia Burkart in her chapter, "Stronger than Love: Louisiana's Sugar Cane Women," presents a portrayal of three black lower-status Southern women. She relies on her case-study research on sugar cane plantations to report on these women who were "born and raised" in this setting. One of the women had left the quarters to build a house through government loans; two had remained on a plantation. Burkart's chapter describes the women and how they viewed life on the plantations and how that life, in the case of the one who moved, compared with the new one.

Beginning with the next chapter, we return to white Southern women and continue to focus exclusively on them throughout the remaining chapters. The first of these, Becky L. Glass's "Women and Violence: The Intersection of Two Components of Southern Ideology," explores the interaction of (1) the attitudes and experiences of white Southern women and (2) Southern attitudes and behaviors with regard to violence. National Opinion Research Center data with a sample of 7,205 cases were used in an effort to understand how the elements of Southern culture affect the self-identity of Southern women and in turn their attitudes toward and experiences in acts of violence.

In their chapter, "Southern White Women Business Owners: Variations on Scripts," Elaine Levin and Lyn Thaxton report on a study they conducted to determine what experiences and personality characteristics might have caused the 15 business-owner Southern women in their sample to differ drastically from their cultural norms and transcend the traditional scripts prescribed for Southern women. Their in-depth semistructured interviews with the women, which were analyzed by the constant comparative qualitative method, included questions on experiences during formative years, career development, relationships with husbands and children, and means of coping with stress.

In the final article, "Southern Women Writing about Southern Women: Jill McCorkle, Lisa Alther, Gail Godwin, Ellen Gilchrist, and Lee Smith," Donna Kelleher Darden demonstrates how contemporary Southern female writers are portraying contemporary Southern women in a number of different settings. Through reviewing the works of five authors and with references to a number of others, she discusses becoming a "new Southern woman" and the pressures to let go of the traditional images and to learn how to substitute others.

And so, beginning with Leslie's antebellum Southern women—both black and white—and ensuing accounts of their trials and tribulations at the mercy of a ruthless patriarchal society on through Tucker's, Hawks and Ellis's, and Brabant's later generations of these Southern women down to the contemporary Southern women portrayed in the final chapters, we find the same qualities manifested, albeit in varying degrees, across classes and throughout the history of women of the South. We see the strength behind the coping mechanism of contemporary Southern women who are facing wrenching changes and conflicting demands in the struggle to discover and maintain an identity of their own.

The message throughout this book is that women of the South—regardless of color or class—personify strength, courage, and survival at any cost.

Caroline M. Dillman

NOTES

1. Raymond D. Gastil, *Cultural Regions of the United States* (Seattle, WA: University of Washington Press, 1975), p. 174.
2. Carole E. Hill, "Anthropological Studies in the American South: Review and Directions," *Current Anthropology* 18:309.
3. Anne Firor Scott, *The Southern Lady: From Pedestal to Politics, 1830–1930* (Chicago: University of Chicago, 1972).
4. Joanne V. Hawks and Sheila L. Skemp, "Introduction," in *Sex, Race, and the Role of Women in the South,* Joanne V. Hawks and Sheila L. Skemp, eds. (Jackson, MS: University Press of Mississippi, 1983), p. xi.
5. Ibid.
6. Karen J. Winkler, "Questioning the Science in Social Science: Scholars Signal a 'Turn to Interpretation,' " *The Chronicle of Higher Education,* June 26, 1985, p. 5.
7. Ibid., pp. 5–6.
8. Ibid.
9. Ellen Glasgow, *Virginia* (Garden City, NY: Doubleday, Page, 1913).
10. Ellen Glasgow, *The Woman Within* (New York: Harcourt, Brace, 1954).

Chapter 1

THE SPARSITY OF RESEARCH AND PUBLICATIONS ON SOUTHERN WOMEN: DEFINITIONAL COMPLEXITIES, METHODOLOGICAL PROBLEMS, AND OTHER IMPEDIMENTS[1]

CAROLINE MATHENY DILLMAN

A glance through the sociohistorical literature on the South and Southerners, both old and new, reveals the usual near absence of women, as is true for most publications in all disciplines. Any mention of women in scholarly works is almost always as an appendage to men. Rarely is there anything of substance about women—about their lives, their activities, and their contributions to society. "Historically speaking," Anne Scott writes, "southern women in the century since 1880 scarcely exist."[2]

Authors responsible for the proliferation of sociological works on the South from the middle to the end of the first half of this century were almost exclusively male.[3] The notable exceptions during that period were Katherine Jocher and Harriet L. Herring, whose works did not focus on women,[4] and Julia Cherry Spruill and Guion Griffis Johnson,[5] whose works will be discussed later. It is interesting to compare the Twelve Southerners who wrote the famous *I'll Take My Stand* in 1930 with the Fifteen Southerners who wrote the 1981 update, *Why the South Will Survive*—all the authors in both the first and the second book are male.[6] Fifty years has not produced much change in gender authorship.

THE LITERATURE ON SOUTHERN WOMEN

It was not until the early 1970s, with the advent of the women's movement, that a book written by a Southern woman about Southern women was recognized as being of scholarly significance and worthy of something more than a brief flicker of local acclaim: Anne Firor Scott's *The Southern Lady: From Pedestal to Politics, 1830–1930.*

In Scott's bibliographic essay, she says that "[m]anuscript sources for a study of southern women are vast and have hardly been touched for this purpose." She also tells us that "[p]rinted sources are vast" from which data can be mined. But then she notes the scarcity of "scholarly publications and unpublished papers bearing on the subject" saying that they "are so few that I can list a high proportion of the total." Earlier in this essay she refers to the scholarly articles and books as "a handful."[7]

That was in 1970. Thirteen years later and much more recently (in 1983) the editors of another publication on Southern women wrote a similar lament in their introduction, "Historians . . . have shown a curious lack of interest in southern women."[8]

Before Scott's book, which has come to be regarded as a publishing event, there were two important works but they had been "lost." The works were Julia Cherry Spruill's *Women's Life and Work in the Southern Colonies* and Guion Johnson's *Ante-Bellum North Carolina.* Scott says, in her discussion of these two books, "One would expect that two such excellent books would have inspired a stream of follow-up studies; but alas, neither of these women was able to secure a regular academic appointment. Neither had graduate students."[9] So in the 1970s, we had access to three major scholarly works (howbeit one gathering dust in library stacks), all covering a lengthy span of time; but they were mainly about educated, or at least literate, women. Hagood's *Mothers of the South,* a rich book but narrow in time frame (the 1930s), does address rural, very poor women and also has recently been "rediscovered" and reprinted.[10]

Two other books reprinted after lying dormant for several decades since their original publication, one in 1926, the other in 1946, give a picture of the lives of Southern women born around the turn of the century. Frances Newman's thinly disguised autobiography, *The Hard-Boiled Virgin,* is described on its cover as "The 1926 novel of an Atlanta woman imprisoned by tradition."[11] Newman herself said she thought it was "the first novel in which a woman ever told the truth about how women feel."[12] Although the protagonist and the author are unique in defying Southern traditions, the book vividly conveys the expected lifestyle of Southern women in that era. Katharine DuPre Lumpkin's book, *The Making of a Southerner,* is described on its cover as "The autobiography of a Southern woman ahead of her time."[13] Both Newman and Lumpkin focus mainly on the lives of educated Southern women from either wealthy families or on those of impoverished gentility.

Lillian Smith, whose *Killers of the Dream* was published originally in 1949, again in 1961, and more recently in 1978, is another example of a female writing about growing up in the South during the first decades of this century.[14] Smith made her mark as a Southern woman daring to expose the racial and sexual overtones of the socialization process of Southerners. Lumpkin, less well known, addresses the same issues through relating the metamorphosis in her views concerning racism. Each of these writers were "without honor in [her] own country," and for most of her life Smith suffered ostracism by the people in her native South.[15]

A more recent scholarly study on Southern-lady women (a term I use to designate Southern women from educated and/or moneyed families) during the 1920s and early 1930s is Jacquelyn D. Hall's *Revolt Against Chivalry: Jessie Daniel Ames and the Women's Campaign Against Lynching*.[16] Once again, we have the history of a group of educated, higher status women, this time focusing on a social issue. Scott, referring to her sources, says the women "who left a mark on the historical record" were "for the most part women of educated or wealthy families"[17]; and all but one of the works reviewed thus far portray mainly educated women from high-status families. All are portrayals of women who reached adulthood prior to the 1930s.

Other works are coming into prominence. Some of these are rediscovered works now being reprinted; others have been written in the last decade. Many address women's lives during the Civil War period, once again those of higher-status women, and one was written by a man.[18] But the three main books mentioned here initially (Scott's, Spruill's, and Johnson's) remain the early classics and with two other major works published in the early 1980s form the main sociohistorical books on Southern women that cover the periods up to the 1940s. One goes beyond this date into contemporary times. The new publications are Catherine Clinton's *The Plantation Mistress* and Shirley Abbott's *Womenfolks: Growing Up Down South*.[19]

Clinton's work fills in the chronological gap between the two books on colonial Southern women and Scott's work on Southern women from 1830 to 1930. In addition, Clinton has been hailed as "the first scholar systematically to apply the new perspective of women's history to the Old South."[20] Abbott gives us for the first time a scholarly work on rural Southern women over a lengthy period of time and one that includes the current generation.

Two other works are extremely important additions to the scant work on contemporary Southern women. *Stepping Off the Pedestal: Academic Women in the South*, edited by Patricia A. Stringer and Irene Thompson, contains articles by and about contemporary Southern as well as non-Southern women—all women in the South who have had or are having to deal with the impact of Southern culture on their lives in the academic world there.[21] *Sex, Race, and the Role of Women in the South*, edited by Joanne V. Hawks and Sheila L. Skemp, includes articles on Southern working women from 1880 to 1950; on the public roles of Southern women; on black women in Washington, D.C., from 1890 to 1920; on the portrayal of Southern women's lives by Southern literary women; and on Southern women's history.

These two publications, curiously, are just about the only ones that include at least some material on contemporary high-status Southern women (Stringer and Thompson) and on lower-status Southern women prior to the middle of this century (Hawks and Skemp). With the exception of Abbott's and Hagood's books, almost all the publications about Southern women's lives before the 1940s focus on Southern-lady women. The situation is reversed after that period. Many recent studies and publications ignore Southern-lady women of the last few decades and those in contemporary times and in their stead focus on Southern black women (e.g., Anne Moody, *Coming of Age in Mississippi*, and Molly C. Dougherty, *Becoming a Woman in Rural [Southern] Black Culture*)[22]; on Appalachian women (e.g., Kathy Kahn, *Hillbilly Women*)[23]; on industrial women (e.g., the oral history project conducted by the University of North Carolina at Chapel Hill and directed by Jacquelyn Hall).[24]

Southern Exposure's special issue entitled "Growing Up Southern," popular enough to have been reprinted in book form, and another special issue entitled "Generations: Women in the South" contain only fragments on the Southern lady, the higher-status white Southern woman, and the more middle-class Southern woman.[25] Such studies and publications on contemporary women in the South include nothing about Southern-lady women and ignore those who form a gray area between them and lower-status Southern women.

A review of works on Southern women would be incomplete without mentioning Rosemary Daniell's *Fatal Flowers* and Florence King's *Southern Ladies and Gentlemen*.[26] Daniell's work, although continuing to be controversial as to its literary merits and its contribution to the body of literature on Southern women, was a real breakthrough in the area of Southern women writing about Southern women—without mincing words, without covering up for the sake of propriety or in defense of Southern culture, without Pollyanna sentimentality, without the author's head in the sand. Though Daniell is misunderstood by many non-Southern readers as representing in her book most if not all kinds of Southern women and though many generalize the women she portrays to include several categories she omits, her work is an important contribution.

Daniell's work was published after King's book, but *Southern Ladies and Gentlemen* was and still is taken mainly as a tongue-in-cheek Southern joke, except by a few female scholars who are studying Southern women. (Just a look at the quotes on the cover will give the perceived tone and mood of the book, e.g., "The best seller that catches Dixie right between the sheets.") Stringer and Thompson's work begins with epigraphs that include excerpts from King's book—they take her work very seriously. Though threads of the culture form the warp and woof of King's book, as well as Daniell's, the real message is missed or dismissed as exaggerated stereotypes. Its popularity was and is based mainly on the humorous manner in which Southerners are depicted, a sort of witty interpretation of the same old media images.[27]

The following sections address the problems that have inhibited, or distorted, research and publications on Southern women and that have contributed significantly to the scarcity of both.

THE CULTURAL TABOO FOR WOMEN WRITERS: THE GLARING OMISSION IN MALE-AUTHORED WORKS

Impediments to the study of Southerners in general and Southern women in particular can be attributed to a number of inherent methodological problems that include lack of accessibility to the population; the tendency of non-Southern researchers to equate Southerners with people living in university or college isolation or in large melting-pot areas like metro-Atlanta; Southerners' attitudes toward outsiders. Even Southern hospitality and ladylike and gentlemanly behavior in interactions with outsiders can get in the way of valid research and mask reality. Some of these inhibitors, however, are part of another stumbling block: definitional complexities. First, though, I would like to discuss a peculiar problem, touched on in the review of books at the end of the last section.

One aspect of so-called popular books like Newman's, King's, and Daniell's and of scholarly works like Scott's, Clinton's, Abbott's, and Johnson's sets them apart from others, particularly those publications on the South that have been written by males. Mary Chestnut[28] bravely addressed this issue, a paramount part of Southern women's lives, a dark, ugly reality that was faced every day and somehow borne in her times: miscegenation and an extreme double standard that was part and parcel of the patriarchal system linking slavery and "woman's place" as its foundation. With the exception of Johnson in her tome written many decades later, few female scholars in this century dared to let the subject appear in their writings on the Old South until the current time of historical enlightenment brought on by the women's movement. One cannot find mention of this everyday part of Old South life even in the universally popular *Gone With the Wind*.[29]

Though Wiley in 1972 did quote in his *Confederate Women* Mary Chestnut's assertions on the subject, most male historians have ignored it. One book, authored solely by men until its most recent edition, is notable for its exceptionality: *The Family in Various Cultures*. As early as the 1950s, these authors spelled out quite clearly in plain language the pervasiveness of miscegenation in the Old South, the sexual exploitation of female slaves, and the resigned acceptance required of white women.[30] Much more recently, in 1982, Bertram Wyatt-Brown in his work, *Southern Honor: Ethics and Behavior in the Old South*, includes a great deal on the subjects of miscegenation and the double standard.[31]

Lillian Smith—considered a deviant and stigmatized because of it—was one of the few women prior to the 1970s to write about the continuation of repression of women's sexuality and exploitation of Southern women in the 20th century. Most female writers did not write about women and sexuality at all. If they dared to do so, ostracism and stigmatization were the results.[32] Now, beginning in the 1970s with Scott, who wrote not only about the pervasiveness of the issue in the 1800s but also about "the half-hidden miscegenation which existed in every Southern community" in the 1920s,[33] it seems we finally have material on this "missing" subject. Female scholars, female writers of popular publications, and reprints of the few earlier "dare-devil" female-authored books are bringing the subject out of the closet.

The importance, therefore, of even the popular works that include this facet of Southern women's lives—whether it be the antebellum version or current-day continuing sexual repression for women and exploitation of them—cannot be overestimated. Without this major facet of Southern's women's lives, the picture remains not only cloudy but distorted.

THE PERSISTENCE AND PERVASIVENESS OF SOUTHERN CULTURE

Inherent in studying the South, Southerners, and/or Southern women is the absolute necessity to recognize and accept the fact that Southern culture is still quite formidable and that there are multitudes who are still promoting the continuity of the culture in spite of all the apparent changes going on around them. Ignorance of this phenomenon can have a tremendously negative effect on research. The importance of this issue is apparent in the literature on the persistency and pervasiveness of Southern culture.

In 1976, the historian, George Brown Tindall, in his book, *The Ethnic Southerners,* analyzed the persistence of Southern distinctiveness and referred to the South as a subculture, pointing out its ethnic and regional identity.[34] A year later, Howard F. Stein and Robert F. Hill in *The Ethnic Imperative* viewed Southerners as a special kind of white ethnicity.[35] Prior to these works, John Shelton Reed included in his work a discussion of Southernness as an ethnicity.[36] He says, "Southerners' differences from the American Mainstream have been similar in kind, if not in degree, to those of immigrant ethnic groups."[37]

All three of these books refer to an earlier work on the subject, Lewis Killian's *White Southerners,* in which he introduces the idea that Southerners can be viewed as an American ethnic group.[38] In other words, this concept of Southerners as a distinct American ethnic group has been presented for more than a decade, and it continues to gain momentum. A more recent book by Reed, *One South,* has as its subtitle, *An Ethnic Approach to Regional Culture;* another by Reed published the following year, *Southerners: The Social Psychology of Sectionalism,* continues the theme, introducing the subject on the first page of the monograph and continuing it as an important thread throughout.[39]

Works that include this concept are not limited to those cited above. And most of these scholars on the South who view Southernness as an ethnicity, refer to Milton Gordon's work to serve as the theoretical, or definitive, basis for their argument.[40]

Wilbur Zelinsky describes the South "as the most aberrant of any [area] with respect to national norms," as "distinct from the non-South," and as "a powerful political and social entity" with a recognized peculiar status.[41] Even *Time,* in its special issue on the South during the Carter era, emphasized the uniqueness of the region and the tenacity of the culture.[42]

Regardless of the differences *within* the South, differences abound between Southernness and the mainstream culture. It is well known that religion permeates Southern culture. Church and family are much more important in the South than in other regions. Reed shows influences of these institutions on Southern children exceeding those on non-Southern children. The school system, he says, remains a weak rival for family and church in socializing Southern children. In addition, Reed's study also shows vast differences in violence and localism.[43] These are just a few of the major differences between Southern and Northern culture. Interestingly, according to both Reed and Tindall, the gaps do not appear to be narrowing with time.

Of course there are traditions in New England; of course there is religiosity in other parts of the country; of course there is family cohesiveness in other groups, particularly ethnic groups. But Southern culture embraces all these aspects and pervades an entire region, not just pockets of certain areas or scatterings here and there. Not only regional traditions, not only extreme religiosity compared with other regions, not only strong family ties, but adherence to the opinions, beliefs, and values of elders, extremely deep regard for kinship networks, and open conservatism on issues of social change create a formidable impediment to becoming a part of the mainstream.

The titles and subtitles of two books summarize the tenacity of Southernness rather succinctly: Reed's *The Enduring South: Persistence in Mass Society* and Carl Degler's *Place Over Time: The Continuity of Southern Distinctiveness.*[44]

At meetings of professional organizations and scholarly seminars and conferences, I have found nationally well-known non-Southern scholars denying the existence or at least the power, of Southern culture. Recently, I was one of several Atlanta professors chit-chatting with a visiting scholar from the Northeast. The before-dinner conversation revolved around courses taught, areas of research, special interests. At the end of my recital of courses, I added something about my work on Southern culture. The visitor remarked to me, obviously assuming my research was limited to that of a sociohistorical nature, "There really isn't any left now, is there?"

Until regional differences are recognized and accepted as reality, research on the South, Southerners, and Southern women can be neither valid nor reliable.

DEFINITIONAL COMPLEXITIES

Before one conducts research on Southern women and/or writing about them in any context, it is imperative to establish definitional parameters. This is not easy—subjectivity, as well as ignorance, get in the way. Problems in this area constitute a methodological impediment and can interfere with the research process itself.

Let me pause here to present a simple definition, simple because it is agreed upon by all scholars on the South and is acceptable to others when brought to their attention. In the context of North-South discussions, North means non-South; Northern, non-Southern, and so on. The latter designations are simply cumbersome for repetitive use. "The North" did originally mean the Northeast, because at that time that was just about the only "other" there was. Also, Southerners use the term *Northerners,* and the designation *Yankees,* to mean any outsider, anyone who is not Southern.

With the concept of Southernness in mind as an ethnicity, as a unique regional entity, how, then, do we define Southerner and, in turn Southern women? What, then, are the specifics of their ethnic group? Who are Southerners? Tindall says "the South *is* the habitat of the quintessential WASP. Is it not, in fact," he goes on to ask, rhetorically and humorously, "the biggest WASP nest this side of the Atlantic?"[45] Reed agrees with the WASP-ness implicit in the term *Southerner* and refers to the common usage of *Southerners* by most researchers, scholars, and other writers to mean *white* Southerners, incorrect though that may be.[46] When speaking of black and white Southerners, writers usually make a point of spelling out both races. Reed also points out that 90% of the white population of the South is Protestant.

Therefore, for all academic and scholarly purposes, Southerner almost always means white, Anglo-Saxon Protestant. Of course, there are others of different racial, ethnic, and religious backgrounds who have lived in the South for generations and consider themselves Southerners. Except for blacks, they are a definite minority.

The most commonly used measure to indicate whether or not one is Southern is that of place of birth or residency, usually over a certain period of time in the person's life ("Where were you living at age 16?" or "Where were you reared?"). One's self-assessment ("Are you a Southerner?") is another frequently used indicator. These may be quite valid criteria, depending upon the study and its purpose. However, such definitions are totally inadequate for dealing with research on Southerners.

Raymond D. Gastil writes "[T]he people of the South are the most 'native' of any region. . . . [N]early all Southerners trace their ancestry in this country back before 1850, and most of them before 1800."[47] It is this question of residency of ancestors that creates the stickiest problem in defining Southerners—and it causes the most disagreements. (It is understood that this criterion comes up after WASP-ness has been established).

I overheard someone ask another person at a professional meeting, "Are you Southern?" The respondent paused, thought a few seconds, and then said, "I guess I am. Sure I am. I've been here over 30 years." Thirty years is meaningless in this context. A person could be living in the South for a lifetime, or could have been born in the South, and yet not be "of the South" if his or her parents were not Southern—the socialization process would simply not be the same.

It would be difficult to find anyone over 30 with more than two generations of only non-Southerners: outsiders came in trickles before World War II and were rapidly assimilated except in special enclaves of particular ethnicities and races.[48] But just for the fun of it, let's consider a third-generation 35-year-old woman, since we are ultimately concerned with Southern women, born and reared in the South of parents whose own parents had no Southern lineage. To use nice round figures, that means our young woman was born around 1950 and her parents were born around 1925. Therefore, her grandparents would have been born in the South around the turn of the century to parents not born in the South.

Now, returning to our young contemporary woman, though she certainly talks with a Southern accent—as did her parents—cooks and serves Southern food at least occasionally, and undoubtedly considers herself Southern, she has never been admonished to remember, respect, and almost revere great-some-bodies (great-great-grandfather, a great-great-uncle) who fought for the Confederacy; her parents never experienced grandparents' stories of the Confederacy and their parents' part in the war; she does not have a storehouse of anecdotes about antebellum days and about the war itself and its aftermath. She has experienced none of the extreme egocentrism inherent in Southern culture nor is her life touched by passing on from generation to generation the specialness of the traditions of a region that was at least for a short time separated politically and economically from the country itself. And she does not have even one male relative who fought and lost a war and, in the process, a way of life.

In studying Southerners—in particular, Southern women—we must, therefore, define Southerners as those who not only consider themselves to be Southern, but who also can trace back to the Civil War many generations of simply being Southern strictly defined. By now most of their original ethnic elements have been so watered down that hardly any of them refer to such origins except in terms of distant ancestors.

In defining Southern women more specifically, we have to start with two terms, *Southern women* and *women in the South*. The problem is that, even though they are distinct terms, they tend to be used synonymously—and thus incorrectly—by Southerners as well as by non-Southerners. Until a few decades ago these terms were, for all practical purposes, synonyms—almost all women in the South *were* Southern women.

Because older times and population composition linger in the minds of many Southerners, they will often say "women in the South" when they mean "Southern women." Northerners, on the other hand, confuse the two terms for another, much more complicated reason. Northern researchers rarely get to know old-time Southern families and traditional Southern women. There are many methodological barriers that contribute to the prevention of their exposure to Southernness and Southerners, and so we really can't fault them for this lack of entrée. However, they uncover "women in the South" in many varieties, women who are simply not Southern as defined by regional scholars. For instance, such researchers find ethnic and racial pockets and write, or present papers, on the diversity of the women in these groups who are fairly new to the

South or who are from the few families that do date back for generations. They also label as "Southern women" many who have been living in the South for a decade or two, women who bear not the slightest resemblance to a Southerner.

Because of the enormity of this population they seek out and study—in comparison to the few Southern-lady women with families in the South for countless generations, whom they might meet and mingle with—it is fairly easy for them to conclude that there is great heterogeneity among the women residing in the South and very few, if any, Southern-lady women. Also, since they lump all women together, regardless of time and generations in the South and regardless of ethnicity, race, and religion—as we have seen, very important criteria for defining traditional Southern women—they ignore the differences between those who are and those who are not traditional Southern women from among the non-Southern-lady women. And so, they begin to use women in the South interchangeably with Southern women, eventually eliminating traditional Southern women of all categories as extinct and thereby rationalizing the two terms to be synonymous.

In an informal, personal survey of those from the general population, I have found that a split-second reaction to the term Southern woman almost universally includes not only the WASP definition but also the Southern-lady image. Whenever we say "Southern woman," almost no one in the white educated middle-class (and upward) pictures, for instance, a female Cuban immigrant to the South, a black Southern woman, or a female Jew who lives in the South. If we say "women in the South," such an array of women should come to mind much more readily than when we say "Southern women." When we use the term Southern women, it should be assumed that the families of such women have been Southerners for generations and that they have been influenced and socialized primarily by Southern culture.

Usually, the term Southern women also means, to many, educated women or those expressing a presence of "gentility," one of the qualities middle- and upper-class Southerners prize most, which, originally, along with family connections, designed high status without having to be wealthy. However, the term also includes lower-status women who meet the other criteria. Many such women live in the rural South, in mill villages, and in Southern Appalachia, and such enclaves are usually more homogeneously populated than are Southern urban and suburban neighborhoods of families of any socioeconomic status.

What about Southern black women? Although the common usage of *Southerners* means white Southerners, technically, Southern black women are certainly included in the term Southern women.[49] Because there is also a "gray" area between the "Southern-lady women" and the "lower-status white Southern women" categories—a huge definitional problem, mainly having to do with subjectivity and perception of other versus perception of self—I have added a category to represent those women who fit neither: "in-between white Southern women." We have, then, the following major categories of "women in the South": black Southern women (there are, incidentally, very few blacks —male or female—in the United States who do not have a Southern heritage), white Southern women (as defined here), other ethnic/racial women (not WASP), and white (WASP) women who are not Southern. Within the category of "white Southern women" are the following subcategories: Southern-lady women, lower-status white Southern women, and "in-between" white Southern women. Certainly many women racially or ethnically different from those designated "Southern women" consider themselves Southern, particularly if they come from families living in the South for generations. But hardly anyone else thinks of them as, or labels them, "Southern women."

Many times I will eagerly attend a session on Southerners or Southern women at a meeting of a professional organization or at a regional conference and find that the titles of the sessions and/or the papers are quite misleading. The study will be on people who happen to live on Southern soil, and there will be no references at all, within the text itself or in the bibliographic material, on the South, its culture, or its people. Carole E. Hill, in her comprehensive review of anthropological studies on the South, refers to the distinction that "should be made between studies *of* the South and studies *in* the South" (emphasis is Hill's).[50] And so I will paraphrase and say that a distinction must be made between studies on women *of* the South and those on women *in* the South. Once definitions are established, it is still no easy matter to conduct research on Southern women. A variety of other methodological problems impede the way.

METHODOLOGICAL PROBLEMS

I want to elaborate on some of the specific built-in formidable obstacles to studying Southerners, obstacles that are inherent in the culture itself. A major one is the incredible wariness and distrust of outsiders by Southerners, especially those in rural and small-town areas. It took George Hicks, in his study of an Appalachian community in western North Carolina, six months' residency before he was accepted well enough to begin his research.[51] In my own experiences of field work in the rural South, it has been difficult for me to gain entry into many homes even though I am a native using a Southern kinship network and accepted kinship credentials and am always accompanied by a local resident for any interview. A second impediment, closely associated with the preceding, is the insider/outsider status hierarchy where even eventual acceptance may still reveal only what the Southerner chooses to disclose to an outsider. And then, the accepted researcher from the outside may be deluded, by the façade of Southern hospitality and the myriad courtesies woven into its fabric, into believing that he or she is indeed "getting to the inside," indeed being successful in obtaining an emic view, in anthropological terms.

Another built-in impediment in studying the American South and its people is the assumption by the outsider that "Oh, well, it really isn't that different." And with that stance, much of the potential research collapses. On the other hand, Southern researchers many times are simply too close to the subject and think similarly, "Oh, well, we really aren't that different." More frequently and far worse, both simply don't know the depth and breadth of the differences.

Although non-Southern researchers and scholars have access to information on the well-being of the South and Southerners (which is mostly negative, especially in the areas of education and health),[52] they rarely have any real understanding of Southern culture or Southerners. Non-Southerners' lack of knowledge about themselves and their own culture relative to Southern culture is a serious impediment to conducting research on Southerners. Compounding this ignorance is a lack of knowledge about Southerners' own relative self-perception. Non-Southerners rarely ever really know or understand much beyond the superficials of Southern culture—and the people expressing it—beyond grits, magnolias, and accents (which most of them believe are always augmented by poor grammar), and what they consider insincerity. Southerners, on the other hand, know very little about North/South differences beyond what they think of as harsh voices, tactlessness, impoliteness, and lack of concern and hospitality.

I will give a simple, almost absurd, example to illustrate the point I am trying to make. I have found that my Southern students who are from small Southern towns and have not travelled extensively are totally ignorant of the fact that iced tea is not served and drunk year round everywhere in the United States and that presweetened tea exists rarely outside the South. On the other hand, my non-Southern students never hear of these two Southern phenomena before moving to the South. Both groups are appalled to learn about each other's ignorance about the regional differences pertaining to this rather minor item. (Southerner: "You never heard of this?"; Northerner: "You didn't know we don't do/have this?") Now if you multiply this example by a large number and throw in some of the major issues, like differences in religiosity, what I am trying to get across becomes clearer.

Impediments to the study of Southern women around the mid-1900s are not exclusively a phenomenon of male-oriented, female-ignored research: research on the South and Southerners in general took a backseat in the decades after the 1940s up until fairly recent years. Wallace, expounding on his theories for the demise of the study of the South at mid-century, speaks of "the notion that the South, as with any other region, is no more. That great homogenizing American melting pot has finally digested even the South, albeit with significant indigestion. We are one people, this explanation proclaims, Americans all."[53] In another vein, he argues, "As the academic job market continues to shrink, we may be in the middle of a variation on [the older] theme. Young scholars are coming into the South, ones whose counterparts 20 years ago would rather have gone to Siberia! Even today [in the 1980s] they come with considerable misgivings. . . . Because the eyes of many of the newcomers are trained northward and westward to the coast, it can be guaranteed that these latest newcomers will not be interested in the South."[54]

A pervasive deterrent to studying the South, Southerners, and Southern women is the influence of the media, which affect the perceptions of mainstream America and in turn, perspectives. George Brown Tindall states on the jacket of Kirby's *Media-Made Dixie*: "The mass media in print and pictures has had so much more influence in shaping popular myths [about the South] than all of the products of scholarship and high culture.''[55] Abbott points to the ''images of rubes and nitwits that pass for Southerners in film and television.''[56]

In referring to that period of little research on the South, in the decades just prior to 1970, Wallace writes, ''What respectable academician of the 1950s and 1960s would deign to be concerned with region, with section, especially with the one called the South? Dixie, as was evident every night on television in the 1960s, remained a backward land filled with the ignorant, one that was an embarrassment to the rest of the nation. Research was not necessary because everyone knew what the South was''[57]—thanks, also, I might add, to radio, the movies, and literary works. Of the latter, Reed has written that Southern fiction is ''filled with cranks, grotesques, and weirdos,'' but, he continues, ''the South doesn't seem to have a great many more than its share.''[58]

I found the same stance among my research colleagues at my California employment setting in the 1970s. In 12 years of work at this ''think-tank,'' I never saw, heard of, read about any research on the South. In later years, when I brought up the subject—why can't we write a proposal for a project on the South—the answer was something like this, ''What is there to study?'' Such a frame of mind among researchers is not conducive to initiating studies in this area.

As we seek ways to overcome the methodological problems discussed here, the necessity to be aware of them and to admit that they are formidable obstacles to research on the South, on Southerners, and on Southern women is first and foremost.

I will end on a more cheerful note by citing evidence of hope. The blossoming of women's research centers in the South[59] and the advent of applying the new scholarship on women to the study of Southern women are signs that the tide is beginning to turn. Granted, it may take a while to turn around the naive mix-up between women in the South and Southern women, and it will take incredible patience and methodological know-how to penetrate the barriers to research on Southern women that have their foundations within the culture itself. And so, in spite of research impediments, of stereotypes and deviants that abound in and are perpetuated by media mythology, and of the omission of Southern women's reality by male scholars, there is hope for research on Southern women that will be both valid and reliable.

NOTES

1. Portions of this article have been included in talks and papers presented at conferences and at the meetings of professional organizations as follows: ''Southern Women in Transition,'' presented at a conference, ''A Fabric of Our Own Making'': Southern Scholars on Women, sponsored by the Women's Educational Equity Act Program and Georgia State University, Atlanta, 1981; ''The Religiosity of Southern Women: Its Effect on Social Change,'' presented at the meeting of the

Mid-South Sociological Association, Shreveport, Louisiana, 1981; "The Making of the Southern Woman: Socialization Then and Now," presented at an invited symposium, Femininity and Feminism in the Deep South, of the meeting of the Southern Anthropological Society, Boone, North Carolina, 1982; "Research on Southern Women in Transition: Definitional Complexities," presented at the meeting of the Mid-South Sociological Association, Jackson, Mississippi, 1982; "Regionalism and Southernness," presented at the meeting of the Southern Sociological Society, Atlanta, 1983; "Southern Rural Parents' Orientation Toward Education and Upward Mobility for Their Children" (session address), presented at the Southern Rural Family Conference at the University of Georgia, Athens, Georgia, 1983; "Researching Feminism in the American South: A Matter of Perspectives and Perceptions," presented at an invited symposium, Anthropology and the Media: Presentations of Feminism, at the meeting of the XIth International Congress of Anthropological and Ethnological Sciences, Vancouver, British Columbia, 1983; "The Problems of the Southern Woman as an Ethnic American," presented at the meeting of the Southern Sociological Society, Knoxville, Tennessee, 1984; "The Special Characteristics of the Rural Southern Family," presented at the Southern Family: Issues in Service Delivery conference, University of Georgia, Athens, Georgia, 1984; "The Interrelationship of Southern Culture, Religion, and Social Change: Its Effect on Southern Women in the Work Force," presented at the Student Honors Program Roundtable of the meeting of the American Sociological Association, Washington, D.C., 1985; "Southern Women: In Continuity or Change?" presented at the Southern Women: Portraits in Diversity conference at Tulane University, New Orleans, 1985.

2. Anne Firor Scott, *The Southern Lady: From Pedestal to Politics, 1830–1930* (Chicago: The University of Chicago Press, 1972), p. 108.

3. See Samuel E. Wallace, "Regional Sociology: The South," *Sociological Spectrum* 1(1981):429–442. Wallace provides a review of this unique period of research and publications on the South. He writes, "In the decade of the 1920s, more than 100 books and monographs were published in the South," (p. 433). In addition, he cites the establishment of institutions for the study of Southern social problems by universities in three states, the founding of several new social science journals and organizations, and in the 1930s the emergence of the agrarian and regionalism positions.

4. For example, see Howard W. Odum and Katherine Jocher, eds., *In Search of the Regional Balance in America* (Chapel Hill, NC: The University of North Carolina Press, 1945) and Harriet L. Herring, *Passing of the Mill Village* (1949; reprint ed., Westport, CT: Greenwood, 1977).

5. Julia Cherry Spruill, *Women's Life and Work in the Southern Colonies* (1938; reprint ed., New York: W. W. Norton, 1972) and Guion Griffis Johnson *Ante-Bellum North Carolina* (Chapel Hill, NC: The University of North Carolina, 1937).

6. Twelve Southerners, *I'll Take My Stand* (1930; reprint ed., Baton Rouge, LA: 1980); Fifteen Southerners, *Why the South Will Survive* (Athens, GA: The University of Georgia Press, 1981).

7. Scott, *The Southern Lady*, pp. 234, 236.

8. Joanne V. Hawks and Sheila L. Skemp, eds., *Sex, Race, and the Role of Women in the South* (Jackson, MS: University Press of Mississippi, 1983).

9. Anne Firor Scott, *Making the Invisible Woman Visible* (Chicago: The University of Illinois Press, 1984), p. 248.

10. Margaret Jarmon Hagood, *Mothers of the South: Portraiture of the White Tenant Farm Woman* (1939; reprint ed., New York: Norton, 1977).

11. Frances Newman, *The Hard-Boiled Virgin* (1926; reprint ed., Athens, GA: The University of Georgia Press, 1980).

12. Ibid., (cover).

13. Katharine DuPre Lumpkin, *The Making of a Southerner* (1946; reprint ed., Athens, GA: The University of Georgia Press, 1974).

14. Lillian Smith, *Killers of the Dream,* rev. and enlarged (1949; reprint ed., New York: W. W. Norton & Co., 1961).

15. I have focused here on publications by Newman, Smith, and Lumpkin as examples. There are a few other books, mostly fiction, that were written by women from the turn of the century on into the early decades of it about women during this period and in some cases during the decades immediately following the Civil War. Space simply does not permit a review of additional works. Two well-known female authors' fictional works that I have not included are those of Ellen Glasgow (e.g., *Virginia* [New York: Doubleday, Page, 1913]) and Kate Chopin (e.g., *The Awakening* [1899; reprint ed., New York: Bantam, 1981]). Scott (*The Southern Lady*, p. 237) has mentioned both as "highly rewarding" in her study of Southern women. Chopin's works are enjoying a revival and reprinting now in the 1980s.

16. Jacquelyn D. Hall, *Revolt Against Chivalry: Jessie Daniel Ames and the Women's Campaign Against Lynching* (New York: Columbia University Press, 1979).

17. Scott, *The Southern Lady,* p. xi.

18. For examples see the following: Ben Ames Williams, ed., *A Diary from Dixie by Mary Boykin Chestnut* (Boston: Houghton Mifflin, 1949); C. Vann Woodward, ed., *Mary Chestnut's Civil War* (New Haven, CT: Yale University Press, 1981); Mary A. H. Gay, *Life in Dixie During the War* (1897; reprint ed., Atlanta: DeKalb Historical Society, 1979); Katharine M. Jones, ed., *Heroines of Dixie: Confederate Women Tell Their Story of the War* (Indianapolis, IN: Bobbs-Merrill, 1955); Bell I. Wiley, *Confederate Women* (Westport, CT: Greenwood, 1975).

19. Catherine Clinton, *The Plantation Mistress* (New York: Pantheon, 1982); Shirley Abbott, *Womenfolks: Growing Up Down South* (New York: Ticknor and Fields, 1983).

20. James M. McPherson, book jacket, Clinton, *The Plantation Mistress.*

21. Patricia A. Stringer and Irene Thompson, eds., *Stepping Off the Pedestal: Academic Women in the South* (New York: Modern Language Association of America, 1982).

22. Anne Moody, *Coming of Age in Mississippi* (New York: Dial Press, 1968); Molly C. Dougherty, *Becoming a Woman in Rural Black Culture* (New York: Holt, Rinehart and Winston, 1978).

23. Kathy Kahn, *Hillbilly Women* (New York: Avon, 1972).

24. The Southern Oral History Project, a study of industrial workers at least 50% of whom were women. The tapes and some transcriptions are now a part of the Southern Historical Collection in the Wilson Library at the University of North Carolina at Chapel Hill.

25. Chris Mayfield, ed., "Growing Up Southern," special issue of *Southern Exposure,* VIII (Fall 1980), and Chris Mayfield, ed., *Growing Up Southern: Southern Exposure Looks at Childhood, Then and Now* (New York: Pantheon, 1981); and Susan Angell, Jacqueline Dowd Hall, and Candace Waid, eds., "Generations: Women in the South," special issue of *Southern Exposure,* IV (Winter 1977). See also

Maxine Alexander, ed., *Speaking for Ourselves: Women of the South* (New York: Pantheon, 1984), an outgrowth of "Generations: Women in the South," called by the editor, "the foremother of the book" (p. xiii).

26. Rosemary Daniell, *Fatal Flowers* (New York: Holt, Rinehart and Winston, 1980); Florence King, *Southern Ladies and Gentlemen* (New York: Bantam, 1975).

27. For other reviews on works about Southern women, see Scott, *The Southern Lady*, pp. 233–237 and footnotes; Anne Firor Scott, "Historians Construct the Southern Woman," in *Sex, Race, and the Role of Women in the South*, eds. Hawks and Skemp, pp. 95–110 and 129–131 (Notes); and Scott, *Making the Invisible Woman Visible*, pp. 173–258.

28. Either Williams, ed., *A Diary from Dixie by Mary Boykin Chestnut*, or Woodward, ed., *Mary Chestnut's Civil War*.

29. Margaret Mitchell, *Gone With the Wind* (New York: Macmillan, 1936).

30. See any of the following editions: Stuart A. Queen and John B. Adams, *The Family in Various Cultures* (New York: J. B. Lippincott, 1952); Stuart A. Queen, Robert W. Habenstein, and John B. Adams, *The Family in Various Cultures*, 2nd ed. (New York: Harper and Row, 1961); Stuart A. Queen, Robert W. Habenstein, and Jill Quadagro, *The Family in Various Cultures*, 5th ed. (New York: Harper and Row, 1985).

31. Bertram Wyatt-Jones, *Southern Honor: Ethics and Behavior in the Old South* (New York: Oxford University Press, 1982). See also F. N. Boney, *Southerners All* (Macon, GA: Mercer University Press, 1984); Boney also includes the subject but not in such detail and at such length.

32. An introductory piece included in the front matter of the reprint of Kate Chopin's *The Awakening* refers to this work as a masterpiece, "which aroused a national scandal for its 'indecency,' " and states the following: "Banned by libraries, it even prevented [Chopin's] admission into the St. Louis Fine Arts Club—even though Kate Chopin was famous for her literary salon, which attracted distinguished artists and writers from all over the country." This is just one example of such ostracism directed at female writers who dared to give the full picture of Southern women's lives.

33. Scott, *The Southern Lady*, p. 199.

34. George Brown Tindall, *The Ethnic Southerners* (Baton Rouge, LA: Louisiana State University Press, 1976).

35. Howard F. Stein and Robert F. Hill, *The Ethnic Imperative* (University Park, PA: The Pennsylvania State University Press, 1977).

36. John Shelton Reed, *The Enduring South: Persistence in Mass Society* (Chapel Hill, NC: University of North Carolina Press, 1974).

37. Ibid., p. 11.

38. Lewis M. Killian, *White Southerners* (New York: Random House, 1970).

39. John Shelton Reed, *One South: An Ethnic Approach to Regional Culture* (Baton Rouge, LA: Louisiana State University Press, 1982); John Shelton Reed, *Southerners: The Social Psychology of Sectionalism* (Chapel Hill, NC: The University of North Carolina Press, 1983).

40. Milton M. Gordon, *Assimilation in American Life: The Role of Place, Religion, and National Origins* (New York: Oxford University Press, 1964).

41. Wilbur Zelinsky, *The Cultural Geography of the United States* (Englewood Cliffs, NJ: Prentice-Hall, 1973).

42. *Time* (Special Issue on the South), September 27, 1976.
43. Reed, *The Enduring South.*
44. Carl N. Degler, *Place Over Time: The Continuity of Southern Distinctiveness* (Baton Rouge, LA: Louisiana State University Press, 1977).
45. Tindall, *The Ethnic Southerners,* p. 8.
46. Reed, *The Enduring South,* p. 3.
47. Raymond D. Gastil, *Cultural Regions of the United States* (Seattle, WA: University of Washington Press, 1975), p. 174.
48. P. J. Dusenberry and T. L. Beyle, *Southern Growth Policies Board Data Book* (Research Triangle, NC: Southern Growth Policies Board, 1978). Many researchers and writers have referred to this phenomenon over the years. Dusenberry and Beyle's work illustrates the dramatic change in immigration into the South beginning in the 1950–1960 period with a trickle (see chart, p. 6). The numbers increased from fewer than 100,000 between 1950 and 1960 to almost 2½ million from 1970 to 1977.
49. Obviously—and unfortunately—this article focuses almost exclusively on white Southern women, which is my area of research. For reviews of the literature on black Southern women and data bases on research and publications on the subject, contact Beverly Guy-Sheftall, Director, Women's Research and Resource Center, Spelman College, and Bonnie Thornton Dill, Director, Center for Research on Women, Memphis State University. In addition, the Special Collections at the Robert Woodruff Library, Atlanta University Center, is an excellent resource for research on black Southern women.
50. Carole E. Hill, "Anthropological Studies in the American South: Review and Directions," *Current Anthropology* 18:(1977)309.
51. George L. Hicks, *Appalachian Valley* (New York, Holt, Rinehart and Winston, 1976).
52. Peggy J. Ross, Herman Bluestone, and Fred K. Hines, *Indicators of Social Well-Being for U.S. Counties* and *Indexes and Rankings for U.S. Counties,* Rural Development Research Report No. 10, U.S. Department of Agriculture (Washington, D.C.: U.S. Government Printing Office, 1979).
53. Wallace, "Regional Sociology: The South," p. 437.
54. Ibid., p. 436.
55. Jack Temple Kirby, *Media-Made Dixie* (Baton Rouge, LA: Louisiana State University Press, 1978).
56. Abbott, *Womenfolks,* p. 6.
57. Wallace, "Regional Sociology: The South," p. 436.
58. Reed, *One South,* p. 178.
59. For example, Women's Research and Resource Center (Spelman College); Duke/University of North Carolina Women's Studies Research Center; Center for Research on Women (Memphis State University); Newcomb Women's Center (Tulane University).

Chapter 2

A MYTH OF THE SOUTHERN LADY: ANTEBELLUM PROSLAVERY RHETORIC AND THE PROPER PLACE OF WOMAN

VIRGINIA KENT ANDERSON LESLIE

For the sake of argument, let us assume that women are human beings[1]—that they are not innately either weak or strong, independent or dependent, intelligent or illogical, virtuous (pure) or licentious. If these assumptions are true, then these questions follow: Why in a certain time and in a certain culture would the ideal, elite white woman be defined as weak, dependent, illogical, and pure? What purposes were being served by defining such an ideal? It is the thesis of this article that the cultural expectations that "Southern ladies" ought to be weak, dependent, illogical, and pure served the purposes of ideology—that it was to keep the ruling gender/class/race ruling; specifically, that this definition-myth was self-consciously used to justify the domination of both Southern ladies and slaves by elite white men.

There is, of course, no such thing as the myth of the Southern lady. However, it is possible to create a myth from a particular perspective. Ann Firor Scott, in her classic study. *The Southern Lady: From Pedestal to Politics, 1830–1930,* used the diaries and letters of elite white women and men in the antebellum South to retrieve an image of the Southern lady as submissive, physically weak, timid, modest, beautiful, graceful, innocent, compassionate, and self-denying.[2] This myth, Scott observes, was at odds with the realities of the lives of plantation mistresses. It represented what they ought to be, not what they were. Assuming that the psychological contortions could be managed, only the great ladies of urban centers could manage to be entirely ornamental. In *The*

Plantation Mistress, Catherine Clinton extrapolates from Scott's theme of contradiction and comes to the conclusion that plantation mistresses were "the slaves of slaves."[3] Anne Goodwyn Jones, in her book, *Tomorrow Is Another Day: The Woman Writer in the South, 1859–1936,* combined the disciplines of history and literature to distill a myth of the Southern lady as the "oxymoronic ideal of the woman made of steel yet marked in fragility."[4]

These images of the Southern lady raise fundamental questions about the relationship between the real and the ideal in the lives of elite white women. How was an ideal defined? If few individuals could actually be Southern ladies, what functions did the ideal serve?

Elite white men sat at the apex of power in the antebellum South. If we assume that the ruling race/class/gender creates ideology in order to justify the status quo, then it is possible to define a myth of the Southern lady and to locate the functions of that myth by examining justifications of the social order by elite white males. For the purposes of this discussion, I have chosen to examine selected texts of three antebellum apologists for slavery: Thomas R. Dew's "Professor Dew on Slavery,"[5] William Harper's "Memoir on Slavery,"[6] and George Fitzhugh's *Cannibals All! or Slaves Without Masters*[7] and *Sociology for the South, or the Failure of Free Society.*[8] These texts were selected for several reasons. First, they are ideological, each was written for a Southern audience, and each had the stated purpose of justifying slavery. Second, the texts fit together chronologically, beginning with Dew's arguments in 1832 that slavery was a positive good, extending through Harper's ethical arguments of 1837, and concluding with George Fitzhugh's thesis that all the world ought to be organized around the benevolent institution of slavery.

THOMAS R. DEW (1802–1846)

Women are precisely what the men make them all over the world.[9]

In Dew's classic article, the justification of slavery assumes the point of view of progressive cultural development:

Slavery gradually fells the forest, and thereby destroys the haunts of the wild beast; it gives rise to agricultural production, and thereby renders mankind less dependent on the precarious and diminishing production of the chase; it thus gradually destroys the roving and unquiet life of the savage; it furnishes a home, and binds him down to the soil; it converts the idler and wanderer into the man of business and the agriculturist.[10]

Dew also assumes an evolutionary point of view when he discusses the relationship between slavery and the position of women.

*In very first remove from the most savage state, we behold the marked
effects of slavery on the condition of women—we find her at once elevated,
clothed with all her charms, mingling with and directing the society in
which she belongs, no longer the slave but the equal and idol of man.[11]*

According to Dew, this elevation of women is the result of the increased
abundance that slavery produces.

*Slavery, we have just seen, changes the hunting to the shepherd and agri-
cultural status—gives rise to augmented productions, and consequently,
furnishes more abundant supplies for man. The labor of the slave thus
becomes a substitute for that of the woman; man no longer wanders
through the forest in quest of game; and woman, consequently, is relieved
from following on his track, under the enervating and harassing burden of
her children. She is now surrounded by her domestics, and the abundance
of their labor lightens the toil and hardships of the whole family.[12]*

If woman is elevated by the abundance which slavery produces, the very
nature of man is changed.

*She ceases to be a mere "beast of burden"; becomes the cheering and
animating centre of the family circle—time is afforded for reflection and
the cultivation of all those mild and fascinating virtues, which throw a
charm and delight around our homes and firesides, and calm and tran-
quillize the harsher tempers and more restless propensities of the male:
Man, too, relieved from that endless disquietude about subsistence for the
morrow—relieved of the toil of wandering over the forest—more simply
provided for by the productions of the soil—finds his habits changed, his
temper moderated, his kindness and benevolence increased; he loses that
savage and brutal feeling which he had before indulged towards all his
unfortunate dependents; and, consequently, even the slave, in the agricultural, is happier than the free man in the hunting state.[13]*

Dew is consequently perplexed when women attack slavery.

*And thus it is a most singular and curious fact, that woman, whose sympa-
thies are ever alive to the distress of others; whose heart is filled with
benevolence and philanthropy, and whose fine feelings, unchecked by
considerations of interest or calculations of remote consequences, have
ever prompted to embrace with eagerness the wildest and most destructive
schemes of emancipation, has been in a most peculiar and eminent degree
indebted to slavery, for that very elevation in society which first raised her
to an equality of man.[14]*

If women are sympathetic, benevolent, and philanthropic and have fine feelings unchecked by considerations of interest or calculations of remote consequences, why should they not be sympathetic to the condition of slaves, even if it is not in their own self-interest?

According to Dew, the elevation of women by slavery is required so that women will raise children with virtue, intelligence, and purest affection.

> *We will not stop here to investigate the advantages resulting from the ameliorated condition of women: her immense influence on the destiny of our race is acknowledged by all: upon her must ever devolve, in a peculiar degree, the duty of rearing into manhood a creature, in its infancy the frailest and feeblest which heaven has made—of forming the plastic mind —of training the ignorance and imbecility of infancy into virtue and efficiency. There is, perhaps, no moral power, the magnitude of which swells so far beyond the grasp of calculation, as the influence of the female character on the virtues and happiness of mankind: it is so searching, so versatile, so multifarious, and so universal: it turns on us like the eye of a beautiful portrait, wherever we take our position; it bears upon us in such an infinite variety of points, on our instincts, our passions, our vanity, our tastes, and our necessities; above all, on the first impressions of education and the associations of infancy.[15]*

Dew places the burden of raising infants to become moral beings squarely on the shoulders of mothers and does so with a certain amount of fear for the powerless child.

If women have great moral power over infants, and consequently the virtues of adults, how is the human family to guarantee that mothers use this power properly?

> *The rule [sic] which women should act in the great drama of life, is truly an important and indispensable one; it must and will be acted, and that too, either for our weal or woe: all must wish then, that she should be guided by virtue, intelligence, and the purest affection; which can only be secured by elevating, honoring, and loving* her *[emphasis is Dew's] in whose career we feel so deep an interest.[16]*

One wonders what is to be feared from a mother who does not exhibit purest affection.

Not only is woman's elevation required so that she will act out of virtue, intelligence, and the purest affection, but her status is a mark of advancing civilization. "The bare name of this interesting half of the human family, is well calculated to awaken in the breast of the generous the feeling of tenderness and kindness. The wrongs and sufferings of meek, quiet, forbearing woman, awaken the generous sympathy of every noble heart."[17] One wonders what these characteristics evoke in the not so generous heart. Dew continues,

> *Man never suffers without murmuring, and never relinquishes his rights without a struggle. It is not always so with woman: her physical weakness incapacitates her for the combat; her sexual organization, and that part which she takes in bringing forth and nurturing the rising generation, render her necessarily domestic in her habits, and timid and patient in her sufferings. If man chooses to exercise his power against woman, she is sure to fall an easy prey to his oppression. Hence, we may always consider her progressing elevation in society as a mark of advancing civilization, and more particularly, of the augmentation of disinterested and generous virtue.*[18]

Dew states that women are required to give up their rights, without a struggle, because their physical weakness and the domestic habits required by mothers incapacitates them for the combat. Combat with whom?

WILLIAM HARPER (1790–1847)

> *There seems to be something in the argument [about slavery] which blunts the perceptions, and darkens and confuses the understandings and moral feelings of men.*[19]

William Harper begins his "Memoir on Slavery" with a set of leading questions:

> *Will those who regard Slavery as immoral, or crime in itself, tell us that man was not intended for civilization, but to roam the earth as a biped brute? That he was not to raise his eyes to heaven, or be conformed in his nobler faculties to the image of his Maker? Or will they say that the Judge of all the earth has done wrong in ordaining the means by which alone that end can be obtained?*[20]

The choice is between slavery and civilization. How does one come to the conclusion that civilization cannot exist without slavery? What does this either/or logic portend for those who are defined as inferior in a slave society—women, children, and black people?

There is a catch for all those who are defined as unable to take care of themselves. If slavery produces civilization, that is, the good, and slavery is based on a trade-off between protection-security and civil-personal liberty, then how one defines civilization becomes crucial. For Harper, "civilization" involves the accumulation of property and the enjoyment of leisure which produces a liberally educated elite and "merely ornamental public institutions," such as "elegant art," and "higher literature," that is, art and literature that are aloof from the "sordidness of trade."[21] According to Harper, "[I]t is better that a part should be fully and highly cultivated, and the rest utterly ignorant."[22] These "highly cultivated" males are in control of the others, and make decisions in everyone's best interest, which they are at liberty to define. Harper argues that this hierarchical arrangement produces affection between the master and his dependents:

> It is not natural that man should be attached to that which is his own [emphasis is Harper's], and which has contributed to his convenience, his enjoyment, or his vanity? This is felt even towards animals and inanimate objects. How much more towards a being of superior intelligence and usefulness, who can appreciate our feelings toward him, and return them? Is it not natural that we should be interested in that which is dependent on us for protection and support? Do not men everywhere contract kind feelings toward their dependents?[23]

How is one defined as dependent? Herein lies a dilemma. Are the utterly ignorant (or in the case of elite white women, partially ignorant) inherently inferior, or are they ignorant-dependent because the preservation of civilization requires that they be kept ignorant-dependent? "Females are human and rational beings. They may be found of better faculties, and better qualified to exercise political privileges, and to attain the distinctions of society, than many men; yet who complains of the order of society by which they are excluded from them?"[24] As for those who do complain, Harper continues:

> I do not speak of the few who would desecrate them; do violence to the nature which their creator has impressed upon them; drag them from the position which they necessarily occupy for the existence of civilized society and in which they constitute its blessing and ornament—the only position which they have ever occupied in any human society—to place them in a situation in which they would be alike miserable and degraded.

In the case of the proper position of women, God has impressed it upon them. However, society may also require that women play a certain role.

> It is said that, of necessity, society must exclude from some civil and political privileges those who are unfitted to exercise them, by infirmity, unsuitableness of character, or defect of discretion; that of necessity there must be some general rule on the subject, and that any rule which can be devised will operate with hardship and injustice on individuals.[25]

For Harper, the choice is between being a blessing and an ornament (mother) without political privileges or being miserable and degraded with political privileges.

Harper links the purity of white women with the sexuality of black women in a very direct and revealing way. For Harper, black women are amoral. In answering the charge that the chastity of slave wives is not protected by law, he states:

> *I answer, as with respect to their lives, that they are protected by manners, and their position. Who ever heard of such outrages being offered? At least as seldom, I will venture to say, as in other communities of different forms of policy. One reason doubtless may be, that often there is not disposition to resist. Another reason also may be, that there is little temptation to such violence, as there is so large a proportion of this class of females who set little value on chastity, and afford easy gratification of the hot passions of men.*[26]

Black women provide white men with willing "prostitutes" and thus preserve the purity of white women.[27] "And can it be doubted, that this purity is caused by, and is a compensation for the evils resulting from the existence of an enslaved class of more relaxed morals?"[28]

For Harper purity of the white female is symbolic. By preserving the absolute purity of white women, society delineates virtue and vice which preserves order: "I have said that the tendency of our institutions is to elevate the female character, as well as that of the other sex, and for similar reasons." However, the master's elevated character does not require purity. He continues:

> *In other states of society, there is no well-defined limit to separate virtue and vice. There are degrees of vice, from the most flagrant and odious, to that which scarcely incurs the censure of society. Many individuals occupy an unequivocal [sic] position; and as society becomes accustomed to this, there will be a less peremptory requirement of purity in female manners and conduct; and often the whole of society will be in a tainted and uncertain condition with respect to female virtue.*[29]

Given that the purity of elite white females compensates for the evils resulting from an enslaved class, then, Harper deduces that slavery produces the greatest good for that greatest number.

> *I am aware that, however often answered, it is likely to be repeated again—how can that institution be tolerable, by which a large class of society is cut off from the hope of improvement in knowledge; to whom blows are not degrading; theft no more than a fault; falsehood and the want of chastity almost venial, and in which a husband or parent looks with comparative indifference on that which, to a freeman, would be dishonor to a wife or child? But why not, if it produces the greatest aggregate of good?*[30]

GEORGE FITZHUGH (1806–1881)

The sentiments of slaveholders are sufficient guarantee of the rights of women, all the world over.[31]

Sociology for the South was addressed to the people of the South and described by the author as an attempt to awaken the South to "the revolutionary tumults, uproar, mendacity and crime in free society."[32] According to Fitzhugh, few Southerners "are aware of the blessings they enjoy, or of the evils from which they are exempt."[33] In the case of *Cannibals All!*, Fitzhugh states that his aim was "to show that Labor makes values, and wit exploits and accumulates them and hence to deduce the conclusion that the unrestricted exploitation of so-called free society is more repressive on the laborer than domestic slavery."[34]

For Fitzhugh, slavery was not a necessary evil but a positive good because it served to subdue competition and thus ensure harmony and order. The liberty of the individual was subordinated to the good of the "social hive."[35] Christian morality could function in such a social order, while it could not in a free society. Fitzhugh wrote:

Christian morality can find little practical foothold in a community so constituted that to "love our neighbor as ourself" or "to do unto others as we would they should do unto us" would be acts of suicidal self-sacrifice. Christian morality, however, was not preached to free competitive society, but to slave society, where it is neither very difficult nor unnatural to practice it. In the various family relations of husband, wife, parent, child, master, and slave, the observance of these Christian precepts is often practiced, and almost always promotes the temporal well-being of those who observe it. The interests of the various members of the family circle, correctly understood, concur and harmonize, and each member best promotes his own selfish interest by ministering to the wants and interest of the rest.[36]

Ruling over this orderly, harmonious social order was the ultimate patriarch, God. His manifestation on earth was, quite logically, the master in a slave society—a person whose character was elevated by slavery so that he was "lofty and independent in his sentiments, generous, affectionate, brave and eloquent."[37]

According to Fitzhugh, this transformation takes place 1) because the master has no equals:

What is more evident, obvious, and axiomatic, than that equals must from necessity be rivals, antagonists, competitors, and enemies. Self-preservation, the first law of human and animal nature, makes the selfish course of action essential to preserve existence. It is almost equally obvious that in the natural, social, or family state, unselfishness, or the preference of others' good and happiness, is the dictate of nature and policy.[38]

2) because all others are his:

A man loves not only his horses, and his cattle, which are useful to him, but he loves his dog, which is of no use. He loves them because they are his. What a wise and beneficent provision of Heaven, that make the selfishness of man's nature a protecting aegis to shield and defend wife and children, slaves and even dumb animals.[39]

and 3) because all others are dependent:

A state of dependence is the only condition in which reciprocal affection can exist among human beings—the only situation in which the war of competition ceases, and peace, amity and good will arise. A state of independence always begets more or less of jealous rivalry and hostility. A man loves his children because they are weak, helpless and dependent; he loves his wife for similar reasons. When his children grow and assert their independence he is apt to transfer his affection to his grandchildren. He ceases to love his wife when she becomes masculine or rebellious; his slaves are always dependent, never the rivals of their masters.[40]

For Fitzhugh, then, harmony, order, and affection depend on hierarchy, dependency, and finally the ownership of all others by a patriarch-master. But what controls such absolute power? According to Fitzhugh,[41] and the modern Southern historian, Bertrand Wyatt-Brown,[42] the answer is public opinion. "Public opinion ["honor" in Wyatt-Brown's terms] unites with self-interest, domestic affection, and municipal law to protect the slave. The man who maltreats the weak and dependent, who abuses his authority over wife, children, or slaves is universally detested."[43] Conversely, Fitzhugh described and condemns the social order in the North:

No slaveholder was ever so brutal as to boast of the low wages he paid his slaves, to pride himself on feeding and clothing them badly—neglecting the young, the aged, the sick and infirm; such a man would be booted from society as a monster. Society hardly tolerates inhumanity to horses, much less to slaves. But disguise the process a little, and it is a popular virtue to oppress free white poor people. Get the labor of the able-bodied husband as cheap as you can, and leave his wife, children and aged

*parents to starve, and you are the beau ideal of a man in England and
New England. Public opinion, as well as natural feelings, requires a man
to pay his slave high wages; the same public opinion commends your [the
North's] cleverness in paying low wages to free laborers, and nature and
conscience oppose no obstacles to the screwing process.*[44]

For Fitzhugh, the surest sign that free society in the North was floundering
was the agitation for women's rights.

*Nothing in the signs of the times exhibits in stronger relief the fact, that
free society is in a state of "dissolution and thaw," of demoralization and
transition, than the stir about women's rights. And yet it is time to work.
Northern newspapers are filled with the suffering of poor widowed needle
women, and the murders of wives by their husbands. Woman there is in a
false position. Be she white, or be she black, she is treated with kindness
and humanity in the slave-holding South.*[45]

When Fitzhugh discusses the proper position of women in the South, he is
concerned with only elite women. His discussion is so theoretical that it ignores
all women who must be physically or morally strong and independent as irrelevant to a discussion of what ought to be. Fitzhugh's theoretical woman is always
present in relation to man, her Lord and Master. "The husband has a legally
recognized property in his wife's services, and may legally control, in some
measure, her personal liberty. She is his property and his slave,"[46] or "Indeed,
all women literally sell their liberties when they marry, and very few repent of
the bargain."[47]

But what if the woman repents of the bargain? What would happen if the
generous sentiments of the slaveholder, grounded as they are in inequality, dependence, and ownership, are trampled upon? "In France, woman draws the
plough and the canal boat. She will be condemned to like labors in America, as
soon as her dress, her education and coarse sentiments fit her for such labors."[48]
Condemned by whom?

*Let her exhibit strength and hardihood, and man, her master, will make
her a beast of burden. So long as she is nervous, fickle, capricious, delicate, diffident, and dependent, man will worship and adore her. Her
weakness is her strength, and her true art is to cultivate and improve that
weakness. Woman naturally shrinks from public gaze, and from the
struggle and competition of life. Free society has thrown her into the
arena of industrial war, robbed her of the softness of her own sex, without
conferring on her the strengths of ours. In truth, women, like children,
have but one right, and that is the right to protection. The right to protection involves the obligation to obey. A husband, a lord and master, whom
she should love, honor and obey, nature designed for every woman, for*

*the number of males and females is the same. If she be obedient, she is in
little danger of mal-treatment; if she stands upon her rights, is coarse and
masculine, man loathes and despises her, and ends by abusing her. Law,
however well-intended, can do little in her behalf. True womanly art will
give her an empire and a sway far greater than she deserves.[49]*

Or, "If she [Harriet Beecher Stowe] sets them [women] to preaching to-day, we
men will put them to the plough, to-morrow. Women would do well to disguise
strength of mind or body, if they possess it, if they would retain their empire."[50]
Again, "Women may wear paddies or bloomers, but if they carry the spirit of
independence so far as to adopt a dress to conceal their sex, they will soon find
themselves in a cage or a prison."[51]

If woman obeys, she has a right to protection, but protection from whom?
Fitzhugh doesn't mention black slave men. What his discussion implies is that
woman must be protected from her "lord and master." Fitzhugh uses the myth
of innate inferiority of women not to justify violence against slaves, but to justify the threat of violence against women, all in the service of an orderly society.

*Marriage is too much like slavery not to be involved in its fate; and the
obedience of wives which the Bible inculcates, furnishes a new threat for
infidelity in petticoats or Bloomers to harp on. Slavery, marriage, [and]
religion, are all pillars of the social forces.[52]*

DISCUSSION

Fitzhugh (F), Harper (H), and Dew (D) collectively define the ideal
Southern lady as physically weak (F, D), delicate (D), soft (F), fickle (F), capricious (F), meek (D), quiet (D), forbearing (D), timid (D), patient (D), ornamental (H, D), cheerful (D), charming (D), animating (D), sympathetic (D),
pure (H), virtuous (H), diffident (F), dependent (F), and obedient (F). She is not
strong (F), hardy (F), or masculine (F); she does not stand on her rights (F);
preach (F); carry the spirit of independence so far as to dress to conceal her sex
(F); or compete with man (D).

These descriptive terms fall into five categories: 1) characteristics that
validate a theory of the innate physical weakness of woman, that is, she is
weak, delicate, soft; 2) behaviors that negate authenticity, that is, she is nervous, fickle, capricious, meek, timid, cheerful, charming, animating, and ornamental, having "fine feelings unchecked by considerations of interest or calculations of remote consequences";[53] 3) traits required by motherhood in a
difficult situation, that is, she is quiet, forbearing, patient, sympathetic; 4) symbolic states, that is, she is pure and virtuous; and 5) behaviors that clearly
acknowledge that someone else is in power, that is, she is dependent, diffident,
and obedient. What can be learned about the functions of this collective myth
from an analysis of these categories?

For Fitzhugh, Harper, and Dew the "fact" that women were physically weaker than men meant that they had to be protected by a man in the public sphere; however, does it not follow that they also had to be protected from a man in the private sphere by not provoking wrath? Fitzhugh states that "if she be obedient, she is in little danger of mal-treatment; if she stands upon her rights, is coarse and masculine, man loathes and despises her, and ends by abusing her."[54] And Dew declares:

> *Her physical weakness incapacitates her for the combat; her sexual organization, and the part which she takes in bringing forth and nurturing the rising generation, render her necessarily domestic in her habits, and timid and patient in her sufferings. . . . If man chooses to exercise his power against women, she is sure to fall an easy prey to his oppression.*[55]

What would be gained by defining the ideal Southern lady as nervous, fickle, capricious, meek, timid, cheerful, charming, and ornamental; "having fine feelings, unchecked by considerations of interest or calculations of remote consequences"?[56] Such a person would be defined as ideally inauthentic, unable to make judgments herself. She would be senseless and consequently, in Anne Jones's words, "ultimately irrelevant."[57] Like a child she would have to rely on someone else to direct her life.[58] But what could be gained by defining the Southern matron as a child-wife? She would be taught not to trust her own judgment, and, if hegemony works, she would learn not to trust her own judgment. She would accept her place in a hierarchical social order.

If one is raised up to be quiet, forbearing, patient, and sympathetic, one who "suffers without a murmur," then we can safely assume that she is headed for a difficult situation. Dew uses these words to define the qualities required by a woman as a mother:

> *Her sexual organization, and the part which she takes in bringing forth and nurturing the rising generation, render her necessarily domestic in her habits, and timid and patient in her sufferings. If man chooses to exercise his power against women, she is sure to fall an easy prey to his oppression.*[59]

Is not the logic of this argument that, because woman can have children, she must have children and she must do so quietly—with forbearance, patience, sympathy, and silence—in order to avoid oppression?

What could Harper have meant when he described woman as pure? From a religious point of view, elite white women might have been described as pure because they were expected to be innocent (ignorant) of evil. From a sexual point of view, the Southern lady, ideally a wife and mother, could not be pure in the sense of being chaste—a virgin. She could be described as pure in the sense of being without lust, and/or she could be described as pure because she was expected to have a sexual relationship only with her husband. Clearly, Harper meant to imply the latter. The former could also be assumed on the basis of the conjecture that if Southern ladies were lustful they would also be demanding, and being demanding of anything, that is, having acknowledged needs, would unbalance the other requirements of the myth.

For Harper the consequences of not being a pure Southern lady were severe: "Here [in the South], there is that certain and marked line, [below] which there is no toleration or allowance for any approach to license of manners or conduct, and she who falls below it, will fall far below even the slave."[60] What state of affairs lies below that of the slave? Why is female purity such an issue, one wonders. Harper answers, "It would indeed be intolerable, if, when one class of society is necessarily degraded in this respect [morals], no compensations were made by the superior elevation and purity of the other."[61] Compensation to whom, one wonders. Harper declares that "the passions of men of the superior caste, tempt and find gratification in the easy chastity of the [black slave] females."[62] Does it not logically follow that it is necessary to have a degraded class of society so that the hot passions of men of the superior caste will not be visited on Southern ladies—all of which assumes that Southern gentlemen cannot contain themselves and that Southern ladies did not enjoy the hot passions of men?

As for the idea of compensation, Harper states, "And can it be doubted, that this purity [of elite white woman] is caused by, and is a compensation for the evils resulting from the existence of an enslaved class of more relaxed morals?"[63] Does it not follow that Southern ladies must be pure as a compensation for the fact that Southern gentlemen are not? Southern gentlemen exercise their hot passions on their property, their "children," with no ethical consequences because of the value placed on the resulting purity of the Southern lady.

Lastly, Southern ladies ought to be dependent, diffident, and obedient. Southern ladies were, in fact, dependent on Southern gentlemen, both their husbands and their male kin. After they married, women were considered "civilly dead." Until the financial panics of the 1850s, their property was not protected (except by prenuptial agreements) from their husband or his creditors. Children were considered the property of their fathers and divorce was rare.[64] A husband was expected to control his wife's behavior and was at liberty to use force within limits.[65] Being diffident and obedient, under such circumstances, would have been an appropriate survival strategy. Power for the Southern lady meant subtle manipulation.

CONCLUSION

Dew, Harper, and Fitzhugh were clearly entangled in a patriarchal model for the organization of society and the family. They argued that this model promised the greatest good for the greatest number, that it maintained order, and that misery was reduced because the patriarch was bound by an ethic of reciprocal duties to care for his family, his dependents, those whom he owned. For his dependents, the consequences of not cooperating in this scheme of reciprocal duties could lead to violence.

A Southern lady who was described as ideally weak, dependent, illogical, and pure would have to be socialized to become attractively disabled and consequently in need of protection. For Dew, Harper, and Fitzhugh, this vulnerability of the ideal Southern lady was used to justify real violence for the sake of social order in the antebellum South.

NOTES

1. Dorothy L. Sayers, *Are Women Human?* (Grand Rapids, MI: Eerdmans, 1971).
2. Anne Firor Scott, *The Southern Lady: From Pedestal to Politics, 1830–1930* (Chicago: University of Chicago Press, 1970), p. 4.
3. Catherine Clinton, *The Plantation Mistress* (New York: Pantheon, 1982).
4. Anne Goodwyn Jones, *Tomorrow Is Another Day: The Woman Writer in the South, 1859–1936* (Baton Rouge: Louisiana State University Press, 1981), p. 4.
5. Thomas R. Dew, "Professor Dew on Slavery," in *The Pro-Slavery Argument* (Philadelphia: Lippincott, Grambo and Co., 1853), pp. 287–490. Dew's article was originally published as "A Review of the Debate in the Virginia Legislature of 1831–1832" in 1832 in Richmond, Virginia, by T. W. White. It was reprinted in 1853 in *The Pro-Slavery Argument* and again in 1860 in a pro-slavery collection called *Cotton Is King and Pro-Slavery Arguments*. All references here are from *The Pro-Slavery Argument*.
6. William Harper, "Harper's Memoir on Slavery," in *The Pro-Slavery Argument* (Philadelphia: Lippincott, Grambo and Co., 1853), pp. 2–174. Harper's article was originally delivered to the South Carolina Society for the Advancement of Learning in 1837 (Faust, 1981:78). It was printed in 1853 in *The Pro-Slavery Argument*.
7. George Fitzhugh, *Cannibals All! or Slaves Without Masters* (Cambridge, Mass.: Belnap Press, 1960).
8. George Fitzhugh, *Sociology for the South, or the Failure of Free Society* (New York: Burt Franklin, 1965).
9. Dew, "Professor Dew on Slavery," p. 105.
10. Ibid., pp. 326–327.
11. Ibid., p. 339.
12. Ibid., pp. 338–339.
13. Ibid., p. 339.
14. Ibid., pp. 340–341.
15. Ibid., p. 341.
16. Ibid.
17. Ibid., p. 336.
18. Ibid., pp. 336–337.
19. Harper, "Harper's Memoir on Slavery," p. 5.
20. Ibid., p. 4.
21. Ibid., p. 22.
22. Ibid., p. 35.

23. Ibid., p. 32.
24. Ibid., p. 7.
25. Ibid.
26. Ibid., p. 40.
27. Ibid., p. 41.
28. Ibid., p. 44.
29. Ibid., pp. 65–66.
30. Ibid., p. 50.
31. Fitzhugh, *Sociology for the South*, p. 216.
32. Ibid., p. iii.
33. Ibid.
34. Fitzhugh, *Slaves Without Masters*, p. 5.
35. Ibid., p. 72.
36. Ibid., p. 30.
37. Fitzhugh, *Sociology for the South*, p. 244.
38. Fitzhugh, *Slaves Without Masters*, p. 217.
39. Fitzhugh, *Sociology for the South*, p. 46.
40. Ibid., p. 247.
41. Fitzhugh, *Slaves Without Masters*.
42. Bertrand Wyatt-Brown, *Southern Honor: Ethics and Behavior in the Old South* (New York: Oxford University Press, 1982).
43. Fitzhugh, *Slaves Without Masters*, p. 25.
44. Fitzhugh, *Sociology for the South*, p. 278.
45. Ibid., p. 213.
46. Fitzhugh, *Slaves Without Masters*, p. 235.
47. Fitzhugh, *Sociology for the South*, p. 272.
48. Ibid., p. 214.
49. Ibid., pp. 214–215.
50. Ibid., pp. 215–216.
51. Ibid., p. 110.
52. Ibid., pp. 205–206.
53. Harper, "Harper's Memoir on Slavery," p. 341.
54. Fitzhugh, *Sociology for the South*, pp. 214–215.
55. Harper, "Harper's Memoir on Slavery," pp. 336–337.
56. Ibid., pp. 340–341.
57. Jones, *Tomorrow Is Another Day*, p. 13.
58. Phyllis Greenacre, "Child Wife as Ideal: Sociological Considerations," *American Journal of Ortho-Psychiatry* 17:167–171.
59. Harper, "Harper's Memoir on Slavery," pp. 336–337.
60. Ibid., p. 66.
61. Ibid.
62. Ibid., p. 41.
63. Ibid., p. 44.
64. Jane Turner Censer, "Smiling Through Their Tears: Antebellum Southern Women and Divorce," *American Journal of Legal History* 25:24–47.
65. Wyatt-Brown, *Southern Honor*, p. 281.

Chapter 3

"MY OL' BLACK MAMMY" IN AMERICAN HISTORIOGRAPHY

PATRICIA MORTON

In contrast to its austerity for the slave, Southern slavery evokes a rich host of images in the American popular mind. From *Gone With the Wind* to *Mandingo* flow these pictures which live on in our heads. As William Van Deburg has noted, the popular media in effect "endorse traditional stereotypes" of "Uncle Tom and his kin."[1] Thus, the culture's most beloved image of Southern slave women lives on much as in Al Jolson's "My Dear Ol' Mammy"—endorsed by her updated Aunt Jemima face.

Providing a steady diet of mammies even with the very breakfast we consume, the pancake box Jemima reveals the modernization and yet continuity of this old-time figure. Some may recall her as the very dark, obese, and grinning image of yesterday. Today she presides still on the product label, lighter and brighter than ever before, but still in bandana and grinning. Simultaneously perceived as both legend and real historical person—as the most devoted of servants—her visual presence tells us the product must be both good and all-American because so steeped in American history. Hence, she is a valuable product status symbol.

As the sociologist John Dollard observed some half century ago in the midst of the Jim Crow era, the mammy served then too as a symbol of worth. But in the 1930s, for Southern whites, it was the claim actually to have a mammy in the family which imparted the status.[2] The mammy was popular as well among American historians during that era. She was cast in their writings on Old South slavery in a uniformly positive light.

Yet in the historiography of today she has become largely invisible. When she figures at all she is quickly dismissed as a racist and sexist stereotype and

35

myth. In Catherine Clinton's words, she is "a trumped-up, not a triumphant, figure in the mythologizing of slavery."[3]

It is worth pausing here to note that while the "Southern Lady" has also been discovered as a pro-slavery myth, she has enjoyed a good deal of attention in the women's historiography of today. From this has emerged the real woman living behind the myth, as a genuine historical personage deserving of recognition, sympathy, and respect.[4] Her inclusion in history contrasts with the mammy's exclusion. While both figures are recognized as mythic, the question of what lies beneath and beyond them has received differential treatment. Hence, it seems time to consider not only the role of myth in the past, but also what role it may continue to play in the shaping of scholarship today. By reviewing the mammy in American history, this article attempts to ascertain how and why this figure has become a virtual historical untouchable.[5]

As Jesse Parkhurst noted in 1938, "because the 'Black Mammy' originated in . . . the period of bondage, she is an acceptable symbol to whites and an unacceptable one to Negroes."[6] Thus, it was in the white-authored story of history that the mammy emerged, commencing in the America of a century ago when history itself was becoming a professional discipline. It was then, too, that racial segregation became institutionalized in the American South. And in the Jim Crow era which followed, the old slave mammy became embedded in American historiography.

Her introduction into this body of literature in the late 19th century may best be discovered in the historical writings of Thomas Nelson Page. This popular Southern author was a convinced white supremacist who warned of the "ever-menacing, ever-growing Negro Question." This "hostile" and "inferior race," he advised in *The Old South,* threatened to destroy "American civilization." Page also wrote from an unself-consciously pro-Southern perspective, presenting this book as correcting distortions of the South's "true history." In this context, he presented the mammy.[7]

She appeared first there as a person of substantial leisure, to be found "in the shade . . . with her little charge in her arms, sleeping in her ample lap." But she was also industrious in her assistance to the plantation mistress in raising the white children. Clearly she regarded her own family with indifference at best, demonstrating a harshness to her children which contrasted with her tenderness to her white charges. But she found ample reward for this devotion to whites since "the young masters and mistresses were her 'children' long after they had children of their own." Moreover, her role in the Big House provided her with "authority . . . second only to that of the mistress and master," and with enduring respect and security as "an honored member of the [master's] family, universally beloved, universally cared for."[8]

Not a professionally trained historian, Page provided no empirical substantiation of the existence of such a slave woman. But the figure he presented forwarded his rehabilitation of the Southern past by portraying slavery as a loving, familial institution. His "Mammy" epitomized the supposed racial intimacy and harmony of an era when blacks knew their place, in contrast with their menacing "uppityness" after emancipation. Such observations may be made from the perspective of today. But it is equally important to recognize that Page presented this figure as strictly factual, emphasizing that the historian must always "tell the truth, the whole truth, and nothing but the truth."[9] Similarly, the mammy would be presented over and over again as factual by a generation of historians in their stories of the Old South that followed.

As professionals, historians liked to see themselves as akin to scientists in their discovery of the objective reality of the past. However, scholarly interest in Southern history stemmed from forces which promoted pro-Southern perspectives. For one thing, the sociocultural changes associated with modernization inspired a widespread nostalgia for a traditional and orderly world. This found expression in the historians' romanticization of the Old South as the best of times and places. Moreover, Southern slavery took on new appeal in the light of contemporary interest in social order and control. Northern concerns with the seemingly mounting tide of disorder were intensified by nativist reaction to the influx of non-Northern European immigrants, and increasing northward migration of Southern blacks had nationalized white concern with the "Negro Problem" by the 1920s. By then the white supremacist South had put its own house in order, while its oppression of the Negro found rationalization in the romanticization of slavery. From these perspectives, slavery had provided a happiness and well-being for both whites and blacks. Although damaged by the institution's abolition, this harmonious order was being restored by the beneficent workings of Jim Crow. In sum, slavery offered a model of racial and social control. As U. B. Phillips argued, it was a school for civilizing the uncivilized.[10]

This Southern historian's portrayal of slavery as a kindly and paternalistic institution dominated the historiography of the Jim Crow era. And in this pro-Southern body of literature, the slave mammy emerged as the epitome of Old South Virtues—but figuring always as an objective historical fact.

Presented repeatedly as factual, the mammy emerged as a taken-for-granted truth for which no substantiating evidence was necessary. Instead, as in U. B. Phillips's 1918 history of slavery, she was herself offered as evidence of the "intertwined" lives of whites and blacks: "If any special link were needed, the children supplied it. The white ones, hardly knowing their mothers from their mammies, had the freedom of the kitchen and the cabins."[11]

In reiterating this point, historical texts such as Frances Butler Simkins' *The South* added such embellishments as that "white children were suckled by black mammies and played indiscriminately with pickaninnies." This picture appeared unchanged even in the 1963 edition of Simkins' history of the South.[12]

Similarly, in the 1964 edition of Clement Eaton's *History of the Old South* (originally published in 1949), the mammy remained devoted to her white family, suckling the white children, and demonstrating that "a much closer integration of blacks and whites occurred during slavery days than . . . in this century.'' Eaton also noted her keen sense of pride in belonging to ''quality folks,'' and her contempt for her own people.[13]

The mammy was a useful prop to the romanticization of the Old South and a particularly useful symbol because of her gender. That sexual racism so intensely tabooed the coupling of a black male and a white female undermined the practicability of presenting black male symbolization of racial intimacy. But again, it is important to note that in these histories the mammy was always presented as a historical fact—indeed, as a fact too self-evidently true to require even footnoting. Yet as the revision of some texts suggests, the reliability of such conventional academic wisdom was in some doubt by the 1960s.

In his 1927 *Oxford History of the United States,* for example, Samuel Eliot Morison wrote that ''there was no physical repulsion from color in the South. White children were suckled by black mammies and played promiscuously with the pickaninnies.'' But according to the 1965 edition, ''there was no physical repulsion from color in the South. White children were suckled by black 'mammies' and played with their children.''[14]

Indeed, during the Civil Rights era the mammy in historiography came often to be enclosed by quotation marks when she was presented. However, she was practically never presented.

In concert with the dismantlement of Southern segregation, post-World War II historians came to manifest an often acute sensitivity to and attack upon the racist stereotypes of their Jim Crow predecessors. They also turned with a newly critical perspective to the reconstruction of Southern slavery. But in the ensuing flood of slavery studies, the slave mammy became all but invisible. However, sources in which she does not figure at all may help illuminate the origins of her new obscurity.

The de-mammification of Afro-American history becomes evident, for example, in John Blassingame's *The Slave Community.* This 1972 book provided a major challenge to the thesis of slaves as ''Sambos'' that had been advanced particularly in Stanley Elkins's 1959 examination of slavery. ''Sambo'' constituted an image of Negro infantilization and, in effect, emasculation. And such an image inspired passionate rejection especially in the context of the black movement's emphasis on racial pride and ''manliness.'' Blassingame's book forcefully confirmed that ''Sambo'' could be dismissed as a racial stereotype. It had originated, he found, as the invention of slaveholders in need of relief from ''the anxiety of thinking about slaves as men.''[15]

Blassingame's book's eloquent reconstruction of slaves as men, however, provided little information about slaves as women, or even as female stereotypes. According to Blassingame, in antebellum literature ''Sambo, Jack, and Nat'' were ''the major slave characters.'' But the ''Mammy'' was a major stock character as well and a figure that cannot be subsumed under that male trio.[16] However, Blassingame and other slavery historians almost without exception treated slaves as if most were men. As Nathan Huggins observed, the new Afro-American history ''saw the function of history . . . [as] closely related to the concept of national myth.'' And to provide ''a myth that defines the black nation'' it was appealing ''to see an Afro-American history as a way to celebrate (and to create) great black men.''[17]

In this context the new slavery studies relegated slave women, when they appeared, to traditional ''feminine'' roles. Moreover, it was all the more necessary to emphasize that slave culture was patriarchal because of the 1965 Moynihan Report, which labeled it as matriarchal. The underlying research on the Negro family, conducted for the Johnson Administration by Daniel Patrick Moynihan, with its subsequent report[18] was intended to be the basis for policy formation. Thus it was taken seriously, and its thesis became immensely controversial.

According to Moynihan, because of slavery's oppressiveness, the slave family became a fatherless, female-dominated, ''disorganized'' institution. Over time, this ''black matriarchy'' had become a self-perpetuating familial pattern which now constituted ''the fundamental source of weakness in the Negro community.'' It lay at the core of the ''tangle of pathology'' from which stemmed a host of social evils such as juvenile delinquency, crime, and welfare dependency. Thus, it imposed ''a crushing burden on the Negro male.'' And so Moynihan seemingly confirmed that the black man was an emasculated ''Sambo'' and was the cause of continuing black inequality. But critics quickly labeled this thesis as the ''myth of the Black Matriarchy.''[19]

In this heated context, historians strove to demonstrate that the father-led black family had not been destroyed by slavery. And in restoring black male authority and ''manliness'' they had little interest in slave women in general. But the mammy was more than irrelevant. Such an image of maternal strength, independence from the black man and slave community, and indifference to her own family was all too complementary to Moynihan's image of black female dominance and damage. Moreover, by the 1960s the association of mammy with matriarchy had been materially forwarded by popular media typecasting. Reshaping the jolly ''Aunt Jemima'' in the image of the bossy ''Sapphire'' stereotype of Amos 'n Andy, the radio and film industry and television had cast mammies as masculinized women who wore the pants in their own families.[20]

Perhaps most stigmatizing of all, the mammy's racial intimacy repute, from black nationalist perspectives, cast her in the enemy's camp. She figured thus in Eldrich Cleaver's warning: ''There is a war going on between the black man and the black woman which makes her the silent ally, indirectly but effectively, of the white man . . . All down through history, he has propped her up economically above you and me. . . . He turned the black woman into a strong self-reliant Amazon and deposited her in his kitchen—that's the secret of Aunt Jemima's bandana.''[21]

The new slavery historiography revealed little of such explicit misogyny. But the new obscurity of the mammy therein constituted, in effect, a political statement about the black identity and racial strategy.

The mammy made but rare and fleeting appearances in this literature. For example, in over 600 pages of Herbert Gutman's *The Black Family in Slavery and Freedom,* she appeared only in an endnote. In this note, Gutman observed that after the abolition of slavery most black female domestic servants were young, unmarried women attempting to supplement the incomes of their parents. As he dismissively noted, this served to contradict the popular stereotype of the old slave "mammy" whose work was a labor of love for the white family.[22]

Certainly Eugene Genovese was alone in presenting the mammy as more than merely a derogatory stereotype and, indeed, as a real woman of history deserving of attention and even respect. In spite of his recognition of her "steadily worsening press," this historian asked what slave woman might live behind the "white legend": "Who were these Mammies? What did they actually do?" In answer Genovese discovered that the legend represented at least a kernel of truth. She did raise the white children and love them, but did not, therefore, withdraw love from her own family. Moreover, this most "important black presence in the Big House" was a figure of considerable power. She served as the plantation mistress's "executive officer or her 'de facto' superior." This role and the devotion of the white family to her made her an authoritative rather than servile figure. Her loyalty to whites did not mean disloyalty to blacks. Instead, she used her power to protect her own kinfolk from hardship and sale and to further the master's attention to the needs of his slaves. In sum, she demonstrated "courage, compassion, dignity, and self-respect" as a "tough, worldly-wise, enormously resourceful woman." Indeed, in this book she was even liberated from her quotation marks. But the racial politics of this era worked strongly against such a positive reconstruction.[23]

Thus, for example, Robert Harris charged that Genovese, like "too many white historians" continued to view "slavery through the slavemasters' lens." He pointed to James D. Anderson for "an incisive critique." According to Anderson, Genovese's "reverence for the Mammy" distorted the coercive basis of slavery and denied the slave's political will to resist. But, he noted, "too much work had gone into the making of the Aunt Jemima image for it to disappear" in response to the black movement's call for a nonracist history. Hence, such historians had changed only the form and not the substance of their old images, just as the pancake box image had been "transfigured by bright and shining colors." In sum, in Anderson's view, "like Aunt Jemima, American scholarship to a large extent became sugar-coated. . . . Though her complexion had been presumably improved, her heart remained the same."[24] And in sum, to reconstruct the "Old Black Mammy" as more than a racist myth has been to risk guilt by association with such an unacceptable figure.

The myth itself, however, has at last inspired some historical attention in concert with the zeal of the new women's historians for unearthing even the most negative images of women. Indeed, as Nina Auerbach has noted, "Gleefully . . . we identified pernicious 'myths' and 'images' of women" in order to slay them with facts.[25] Thus, the "Mammy" has now been discovered as not only a racist but also a sexist myth which underpins the oppression of not only black but also white women.

Some have emphasized the myth's damage to Afro-American women. As Karen Sue Warren Jewell argues, for example, it has perpetuated their typing as suited only for menial service to whites. As Mae King writes, it has defeminized black womanhood in a way that has propped up the "power distance" between whites and blacks. As Bell Hooks observes, "it epitomized the ultimate sexist-racist vision of ideal black womanhood—complete submission to the will of whites . . . the embodiment of woman as passive nurturer; a mother figure who gave all without expectation of return."[26]

In other studies the "Mammy" has emerged as a weapon of patriarchal politics that has been oppressive to all women. In Barbara Christian's view, for example, the myth was an outgrowth of the repressive, patriarchal cult of the Southern Lady. The cult prescribed the role of the plantation mistress: to display her husband's status and power by her freedom from work and her decorative and moral attributes and to provide numerous offspring for the patriarchy's perpetuation. But these roles and her unacknowledged one as plantation manager contradicted her supposed leisure, delicacy, and ornamental function. Hence, in practice she needed and was provided with the assistance of a real slave mammy. But for the "Lady" to be a credible ideal of Southern womanhood also required an idealized servant companion, assigned complementary moral qualities and contrasting physical attributes. Hence, the "Mammy" became a major stock character in Southern fiction, one whose attributes of devotion and piety reinforced the image of white womanhood as the flower and epitome of Southern virtue. And that she always figured in this literature as tough, ugly, and masculinized highlighted the ultrafemininity assigned to the "Lady." Thus, the mammy myth propped up the patriarchy's depowering pedestalization of Southern white womanhood. In Christian's words, "The image of the Mammy, then, cannot be seen in a vacuum; she is a necessary correlate to the lady. If one was to be, the other had to be."[27]

Catherine Clinton has denied any objective, historical existence to the mammy. Since antebellum primary sources provided no "hard evidence" for her reality, in Clinton's view she was but a mythical creation "of the combined romantic imaginations of the contemporary southern ideologue and the modern southern historian." The myth answered abolitionist images of hapless slave women pursued by rapacious masters by presenting the master-slave relationship as desexualized. And presenting black female strength, it thereby confirmed that the black male was an emasculated "Sambo" suited only for slavery. At the same time, the image of the white male suckling at black breasts also reduced the black woman to a body to be milked in a way that promoted the dichotomization of Southern women into white ladies and black whores. By associating deviation from the "Lady" role with the stigmatization of black womanhood, such polarization propped up patriarchal control of white as well as black women.[28]

As a truly multipurpose myth, the "Mammy" has also been decodified by Deborah White. In her view the myth grew first as a counterimage of the "Jezebel" stereotype of the slave woman as inherently sensual and promiscuous. The latter image was useful in countering the antislavery charges of white sexual exploitation of black women. But it also contradicted the South's taboos against miscegenation and its cult of female purity. Hence, the "Mammy" image cast the good slave woman as maternal, old, and thoroughly desexualized. Moreover, it complemented the growth of the ideology of domesticity which prescribed feminine roles as extensions of motherhood and family. Thus, as "the personification of the ideal slave and the ideal woman, Mammy was an ideal myth of the patriarchal tradition."[29]

While focusing on the myth, however, White does ask if it might represent any objective, historical reality. In answer she argues that while it was true that most slave domestics were female, in the Big House it was several such women who shared the various tasks attributed by legend to the mammy. Moreover, the plantation mistress herself did much of the work assigned by myth to the mammy. In sum, "female household service does not square with the Mammy legend."[30] And in sum White has arrived at essentially the same conclusion as other women's historians: that mammy was a myth rather than a reality. Indeed, in American historiography at least, the mammy has been thoroughly transfigured from historical fact to historical fiction and fallacy. This transfiguration, however, seems itself—to recall Anderson's words—to be based upon form rather than substance. Certainly it has been based upon little or no new research and evidence. With the exception of White's somewhat more extended discussion, any recent attention to the mammy adds up to but a few textual pages in total.

White suggests that the historian faces a dilemma in studying the objective reality of a figure that seems discoverable largely only in the same sources that transmitted the mammy legend. Hence, the difficulty of examining this figure without adding credibility to the myth.[31] This is both a perceptive insight, and one which reveals the prevailing consensus that the myth, in effect, cannot be credible. Because so racist and sexist, it must be a fiction and a fallacy. In this context, any real, historical women living behind it would be a discovery no one would wish to make.

The problem does not seem to lie in a dearth of reliable sources, although slaves, in general, have been unable to speak to historians for themselves. But that they could not leave their own written record has not deterred the historians' discovery of them. Instead, the slave experience has richly been reconstructed, as Van Deburg has observed, "as a triumph of the human spirit over adversity."[32] Nor have slave women remained marginalized figures. They emerge in the new black women's historiography in a variety of roles ranging from workers and mothers to black nationalist and feminist forebears.[33]

American historiography has in the past assigned to Afro-American women, in Michele Wallace's words, "a hell of a history to live down."[34] The mammy myth was woven into and out of that historical story. The matriarchy emerged from it too. But it seems increasingly possible to transcend the confines of the matriarchal mythology. Certainly the slave woman's strength, and her centrality to black triumph over adversity, emerge ever more clearly in today's historiography. It seems time now to explore more freely her diversity so that she may be discovered as a multidimensional, fully human woman of the Southern past.

The "Ol' Black Mammy" may, in fact, represent no objective reality. This answer, however, is uncertain because the question remains essentially unasked. What is clear is that the scholarly will and ability to ask is limited by rightful condemnation of the images identified as surrounding her. But the popular culture's "Aunt Jemima" easily survives the stigma of scholarly dismissal. And so long as we fail to ask freely the historian's questions—did the slave mammy exist and, if so, who was she—we reveal only the enduring power of a myth with so much history to live down that it continues to shape the writing of history today.

NOTES

1. William Van Deberg, *Slavery and Race in American Popular Culture* (Madison, WI: University of Wisconsin Press, 1984), p. 158.
2. John Dollard, *Caste and Class in a Southern Town* (1937; reprint ed., New York: Doubleday Anchor Books, 1957), p. 82.
3. Catherine Clinton, *The Plantation Mistress: Woman's World in the Old South* (New York: Pantheon Books, 1984), p. 202.
4. Ibid. See also, for example, Anne Firor Scott, *The Southern Lady: From Pedestal to Politics 1830–1930* (Chicago: University of Chicago Press, 1970), and Jean E. Friedman, *The Enclosed Garden: Women in the Evangelical South, 1825–1885* (Chapel Hill, NC: University of North Carolina Press, 1985).
5. Today's scholarly custom of enclosing the mammy within quotation marks signifies she is regarded as a stereotype representing no objective historical reality. This article follows such a custom only when explicitly referring to the mammy in that light. For discussion of the role of myth in the writing of history see, for example, Peter Munz, *The Shapes of Time: A New Look at the Philosophy of History* (Middleton, CT: Wesleyan University Press, 1977), pp. 113–150.
6. Jesse Parkhurst, "The Role of the Black Mammy in the Plantation Household," *Journal of Negro History* 23(1938):349.
7. Thomas Nelson Page, *The Old South* (1889; reprint ed., Chautauqua, NY: The Chautauqua Press, 1919), pp. 320, 342, 291.
8. Ibid., pp. 149, 165, 156.
9. Ibid., p. 273.
10. Ulrich Bonnell Phillips, *American Negro Slavery* (1918; reprint ed., Baton Rouge, LA: Louisiana State University Press, 1966). On the interest of historians in slavery, see Van Deburg, *Slavery and Race in American Popular Culture.*
11. Phillips, *American Negro Slavery,* p. 313.
12. Francis Butler Simkins, *The South, Old and New, A History, 1920–1947* (New

York: Alfred A. Knopf, 1947), pp. 63, 45; compare with Francis Butler Simkins, *A History of the South,* 3rd and revised edition of *The South, Old and New,* with different title (New York: Knopf, 1963), p. 126.

13. Clement Eaton, *A History of the Old South* (1949; reprint ed., New York: Macmillan Co., 1964), p. 259.

14. Samuel Eliot Morison, *Oxford History of the United States* (New York: Oxford University Press, 1927), p. 8; Samuel Eliot Morison, *Oxford History of the American People,* revised ed. (New York: Oxford University Press, 1964), pp. 5–6.

15. John Blassingame, *The Slave Community: Plantation Life in the Antebellum South,* revised edition (New York: Oxford University Press, 1979), p. 230; Stanley Elkins, *Slavery* (Chicago: The University of Chicago Press, 1959).

16. For example, Barbara Christian, *Black Women Novelists: The Development of a Tradition, 1982–1976* (Westport, CT: Greenwood Press, 1980), pp. 10–12; Blassingame, *The Slave Community,* p. 224.

17. Nathan I. Huggins, "Afro-American History: Myths, Heroes, Reality," in *Key Issues in the Afro-American Experience,* Vol. I, Martin Kilson and Daniel Fox, eds. (New York: Harcourt Brace Jovanovich, Inc., 1971), pp. 11–12.

18. Daniel Patrick Moynihan, "The Moynihan Report: The Negro Family: The Case for National Action," in *The Moynihan Report and the Politics of Controversy,* Lee Rainwater and William Yancey, eds. (Cambridge, MA: Massachusetts Institute of Technology Press, 1965), pp. 39, 124.

19. Ibid., pp. 29, 75. The sociological controversy is presented in Rainwater and Yancey's book; the historical controversy is indicated, for example, in Eugene Genovese, "The Slave Family—Women—A Reassessment of Matriarchy, Emasculation, Weakness," *Southern Voices* 2(1974):9–66.

20. See for example, Karen Sue Warren Jewell, "An Analysis of the Visual Development of a Stereotype: The Media's Portrayal of the Mammy and Aunt Jemima as Symbols of Black Womanhood" (Ph.D. diss., Ohio State University, 1976); and Edward Mapp, "Black Women in Films," *The Black Scholar* 4(1973):42–46.

21. Eldridge Cleaver, *Soul on Ice* (New York: Delta/Dell Publications, 1968), p. 162.

22. Herbert Gutman, *The Black Family in Slavery and Freedom, 1750–1925* (Vintage Books/Random House, 1977), Note 7, p. 632.

23. Eugene Genovese, *Roll, Jordan, Roll: The World the Slaves Made* (New York: Vintage Books, 1976), pp. 353–361.

24. Robert Harris, "Coming of Age: The Transformation of Afro-American Historiography," *Journal of Negro History* 67(1982):114, 120; James Anderson, "Aunt Jemima in Dialectics: Genovese on Slave Culture," *Journal of Negro History* 61(1976):99.

25. Nina Auerbach, *Woman and Demon: The Life of a Victorian Myth* (Cambridge, MA: Harvard University Press, 1982), pp. 2–3.

26. Jewell, "An Analysis of the Visual Development of a Stereotype"; Mae King, "The Politics of Sexual Stereotypes," *Black Scholar* 4(1973):12–23; and Bell Hooks, *Ain't I a Woman: Black Women and Feminism* (Boston: South End Press, 1981), p. 84.

27. Christian, *Black Women Novelists,* p. 12.

28. Clinton, *The Plantation Mistress,* pp. 201–202.

29. Deborah White, *Ar'n't I a Woman: Female Slaves in the Ante-Bellum South* (New York: Norton, 1985), p. 58. For her discussion of these images, see pp. 27–61.

30. Ibid., p. 56.
31. Deborah White, "Ain't I a Woman? Female Slaves in the Antebellum South" (Ph.D. diss., University of Illinois, 1979), p. 246.
32. Van Deburg, *Slavery and Race,* p. 140.
33. The discovery of slave women commenced with Gerda Lerner, ed., *Black Women in White America: A Documentary History* (New York: Vintage Books, 1973). Since then, black women's history has become an exploding field and fully inclusive of slave women. See for example, Jacquelyne Jones, " 'My Mother Was Much of a Woman': Black Women, Work, and the Family Under Slavery," *Feminist Studies* 8(1982):235–267; Angela Davis, "The Legacy of Slavery: Standards for a New Womanhood," in *Women, Race and Class,* Angela Davis, ed. (New York: Vintage/Random House, 1983), pp. 3–29; and Deborah White, *Ar'n't I a Woman.* For freed slave women, see Suzanne Lebsock, *The Free Women of Petersburg: Status and Culture in a Southern Town, 1784–1860* (New York: W. W. Norton & Co., 1984). For a theoretical discussion of the historical relationship of slavery to patriarchy, see Gerda Lerner, "Women and Slavery," *Slavery and Abolition* 4(1983):173–197.
34. Michele Wallace, *Black Macho and the Myth of the Superwoman* (New York: Warner Books, 1979), p. 133.

Chapter 4
TOWARD AN UNDERSTANDING OF THE QUADROON SOCIETY OF NEW ORLEANS, 1780–1860

MARY GEHMAN

New Orleans 1988—two black women are overheard chatting on the bus:
"You know Clothilde, the high yellow woman, the pass-en. From the Seventh Ward, you remember? Her momma, Miss Sophia, always wear a chin-ya, *you* know!"

"Ah, the Creole. She went to St. Mary's. Sure. She the one used to make good yacamein, no?"

The tourist turns with a quizzical expression to catch a glimpse of the two friends as they leave the bus. Are these women speaking English? Yes and no. Their references to "high yellow" (light-skinned), "pass-en" (pass for white), Seventh Ward (area of the city), "chin-ya" (head scarf), Creole (person of mixed blood), St. Mary's (girls' Catholic school), and "yacamein" (turtle soup) are common to native Orleanians, especially those in the black community. To explain them to an outsider, however, requires patience and a big step back into the history of New Orleans, its women, and the society called the "Quadroons," free women of color who served as mistresses for French men from the late 1700s up to Civil War times.

Although the influence of these women of a century and a half ago is as subconscious as the terms so casually exchanged by the two friends on the bus, it is profound, far reaching, and yet clouded with misunderstanding and obscurity. Since no written records or history of the quadroons exist, their legacy is largely one of conjecture, rumor, and romanticism.

Even the semantics of race in terms of these women and their descendants is a difficult matter. The term *quadroon* was originally used to describe anyone having one-fourth black blood. Since the early days of New Orleans the word has been used sometimes as that definition; more often, however, as a collective name for black women who were mistresses of French settlers. It is rare to read about quadroon men—although there were many one-fourth black-blooded males; the term is used almost exclusively for women. The word *Creole* meant originally anyone born in the Louisiana Territory. The term *criollo* from the Spanish word for "mixed" applied to the various racial combinations found in Louisiana in the early years: French-Spanish, French-African, African-Indian, and so on. "Creole society," however, referred to the French settlers and their immediate families. Through two and a half centuries the term *Creole* has come to mean light-skinned blacks, the descendants of the quadroons and other European and African liaisons.[1] Today one never uses the term *quadroon* but rather *Creole*.

The quadroons are mentioned in a number of traditional histories of the city. The German Duke of Saxe-Weimar-Eisenach visited America in 1825 and wrote enthusiastically of his experience with the quadroons of New Orleans. "The quadroon women," he writes, "coquetted with me in the most subtle and amusing manner." To the duke these women were "the most beautiful women in the world."[2]

Around the same time, an anonymous English traveler is quoted as comparing the quadroons with high-class Hindus. He tells of their "lovely countenances, lips of coral, teeth of pearl, full, dark liquid eyes and their sylph-like figures."[3]

Harriet Martineau mentions the quadroons in her book, *Society in America,* published in 1837. She notes, "The quadroon girls are highly educated, externally and are, probably, as beautiful and accomplished a set of women as can be found. Every young man early selects one and establishes her in . . . her own house."[4]

These popular historical accounts also go on to describe the lavish quadroon balls given to introduce the young available quadroon women to their prospective French lovers. Some authors mention the second row of loges at the famous French theaters being reserved for the quadroons, who "because of their richness of dress and eccentricity attracted all the glances."[5] Reportedly the first quadroon ball was held in 1805 for women of color and white gentlemen. The ballroom on St. Philip Street had held dances there for blacks since 1799.

Duels came to be associated with quadroon balls. Historian Herbert Asbury states, "More duels probably originated there than at any other place in New Orleans, for the Creole [Frenchman] was even quicker to resent a fancied slight or insult to his colored mistress than to his white wife or fiancee."[6]

From the earliest days of the Southern novel the quadroon has been a favorite staple. In 1856 Captain Mayne Reid wrote *The Quadroon,* a romantic novel.[7] During that same era George Washington Cable and Grace King, both New Orleans natives, published a number of short stories and novels about the Creoles of Louisiana among whom the quadroon figured strongly.[8] William

Faulkner used a quadroon woman from New Orleans as an influential character in *Absalom! Absalom!* in the early 1930s, Edward Larocque Tinker wrote the locally popular *Toucatou* in 1928, and more recently Anne Rice has published *The Feast of All Saints,* a novel depicting the daily life of a quadroon.[9]

The image of the quadroon that emerges from these fictional treatments is one of a rather stoic and ambitious woman who accepts her fate as the mistress of a French man, schemes to have her children by him rise to a higher standard of living, and is cut off from the men of her own race. How much of this is romanticism and how much authentic historical truth is impossible to determine.

Arthé Agnes Anthony finds that there are obvious limitations in the observations of travelers and visitors in that they tend to "be superficial with an emphasis on the unusual." They should be considered, she writes, as the interpretation of outsiders biased by the prejudices of their times. The value of such observations is suspect and can best be viewed as how others saw the free Negro community of that day.[10]

What *is* known about the quadroons is that there was a significant community of free women of color in New Orleans from the earliest days; that some of these women became mistresses of French men; that they could not marry their French lovers due to the ban on miscegenation; that some of these women were given houses, property, and financial support by their French lovers; that children were frequently born to these liaisons; that these children usually received their father's French surname and, in some cases, were educated and received indirect inheritances from their father; that some of these quadroons never married but were faithful to their French lover long after he had taken a French wife; that the French wife was often aware of her husband's quadroon mistress; that the quadroon system ended with the Civil War.

Information crucial to understanding who these quadroon women were but that is *not* known includes what the exact size of the quadroon community was; what the women's names and their birth and death dates were; where they lived; what professions they had; what their medical history was; what their social life among their own people was like; how the term *quadroon* came to be applied to these women; how many actually became mistresses of French men; how long these liaisons lasted on the average; the extent to which the quadroons were educated; how they perceived themselves in terms of the black community (slave and free) in New Orleans at the time; what their attitudes were toward their French lovers; how the quadroons felt about being mistresses of these men; what their attitudes were toward men of their own race; what their aspirations were for themselves and their children; how they supported themselves in cases where their French lovers discontinued the relationship; to what extent French men supported their families of color; how many instances of the romantic relationship between the quadroon and the French man were more meaningful to the man than was his relationship with his French wife.

In other words, a lot less *is* known about the quadroons than what is *not* known, and we have a very fragmented and incomplete picture of who these women were. What we don't know is of greater importance than what we do know, making it virtually impossible to understand them, judge them, or gain a meaningful and accurate image of them. They are truly a shadowy and nearly missing link in New Orleans history, in the history of black people of the South, and in the history of American women, in particular Afro-American women. Gerda Lerner in her comprehensive documentary history *Black Women in White America* gives not even passing mention of the quadroons. Chapter 1 is titled "Slavery: Purchase and Sale"; the book proceeds from there as if *free* women of color never existed.[11] This is typical of most treatments of black history, whether for lack of material on such groups as the quadroons and Creoles of color or for lack of awareness that they constituted a significant sector of the black population of the South.

The blackout on knowledge and documentation of the quadroons is due to several factors. To begin with, we have no idea how many of these women could read and write. There are records showing that as early as the 1730s the Ursuline nuns in New Orleans took some black girls into their convent school. By the 1840s the Sisters of the Holy Family, an order of black nuns founded in New Orleans by the daughter of a quadroon, Henriette DeLisle, were operating a school for the children of free persons of color. Since historical references to the quadroons show them as French speaking, cultured, and intelligent with professions such as hairdresser, dressmaker, nurse, and guest house proprietress, it is fair to assume that at least some of these women had a rudimentary education.

Second, we do not know what became of any written mementos left by either the quadroon or her French master-lover. It is totally understandable that upon the death of the French man his white family would have destroyed any and all evidence of his relationship with a woman of color to hide it from future generations of his white family. If the family of the quadroon kept any mementos, they have not surfaced in libraries, archives, or special collections. Quite possibly they were not carefully saved, especially after the Civil War when one's fraction of white blood was no longer an issue in racial identity.

A third consideration is that documents such as birth, marriage, and death records were kept in the early years by the parish priest. It is common knowledge that priests were not above being persuaded to alter facts and records for the proper monetary inducement. Therefore, many of these records are not accurate regarding race. To this day the records of the Sisters of the Holy Family, the black nuns, are closely guarded for fear that disclosure of whose ancestors attended their school and orphanage might cause problems for families who have long passed for white.

For these basic reasons there is literally no historical documentation available on the quadroons. In 1890 Charles Gayarré, eminent Louisiana historian of French Creole descent, ruminated that "it is quite impossible to find a sketch of the quadroons that is carefully and truthfully drawn." He encouraged his contemporaries to consult the few elderly people who remember "the days of the so-called quadroon domination'' because, as Gayarré pointed out, ''the picture they paint is far different from that which one sees in all printed accounts.''[12] To the regret of subsequent generations, his advice apparently was never followed, for there is no account of such interviews ever having been made.

It was not until the 1970s in the aftermath of the civil rights movement and the election of the first black mayor in New Orleans—Ernest Dutch Morial, the descendant of a Creole family of color—that New Orleans blacks began seriously to study the role and contributions of free people of color in the city's history. The main source for such study was a book *Our People and Our History* by Rudolphe L. Desdunes, a black Creole of New Orleans who wrote his book in French in the early 20th century. His French Creole, the language spoken by the black Creole community, was not translated into English and published until 1973.[13]

Desdunes does not single out the quadroon women, but he lauds the black Creole women in general for their piety and charity, their generous services to the church, their feeding of the poor, and their role as ''nursing women'' to victims of frequent yellow fever epidemics.[14]

An interesting aside not developed by Desdunes or other scholars but questions well worth raising are: why were the women of color such reliable nurses to yellow fever victims and why were they not afraid of contracting the fever themselves? Apparently they were not, for blacks in general counted far fewer casualties during the epidemics in New Orleans. This was due, reportedly, to the sickle-cell trait, known to guard against yellow fever in Africa. This fact of nature gave the quadroons and other persons of color a distinct advantage over whites in 19th-century New Orleans and explains the figure of the quadroon as nurse in local history and literature.[15]

Using Desdunes's book as a base, Gilbert E. Martin in 1981 became a political mouthpiece with his book *Creoles: A Shattered Nation* that called for the recognition of Creole as a nationality and the French Creole language as a legitimate language of New Orleans.[16] Martin protests the ''extensive efforts that have been exerted toward creating a white monopoly on the term Creole.'' He insists that ''without our history in its true perspective, we shall continue . . . not knowing who we are, where we came from . . . where we are heading, and the whys behind it all. As it stands today we are in every respect a shattered nation.''[17]

Martin's call for a complete history of the Creoles of color runs into the same snag on the question of the quadroons. In his discussion of these elusive women he notes that not even the census of the early days of New Orleans can be relied upon. ''There has never been an accurate racial census in the state of Louisiana,'' he writes. ''How could there be 1,500 unmarried 'women of color, all free' in the colony in 1788 when the census of 1785, only three years earlier, counted 1,303 free mulattos all total?''[18]

As a further complication, Martin observes that the source for the census reports also mentions that, ''many of these women were quadroons or even lighter in color." Martin adds that "a person lighter in color was considered an octaroon [sic] (one-eighth Negro blood), and according to the 1785 census, quadroons and octaroons [sic] were counted as white. How could one census count them as white and another count them as 'colored' and both be accurate?"[19]

Martin's book has not made much headway on the subject of documenting the Creoles of color. Since 1981 there have been several papers about the Creoles written and presented by the scholars but nothing substantial in terms of Martin's claim to nationhood. Toni Jones, who conducts the Black Heritage Tour of New Orleans, has noted that many local blacks on her tours do not feel comfortable hearing about and discussing the quadroon system. It seems to them something to be ashamed of. But Jones says she thinks it is an essential element of local black heritage and that her interpretation of it is one of pride, since the quadroon women took the situation they were given and made it work to their advantage. "Black women are still doing that today," she says, "taking a bad situation and making something good of it."[20]

Contradictory statistics aside, there is good reason to believe that free women of color greatly outnumbered men in that category from the earliest days of New Orleans and that but for the quadroon system it is possible that few would have had the opportunity to raise children. The more that becomes known about this unique group, the more it appears that the quadroon system was perhaps a mutually beneficial arrangement between free women of color with few prospects of marriage and young French men who had no other sexual outlet until their mid-20s when they were expected to have a legitimate French family. Because white women were very scarce during the 1700s, many of these men had no one to marry.[21]

Free people of color in New Orleans derived from two groups: freed slaves and free immigrants from the West Indies. The Code Noir, or Black Code, that governed the treatment of slaves by their masters in Louisiana was established in 1724, six years after the city's founding, and provided for slaves being freed in two ways—purchasing their freedom or being set free by their master, a custom relatively common by masters on their deathbeds in gratitude to faithful slaves.

There were not many male slaves in New Orleans as the lack of plantations left little demand for males. At most a family estate owned a coachman, a stableman, and a butler or two. The care of the house and family was largely the responsibility of slave women. Consequently it is believed freed slaves tended to be predominately women.

The influx of both whites and free blacks from Santo Domingo to New Orleans in the late 1700s during the slave uprisings led by Toussaint L'Ouverture created a community of French-speaking people of color who, once they reached Louisiana, could no longer be held as slaves. As most black men either were killed in the uprisings or stayed on to help continue the fight, it was predominantly women and children who managed to escape and make their way to New Orleans.

For nearly a century the community of free people of color thrived quietly in New Orleans. Or at least there is no information to the contrary. The men were artisans and craftsmen, well respected and given every right of a white man except they could not vote nor hold public office and they had to be careful to always add to their signature in any legal matters the notation "f.m.c." (free man of color). Some of these men amassed fortunes and even owned slaves.[22]

The free women of color, outnumbering the men in their group, early on became a threat to white women. Unbridled by the strict decorum and chaperones of the young French women, the free women of color were in a position to be openly flirtatious toward men in general and to be more sensual in their dress and demeanor. As early as the late 1780s it had reached the point where a law had to be passed branding these women as inferior. The "tignon law" (also called "chignon law") prohibited women of color from wearing hats in public. Since a woman could not appear in public without her head covered, this would have logically left the free women of color with resorting to wearing the bandana, a symbol of the black slave mammy. Making the best of the situation the free women of color cleverly adapted their tignons (or head scarves) by choosing fabrics in beautiful colors and piling them high on their heads like turbans. As a final touch they slipped jewels and feathers into the folds of their tignons, thus managing to still appear elegant and stylish, despite the law meant to stigmatize them.[23]

At what point young French men began to practice the custom of "placage," or concubinage, with these women is not clear, but there is evidence that it began early on and was perhaps the continuation of the French-Spanish custom in the West Indies where liaisons of white men with black and Indian women were more or less accepted.

Gayarré suggests that in 1890 this system of concubinage in New Orleans kept common prostitution out of the city in the early years. He comments that with the late arrival of "the first white women, professionally corrupt, who came from the North . . . what had been open concubinage, deplorable indeed, but restricted within some limits of decency, became a secret, unbridled and coarse libertinism."[24]

French girls in New Orleans were married off at age 14 or 15 to husbands —often their first or second cousins—preselected by both families to keep blood lines pure and family estates intact. Given these marriages of convenience and the fact that French women spent the majority of their adult lives pregnant in order to have two or three surviving sons, it can be assumed that the French men sought romance and intimacy elsewhere, namely with their quadroon mistresses. The French men did not marry until their mid- to late 20s when they had the experience and the money to support a family and run the family business. Although they are reported to have been attentive to their wives and children, these men were also known to spend much of their time in offices, cafés, and gambling houses. It is not inconceivable that the young free woman of color with whom the French man sowed his wild oats prior to marriage remained in some instances his true love and that he made frequent visits to her and their children. There are accounts where in the French opera a man's white family occupied the upper loge, while his colored family sat in the loge below.

What this system did to create animosity and despair between the two families is left to conjecture, as there are no first-person accounts. But it is easy to imagine that both classes of women endured with uneasy acceptance a system into which they had been born and over which they had little if any control.

A present-day descendant of the quadroon system is Aline St. Julien, an outspoken civil rights and black pride advocate and New Orleans native. In a booklet she wrote in 1977 called *Colored Creole: Color Conflict and Confusion in New Orleans,* she tells what it was like to be light-skinned enough to pass for white during the years of desegregation and civil rights demonstrations and the consequent identity crisis that she faced. She concludes in a matter-of-fact statement which is a culmination of her background: "Being a Colored Creole-Catholic Negro-Afro-American has brought me through the struggle of finding my true identity. All of these, race, class, and religion has made me Black. Thank you, God. Salaam."[25]

The true history of the quadroons may never be known. A hundred years removed from the last living quadroons leaves us no choice but to piece together the few vague references available and to read between the lines of the romanticized versions of their lives. Like St. Julien, we are wise to acknowledge their presence among us as Southern women and to recognize that our identity today is inextricably interwoven with theirs.

NOTES

1. Joseph G. Tregle, "On that Word Creole Again: A Note," *Louisiana History* (1982): 193–198. For a detailed study of the subject see Virginia R. Dominguez, *White by Definition: Social Classification in Creole Louisiana* (New Brunswick, NJ: Rutgers University Press, 1986).
2. Mary Scott Duchein, "Research on Charles Etienne Arthur Gayarré" (master's thesis, Louisiana State University, 1934), p. 118.
3. Ibid.
4. Ibid., p. 120.
5. Ibid., p. 128.
6. See Herbert Asbury, *The French Quarter* (New York: Knopf, 1936), p. 134.
7. Mayne Reid, *The Quadroon* (New York: Robert Dewitt, 1856).
8. For example, see George Washington Cable, *Old Creole Days* (New York: Charles Scribner's Sons, 1879), *The Grandissimes* (New York: Charles Scribner's Sons, 1880), and *Madame Delphine* (New York: Charles Scribner's Sons, 1881); Grace King, *Monsieur Motte* (New York: A. C. Armstrong & Sons, 1888), *Tales of a Time and Place* (New York: Harper, 1892), and *La Dame de Sainte Hermine* (New York: Macmillan Co., 1924).
9. William Faulkner, *Absalom! Absalom!* (New York: Random House, 1936); Edward L. Tinker, *Toucatou* (New York: Dodd, Mead & Company, 1928); Anne Rice, *The Feast of All Saints* (New York: Simon and Schuster, 1979).
10. Arthé Agnes Anthony, "The Negro Creole Community in New Orleans,

1880–1920: An Oral History'' (Ph.D. diss., University of California, Irvine, 1978), pp. 8–9.

11. See Gerda Lerner, *Black Women in White America: A Documentary History* (New York: Vintage, 1973).

12. Duchein, "Research on Charles Etienne Arthur Gayarré," p. 148.

13. Rudolphe L. Desdunes, *Our People and Our History* (Baton Rouge, LA: Louisiana State University Press, 1973).

14. Ibid., pp. 97–98.

15. See David Connell Rankin, "The Forgotton People: Free People in New Orleans, 1850–1870" (Ph.D. diss., Johns Hopkins University, 1976), p. 33, where he notes that Louisiana blacks were resistant to yellow fever because it was endemic to Africa, but they did suffer from smallpox and cholera. The author of this paper is not aware of any documentation for the sickle-cell trait's guarding against yellow fever, but several local physicians have stated that the sickle-cell trait is considered one of the possible reasons why yellow fever is rare among blacks.

16. Gilbert E. Martin, *Creoles: A Shattered Nation* (New Orleans, LA: Glbert E. Martin, 1981).

17. Ibid., p. 8.

18. Ibid., p. 123.

19. Ibid., pp. 124–125. Arthé Agnes Anthony has challenged the statistics and the romanticized image of the quadroons on pp. 7–8 of "The Negro Creole Community in New Orleans, 1880–1920."

20. Personal conversation with Toni Jones.

21. See John W. Blassingame, *Black New Orleans, 1860–1880* (Chicago: University of Chicago Press, 1973), pp. 7–8, where he discusses the large discrepancy in male-female ratios among whites and free blacks in early New Orleans.

22. See Desdunes, *Our People and Our History*. Much of the book is devoted to names and contributions of wealthy free men of color in New Orleans. Blassingame also mentions them as a group in *Black New Orleans, 1860–1880* (pp. 10–15).

23. The term *chin-ya* for head scarf used by some black women today in New Orleans derives from the French word *chignon* or *tignon*. Several histories mention the tignon law; for example, see *Beautiful Crescent: A History of New Orleans* by Joan Garvey and Mary Lou Widmer (New Orleans: Garmer Press, 1984), p. 99.

24. Duchein, "Research on Charles Etienne Arthur Gayarré," p. 143.

25. Aline St. Julien, *Colored Creole: Color Conflict and Confusion in New Orleans* (New Orleans, LA: Ahidiana Hobari Press, 1977), p. 10.

Chapter 5

LORRAINE HANSBERRY AS VISIONARY: BLACK AND WHITE ANTEBELLUM SOUTHERN WOMEN IN CONCERT

ELIZABETH BROWN-GUILLORY

Lorraine Hansberry, who was born in 1930 and died in 1965, was the first black playwright, and the youngest of any color, to win the coveted New York Drama Critics Circle Award for *A Raisin in the Sun*.[1] However, *The Drinking Gourd*, a much lesser known Hansberry play, deserves serious critical treatment because of her atypical portrayal of Southern black and white women.

In *The Drinking Gourd*, written in 1960, Lorraine Hansberry levels an indictment against slavery because it dehumanized whites as well as blacks. Hansberry drives home the point that whites, too, were victims of the system. Margaret Wilkerson makes a poignant remark when she comments on Hansberry's message in this drama, *"The Drinking Gourd* explores the brutalizing effect of the U.S. slave system on all who were a part of it—master, mistress, overseer, slave. Hansberry shows how that system, set in relentless motion by greed and exploitation, is a leaderless, irresistible force that is unresponsive even to those in power who would mediate its terrifying effects."[2]

This costume drama centers around an ineffectual slave master, Hiram Sweet, who is powerless to prevent his avaricious son, Everett Sweet, from destroying what it has taken Hiram his whole life to build: a profitable plantation manned by slaves who are supposedly treated humanely. Maria, the slave master's wife, sides with her son and helps Everett to ''rule'' without the father's knowledge or permission. Rissa, the black mammy, transforms into a militant woman when her son, Hannibal, has his eyes gouged out for learning to read, an order given by Everett Sweet.

Hansberry in writing *The Drinking Gourd* did not succumb to lambasting unfairly all white Americans. This play does not depict whites as ruthless beasts bent on blindly heaping abuse upon blacks. Instead, and particularly intriguingly, Hansberry depicts a black woman who truly cares for her master and gets along fairly well with his wife. One must view the messages of this play as special, given that Hansberry wrote this costume drama at a time when artists like Baraka were promoting ritualistic killings of whites in popular black drama.[3]

Hansberry, particularly in her characterization of the two Southern women in *The Drinking Gourd*, asks America to see the humanity in all. Blacks are portrayed as passionate, rational seekers of freedom and whites are depicted as victims of a system that they created. Hansberry's unique, significantly insightful, and perhaps controversial view of the slave South with its capitalistic tenacles dehumanizing all begs to be recovered because it is a compelling drama. Her fairness, mildness of temper, and uncommon treatment of oppressed black and white women deserve further study, regardless of the fact that this drama may be perceived as propagandistic and political.

The Drinking Gourd merits serious critical treatment because of its compellingly fresh mix of wit and wrath, imagination and history, and misery and poetry surrounding the two Southern women in the play. Essentially, these two women are symbiotic links; Maria, the big missy, and Rissa, the black mammy, are as dependent upon each other as the slave institution which Hansberry attacks depends upon the labor of blacks.

Big Missy, Maria Sweet, is no vicious, insecure, paranoid woman who fears that Rissa, the Black Mammy, will usurp her position as wife and first lady of the plantation. Instead, she and Rissa are very much alike in their devotion to Hiram. They both are very concerned about Hiram's failing health and his blatant stubbornness about following the doctor's orders. Maria says to the family doctor, "He's been eating salt again, too, Macon. I declare, I can't do a thing with him."[4]

Similarly, Rissa pampers Hiram and demonstrates genuine concern for her master when he snidely remarks that there wasn't enough salt in the greens. Rissa tenderly replies, "There was all you gon a get from now on. . . . If you aiming on killin' yourself Marster Hiram, don't be askin' Riss to hep you none 'cause she ain't gonna do it."[5] When Hiram accuses her of eavesdropping on Doc Bullet's orders for a reduction of salt, Rissa quips, "I don't have to lissen to no other folks' conversations to see h'you ailin'. You sittin' there now, white as cotton, sweatin' like you seen the horseman comin'. Lord, you one stubborn man. I spec you was allus the most stubborn man I ever come across."[6] Rissa comes from a line of black women who accepted slavery as a way of life and who felt a strong attachment and even loyalty to the white family, very much as is the case with Vyry in Margaret Walker's *Jubilee*.[7]

Rissa cares and protects her master because he represents to her the only type of life and security she knows, and he has always been kind to her, as she says at one point in the play. Hansberry, with the name Hiram, suggests that not only is Hiram the high or head ram on the plantation, but that he is also of a higher realm than the average slave owner in that he does not initiate or condone cruelty. There are many who would like to believe that all slaves were rebellious and spent their whole lives battling to escape. However, Hansberry's research combined with stories told to her by her Southern grandmother led her to depict a slave woman who is content, or who is at least not openly rebellious, only until her family is threatened, an image which contradicts the stereotypical "contented" slave syndrome.

The missy and mammy in *The Drinking Gourd* also share the responsibility of controlling their sons, one white and the other black. Hiram and Maria's son, Everett, is eager for his father to relinquish the responsibility of master. Everett is anxious to revamp his father's old ways of managing a plantation. Maria, however, constantly holds Everett in check when he threatens to force Hiram into retirement or when he taunts Hiram about his ineffectuality as plantation and slave owner. Once when Everett chides his father, Maria shouts, "I think that will do, son."[8] Maria knows a bit about reverse psychology, so she comes up with a strategy and Everett agrees to go along with it when Maria says:

> *You must take over the running of the plantation.—no—listen to me, and you must make him believe you have done no such thing. Every night if necessary you must sit with pencil and pad and let him tell you everything he wishes. And then—well, do as you please. You will be master then. But he will think that he still is, which is terribly important.[9]*

Like the leader that he isn't, he obeys his mother's command. Maria, unquestionably, controls her weak son; she does so very easily because of his blind greed and eagerness for what he considers the soft, rich life of the plantation owner. In forcing Everett to suppress his thoughts, Maria works to allay her husband's fears of being dethroned, thus preventing him from having the heart attack of which he has been warned.

Rissa, like Maria, has a son. Hansberry only nebulously suggests that Rissa's son is the child of her slave master, Hiram. This son, Hannibal, who resembles the great African general of the same name, also has to be kept in check, though he is not as easily controlled as Everett. Hannibal, rebellious and resentful of his enslavement, breaks equipment and leaves as much work undone as possible. Rissa, aware that Hiram can be pushed only so far before he is forced to punish her son, serves as a mediator as does Maria. Rissa says, "I done tol' you so many times, that you a slave, right or not, you a slave."[10] Hannibal, a field hand who has been abused physically by overseers and who resents his mother's docility, subservience, and complacency, lashes out at Rissa:

*And I tell you like I tell Coffin [the plantation Uncle Tom]—I am the only
kind of slave I could stand to be—a bad one! Every day that come and
hour that pass that I got sense to make a half step do for a whole; every
day that I can pretend sickness 'stead of health; to be stupid, 'stead of
smart, lazy 'stead of quick—I aims to do it. And the more pain it give* your
Marster and the more it cost him—the more Hannibal be a man![11]

Rissa, however, tries to minimize Hannibal's disgust for Hiram and
slavery by begging Hiram to take Hannibal out of the fields and to make him a
house servant. She humbles herself to get what she feels is a better life for her
son. Rissa says to Hiram, "Marster, a promise is a promise! And you promise
me when that boy was born that he wasn't never gona have to be no field
hand."[12] With some convincing, Hiram agrees to elevate Hannibal, a decision
that he is aware will benefit him. Hiram shouts, "All right, for God's sake!
Anything for peace in this house."[13] Again, Rissa, like Maria, manages to dif-
fuse potentially explosive sparks between father and son. However, it is important to note that though both women exert power over their sons, neither of these
women has the power to make any significant decisions on her own.

Hansberry's Rissa and Maria are not stereotypes, for they work together
apparently without vengeance, violence, and subtle or covert hatred. Hansberry
depicts Maria as a white woman who closes her eyes and refuses to dignify her
husband's infidelity. Only once in the play does Maria show any signs that she
is jealous of Hiram's ralationship with Rissa: the time Hiram agrees to make
Hannibal a house servant. Even in this instance, Hiram silences her immediately.

It does not seem normal that Maria and Rissa should get along so well, but
the circumstances of the play suggest that they had little choice. Maria tolerates
Rissa because she knows Hiram will have it no other way and because she
knows that Rissa is loyal and has always done what Hiram ordered her to do.
Hansberry's research in writing this play led her to believe that during slavery
there were women such as Maria and Rissa, and her statement is that these
women were both powerless under the slave system. Noteworthy is that, while
Hansberry levels an indictment against slavery, she looks deeply and compas-
sionately in the souls of all caught up in the system and shows their strengths
and weaknesses.

Hansberry snips any threads of stereotype when she has Rissa undergo a
metamorphosis; she becomes a dynamic and articulate militant mammy, unlike
anything depicted in Faulkner's *The Sound and the Fury*, Hellman's *The Little
Foxes*, McCullers' *The Member of the Wedding*, Walker's *Jubilee*, or Hughes'
Mulatto.[14] Rissa's militancy comes as no surprise when one bears in mind that
this costume drama was written in 1960 by a sociopolitical activist who claimed
that her grandmother told her of women who took life-threatening risks under
the slave system.

Rissa's militancy is best seen when, at the end of the play, Hiram comes to apologize to Rissa whose son's eyes have been dug out: "I had nothing to do with this. I—some things do seem to be out of the power of my hands after all."[15] Instead of humbly backing into a corner, Rissa—for the first time presumably—stares Hiram in the eye and cynically says, "Why, ain't you Marster? How can a man be marster of some men and not at all of others?"[16] When he tells her she has gone too far, Rissa seethes with anger as she retorts, "What will you have done to me? Will your overseer gouge out my eyes too? I don't spect blindness would matter to me. I done seen all there was worth seein' in this world—and it didn't 'mount to much."[17] It is evident in this scene that Rissa is, as her name suggests, a risk-taker. Rissa is bolder than most of her counterparts in recent American literature.

Maria, like Rissa, is atypical. Maria is very different from Big Missy in Margaret Walker's *Jubilee,* who pathetically deteriorates mentally and physically after the death of her husband. In *The Drinking Gourd,* however, there is evidence that Maria will adjust and continue to have her hand in the running of the plantation through her influences over the new master, a young man who is not so sweet, Everett Sweet.

Lorraine Hansberry's *The Drinking Gourd* has two female characters whose lives are interwoven and dependent upon each other for survival. Both women have a keen understanding of the politics involved in running a plantation; they both know that their survival and the happiness of their children depend on how well they give Hiram what he requires of them. They are neither antagonistic nor jealous, to any significant degree, of each other; instead, they are two Southern women who work to keep the lid on the bubbling pot—a pot which contains white and black links, a family which is made up of master, missy, mammy, legitimate, and illegitimate children.

In closing, Lorraine Hansberry's *The Drinking Gourd,* now 27 years old, deserves additional serious critical treatment. The two Southern women, Maria and Rissa, merit further exploring because they embody the essence of the play. Hansberry writes of the politics in which Maria and Rissa engage in order to survive, just as Margaret Walker does in *Jubilee* and Katherine Anne Porter does in *The Old Order.* Hansberry, like Walker and Porter, portrays strong black and white women acting in concert.

NOTES

1. Margaret B. Wilkerson, "The Sighted Eyes and Feeling Heart of Lorraine Hansberry," *Black American Literature Forum* 17(Spring 1983):8.
2. Margaret B. Wilkerson, "Lorraine Hansberry: The Complete Feminist," *Freedomways* 19(1979):242.
3. Amiri Baraka was one of the leading playwrights of the Black Power Movement in the 1960s whose works advocated the ritualistic killing of oppressive whites. Most notable of his works are *Dutchman, The Slave,* and *The Toilet.*
4. Lorraine Hansberry, *The Drinking Gourd,* in *Lorraine Hansberry: The Collected Last Plays,* ed. Robert Nemiroff (New York: Random House, 1972), p. 180.

5. Ibid., p. 186.

6. Ibid.

7. Margaret Walker, *Jubilee* (Boston: Houghton Mifflin, 1966).

8. Hansberry, *The Drinking Gourd*, p. 182.

9. Ibid., p. 190

10. Ibid., p. 201.

11. Ibid. Reprinted by permission of Random House, Copyright © 1972.

12. Ibid., p. 187–188.

13. Ibid., p. 188.

14. William Faulkner, *The Sound and the Fury* (New York: Random House, 1929); Lillian Hellman, *The Little Foxes* (New York: Random House, 1939); Walker, *Jubilee;* Langston Hughes, *Mulatto,* in *Five Plays by Langston Hughes,* ed. Webster Smalley (Bloomington, IN: Indiana University Press, 1968).

15. Hansberry, *The Drinking Gourd*, p. 215.

16. Ibid.

17. Ibid.

Chapter 6

GROWING UP FEMALE, WHITE, AND SOUTHERN IN THE 1850s AND 1860s

KATHRYN PALUMBO

The diaries, letters, and memoirs of antebellum women present a portrait of Southern life unlike the popular mythology of Scarlett O'Hara and Tara. One such memoir was written in 1930 by Nancy Keil Ivey, who spent most of her life in the town of Milledgeville, Georgia.[1]

Milledgeville, which was at one time the state capital and for a short period the seat of government for the Confederacy, is in the center of the state. During Nancy Keil's childhood in the 1850s and early 1860s the town was a bustling commercial and governmental city and was easily accessible to the coastal cities and Atlanta by train. In 1850 the city had a population of just over 8,000; the majority were blacks, some of whom were free.[2] A significant number of the white residents were political refugees of a recent Irish rebellion. Most households, white and black, consisted of extended families.

Many local plantations produced large amounts of cotton, grain, and livestock. The wealthiest family, the Harrises, owned the cotton gin, grist mill, grain storage facilities, the most acreage, and the greatest number of slaves. Other white and free black families farmed. Several of the free black men had established successful businesses in town, which were frequented by all of the town's residents. Of those white families who owned slaves, most had fewer than 20. This would prove to be fortuitous once Sherman's army reached the town since, during his March to the Sea, he would order to be burned all plantations with 20 or more slaves.

Nancy's memoirs span the years following her birth in 1848 to the 1930s.

Of particular interest here is her commentary regarding the Civil War and the years of Reconstruction. Alternately referring to the war as "the War of Northern Agression," "the War of the '60s," and the "War Between the States," she presents a picture of female life in Georgia that is as revealing for what it omits as for what it states. Written in polite prose, Nancy says little about the issue of slavery. Her one inclusion involves the train trip her family made when moving from North Carolina to Georgia before the war.

> *I had never seen a train before—there were not so many railroads then. When we boarded the car, we found it full of negroes. The conductor made room for us till we reached the next station, when we changed for the right car. The negroes were being brought from the north to sell to the South. A woman in that car of negroes was singing, "Home Sweet Home." I thought it was the most beautiful and pathetic singing I had ever heard.[3]*

Although the Keils had owned slaves in North Carolina, they were sold before the move to Georgia. While Nancy's sentiments toward the "pathetic" situation of the black occupants of the railroad care is obviously heartfelt, there is no evidence that she gave the matter of slavery much intellectual consideration. Slavery was a given in her time and place. Her lack of text regarding blacks may be a reflecton of her community's racist attitude toward the status of blacks and of an unwillingness to face the issue as a moral one.

Commenting on her grandmother's memoirs, Frances Ivey Pomazal noted: "The family's most unreconstructed Southerner, however, was my father's mother. . . . Even when past the age of eighty she would not permit Abraham Lincoln's name to be mentioned in her presence."[4]

Nancy continued to describe her family's train trip to Georgia and discussed the ambiguous social status of those who promoted the trade in slaves:

> *I guess the speculators were in charge of the train. I remember those speculators, my childish terror, next to his Satanic Majesty. My mother often said to me, "If you don't wear your bonnet the speculators will get you." They caused me to be particular not to get sunburned, as I thought they wanted all dark-skinned people. And in the long ago it was the ambition of the white race to be fair and not get sunburnt. Little girls were constantly admonished to wear bonnets for that purpose.[5]*

Nancy's comments about the "speculators" bring to mind images of more contemporary older Southern women, strolling on sunny, summer afternoons holding parasols over their heads in carefully gloved hands. The term, *speculator,* is an interesting one. Devoid of connotation regarding the buying and selling of human lives, it is a polite term. Nancy's statement that she thought the speculators dealt in "all dark-skinned people" is revealing. Perhaps discussion of black men and women as a race of humans was a forbidden topic in the Keil household. Yet, Nancy's fear of the speculators points to a young child's realization that such men did deal in the trade of men, women, and children with dark skin tones.

The six Keil girls were joined by a brother born in 1861. Eliza Keil, Nancy's mother, never recovered from the birth and died in the same year. Nancy's father, Caswell, leased shares to his farm and opened a grocery business in town where he moved his family. And then the Civil War began.

Caswell enlisted with the local militia and left the children in the charge of a hired, white nanny. The nanny and her family moved into the Keil home. The children began to receive home tutoring from the wife of the secretary of state, Mrs. N. C. Barnett. In the book *Confederate Women*, Bell Wiley notes that home tutoring and school teaching were new professions for Southern women during the war years. Before the war, teaching had been a male profession, although some "subscription schools" employed "Yankee school marms."[6] With the men and school marms gone, Southern white women found themselves needing steady income and having to teach the children. Also they had to perform a number of duties, on and off the farms, jobs that had been formerly designated as unladylike and that had been done behind the scenes, unacknowledged and unrewarded.[7]

The Secession Conference of 1861 held in Milledgeville (the capital at that time) made a lasting impression on Nancy. A torchlight parade was a spectacle that involved the total white population of the town. Candles were lit in windows and affixed with copper holders made especially for the occasion by a local craftsman. The belief was that secession would be successful and a war would be brief.

The Baldwin Blues, formed a few months earlier to enforce a curfew upon black residents following an outbreak of vandalism and arson, were the first militia to leave Milledgeville.[8] Nancy wrote of their departure:

> *Many families were represented in that company. A big crowd of men, women, and children were at the depot the morning of their departure to bid them farewell and Godspeed. To whip the Yankees and return home soon was the consummation devoutly wished for. The parting was sad as the fervent "Goodbye and God bless you," with endearments and encouragements could be heard amid the stir and bustle. When the train . . . came rolling into the depot puffing and blowing, we saw fastened in front of the engine a large broom. A lady standing by me remarked, "That's the broom of destruction." I suppose it was emblematic of what they expected to do—sweep off and away the Yankee invaders.[9]*

Of the 71 men who left that day, only 7 remained with the regiment by the time it reached Appomatox. Many died, some deserted. During the four years of fighting, the town sent 152 additional men to the company which became the

Fourth Regiment of Georgia Volunteers.[10] The last year of the war, healthy male convicts from the Milledgeville State Prison were offered clemency and $50 to join the regiment.

The roles of Southern white women during the war years were innumerable. The women of Milledgeville established a Soldiers' Relief Fund and raised enough money to open a hospital with a staff of 11 surgeons.[11] The women served as volunteer nurses, as well. The hospital, which contained a hundred beds, functioned until shortly before Sherman's invasion.[12] The women operated a munitions factory within the walls of the state prison. They supplied a total of 1500 garments for the Fourth Regiment.[13] The cotton gin and grist mill continued to function, run by women and slaves.

The women of Milledgeville and elsewhere learned to find substitutes for goods and products which became unavailable, particularly during the blockade. The Keils' situation was not unique.

"Hard times and worse coming" was a common expression at that time. Some much used articles could not be had on account of the blockade, so we got busy getting substitutes. I've spent many an hour cutting and drying sweet potatoes used for coffee. I became an expert molder of tallow candles when sperm ones could not be bought. Even matches were hard to get, though they did get to making them in our Dixieland. We made and wove homespun dresses, gladly and proudly.[14]

Life in Milledgeville became increasingly difficult, particularly for farming families, both black and white. During Good Friday church services in 1863, a number of poorer members of the community raided local groceries and food warehouses in a "bread riot." Such riots took place in Richmond, Augusta, Macon, Petersburg, and other Southern towns. Inflation had forced the prices of necessities beyond the purchasing power of most families. In *Heroines of Dixie,* edited by Katherine Jones, a letter written by Sarah Lawton of Richmond, Virginia, listed the groceries she purchased during a week and their prices: "a peck of green peas—$12.00, two heads of lettuce for $1.50 each, butter at $12.00 a pound and snap beans for $10.00."[15] Nancy Keil made no mention of whether her father's grocery store was still operating during the war, but the family was in fair financial circumstances. The Keil children's paternal uncle was responsible for household expenses and maintenance of land holdings. While Uncle Nathan did poorly with money, he did keep title to the land which proved beneficial to the sisters following the war.

News from their father was sporadic. Occasionally, Caswell Keil was able to send money home to his children. Nancy recalled the eagerness with which she awaited news and money from her father.

Whenever he was paid off he would send us a little money to spend any way we wished. One time with my little bit I bought a cameo pin. I surely

needed something else more than that pretty pin. However, that was what
I wanted. I really did get a lot of pleasure and service too out of it. I had it
for many years and finally lost it.[16]

Caswell Keil caught typhoid fever during the Battle of the Wilderness and
died on June 7, 1864. The loss of their father changed the direction of the
children's lives. After his death, the six girls (the infant brother had died) were
divided among neighbors and lived away from the family home. Throughout the
remainder of her memoir, Nancy's steadfast devotion to a sense of family proves
to be a motivating factor in her life. The demise of her childhood home, family,
and the South's "lost cause" was tightly woven in her memory.

As I recall at that time our situation might be summed up thusly; no father,
no mother, no relatives in hundreds of miles except an uncle and some
interested people and a few friends. Finances were also limited. Most
everyone was in straitened circumstances, owing to the war maintenance.
The property, left in trust, for our maintenance by my father, was not
properly managed.[17]

During the cold November of 1864, General Sherman and 65,000 Union
troops descended upon the small town. The population had swollen with the
presence of Atlanta refugees. With the men gone to fight and the seat of the
Confederacy moved to Richmond, the only ones left in the town were the elderly, women, children, slave families from surrounding farms, and one Confederate soldier home on furlough. Although Sherman placed officers in many
of the Milledgeville homes to discourage vandalism, such efforts did little good.
The railroad, cotton gin, grist mill, and plantations on which 20 or more slaves
were owned were destroyed. Hungry soldiers raided farms, smokehouses, and
kitchen larders. One white woman was raped. No record exists of any possible
rapes of black women. Local legend insists Sherman ordered molasses to be
poured into the Methodist Church's pipe organ and that he slept in the former
governor's wife's bed with his boots on his feet. Another story details the arson
of the state prison by Union soldiers. However, historian James Bonner has
discovered that the fire was most probably set by a female inmate indicted for
the murder of her husband. Following the fire, the inmate attached herself to an
Indiana regiment and earned her money as a prostitute.[18]

Nancy was 16 during the invasion. She described the Union troops as
"vandal hordes."

The entrance of (federal troops) into the city struck terror into the hearts
of women and children and what few men were left. After three days of
plundering, destroying and carrying out their orders of destruction in ac-
cordance with Sherman's definition of war, the last of them passed on
across the river and burned the bridge.[19]

Destitute and homeless, former slaves tried to follow Sherman's troops across the bridge. Many hoped to remain with the Union soldiers until they reached the coast and, eventually, continue to the North. Sherman knew the slaves would be a burden and slow down his March to the Sea. To circumvent the problem, he ordered the burning of the bridge and the river ferries. (Many of the descendants of slaves left on the banks of the river live in Milledgeville today. A number of white and black families share the identical surnames and branches of various family trees.)

Several days after the departure of federal troops, a Confederate brigade rode through town and confiscated whatever food and livestock remained. The town was in shambles with no method of transportation available to bring food, medical supplies, or building materials. White citizens did, however, find a way to insure the use of former slaves by instituting a loitering fine on blacks that could be paid by the purchasing of indentured labor. Nancy wrote a description of the failure of the Confederacy.

> *After four years of War between the States, it was ended. The cruel war of untold agony and privation was over. The struggle given up, the inevitable accepted. Hopes and ambition buried in the grave of the Confederacy. The returned soldiers were esteemed for what they tried to do, even though they failed. They were heroes all and were given preference as a popular song of the times says of them. I quote one verse from memory: "I would like to change my name, And settle down in life; here's a chance for some young man, Who's seeking for a wife; But he must be a soldier, A veteran from the war, Who's fought for Southern rights, Beneath the bars and stars."[20]*

In 1865 Nancy "quituated [was graduated]" from a local secondary academy. Because of the family's financial status, she accepted a position as a teacher for a family in Emanuel County, 60 miles from home. Employed as a teacher for the next five years, Nancy found the experience unsatisfactory and returned to her uncle's home. "I felt that I had a claim on uncle anyway, he not having done for us what my father had expected him to in the preceding years."[21] Nancy met a young man, James Ivey, from a prominent Milledgeville family. The Iveys claimed kinship to Martin Van Buren, but had been in a tenuous position during the war as several were Quakers. Nancy and Jimmy began to court and were married on December 21, 1871. The Iveys and Nancy's sisters spent the next few years trying to farm. They were not successful, although they did acquire additional property to add to their holdings, Jimmy began to do carpentry work, two of Nancy's sisters married, one became a teacher, and two others started a millinery business. Nancy and Jimmy's family grew to include five children of their own. Four nieces and nephews came to live with them following the death of Nancy's sister, Emma.

Sister Mattie's millinery business did quite well and she talked her brother-in-law into starting a real estate and construction business with the use of her capital. The business thrived. Mattie and Jimmy arranged to lease their farmland's timber and found it to be a lucrative enterprise for the next 40 years.

Nancy offered no comments on the political climate of Reconstruction. A period of turmoil in Georgia history, its absence is glaring. Missing, also, is any commentary on the presence of the Klu Klux Klan in Milledgeville. Nancy focused her attention on family matters rather than politics. The years of the war had taken a dramatic toll on Nancy's childhood. The bitterness her great-grandchildren remember may have been a reflection of those hardships.

Memoirs such as Nancy's breathe life into the stories one hears about the Civil War and the Reconstruction aftermath. They offer the history student an examination into the myths and realities of life in the South during the later half of the 19th century. They chronicle changes in transportation, language, entertainment, family structure, land use, and women's work. Gertrude Stein once said the true history of war would only be known when women's stories were told. Nancy's tales of the women's battles during the war and Reconstruction cast light upon this endeavor.

NOTES

1. Nancy Keil Ivey, *Memories* (Unpublished manuscript, 1930).
2. Census of Baldwin County, Georgia, 1850.
3. Ivey, *Memories*, p. 2.
4. Frances Ivey Pomazel, "Southern Memorial," *The Peacock's Feet* 9 (Spring 1984), p. 13. Additional personal information for this article was obtained through interviews with Nancy Keil Ivey's great-granddaughter, Priscilla Pomazel, in 1986.
5. Ivey, *Memories*, p. 3.
6. Bell Wiley, *Confederate Women* (Westport: Greenwood Press, 1975), p. 147.
7. See Catherine Clinton, *The Plantation Mistress* (New York: Pantheon, 1982).
8. Leola Selman Benson, *History Stories of Milledgeville and Baldwin County* (Macon, GA: J. W. Burke Co., 1943), p. 49.
9. Ivey, *Memories*, p. 4.
10. James Bonner, *Milledgeville: Georgia's Antebellum Capitol* (Athens, GA: University of Georgia Press, 1978), p. 159.
11. Ibid., p. 167.
12. Ibid., p. 160.
13. Benson, *History Stories of Milledgeville and Baldwin County*, p. 49.
14. Ivey, *Memories*, pp. 4–5.
15. Katherine Jones, editor, *Heroines of Dixie: Confederate Women Tell Their Story of the War* (Indianapolis, IN: Bobbs-Merrill, 1955), p. 301.
16. Ivey, *Memories*, p. 4.
17. Ibid., p. 4.
18. Ibid.; Bonner, *Milledgeville*, p. 179.
19. Ibid., *Memories*, p. 5.
20. Ibid., p. 5.
21. Ibid., p. 7.

Chapter 7

THE CIVIL WAR AND BLACK WOMEN ON THE SEA ISLANDS

CAROLYN E. WEDIN

The opening shots of the American Civil War on 12 April 1861 began a progression of events which were to throw together a Northern white woman, Laura Mathilda Towne, and many Southern black women on the Sea Islands of South Carolina in a pressure cooker of hardship, rumors of war, war, and human struggle. In response to a call from the federal government to send agents to assist with newly freed slaves, Towne was one of several score who came from the North during the years of the Civil War, arriving at Port Royal Island, 55 miles south of Charleston, on 15 April 1862 with a large store of provisions from Philadelphia. She remained on St. Helena Island through the war, through Reconstruction, until her death in 1901, leaving a legacy of medical care and educational innovation and establishment (Penn School); leaving, too, a written legacy in her letters and diary of 1862 to 1864, first published in 1912.[1]

The history of St. Helena Island has been told in powerful detail in Edith Dabbs's *Sea Island Diary,* and the history of the "Port Royal Experiment" in Willie Lee Rose's excellent *Rehearsal for Reconstruction,*[2] but directly from Towne's letters and diary the reader is granted a powerful view of the lives of history's inarticulate, in this case those who have borne a triple discrimination in historical records: as blacks, as women, and as illiterate. The women Towne met, and sympathized with, and lived with are those whose story has never been told in their own words. In Towne's words, we come close.[3]

In Beaufort, South Carolina, access city to the islands off the coast, upon her arrival on the steamship *Oriental,* Laura Mathilda Towne is introduced to the sights and sounds of the Sea Islands: "the tide [rising] over sandy, grassy flats," "sands . . . full of fiddler-crab holes" and "negro children with tubs on their heads, crabbing,'' boats passing by frequently, ''the negro rowers singing their refrains.''[4]

She is introduced, too, to the ''aristocratic'' of the ex-slaves, those whose lives in slavery were not so bad that they are convinced that the new freedom is better. She describes two of the women of the ''colored aristocracy,'' who had ''lived in the best families, never did any work to speak of, longed for the young ladies and young 'mas'rs' back again, because April was the month they used to come to Beaufort to have such gay times.''[5]

Out of Beaufort and onto the Oaks Plantation on St. Helena Island where she will begin her own work, Towne begins to encounter women with other experiences of slavery and other needs than simply to be around white women. In the midst of salt water (at high tide), towering pines, whitewashed Negro quarters, ''Pride of China'' and fig trees, vegetable gardens, stables, pig-pens, lie the cotton fields where all but a few women and girls, ''unfit for the field,'' must work, now for federal government pay or rations.[6] From one of the black women on the plantation, Susannah, Towne learns something of life as a slave before the war, and of the uncertainty facing the slaves in their transition from taking care of white masters to white Northern soldiers and philanthropists. Susannah had had a hard master

> who gave no shoes, salt, molasses, or Sunday clothes—neither would he allow the field hands any meat. . . . Susannah once raised some pigs and her master threatened to shoot them. ''No massa, you cawnt do it. What can I do for our children's winter shoes and our salt if our pigs are shot? You cawnt do it—you cawnt do it.'' . . . He used to buy and sell as suited him. Susannah's three boys (all she raised out of twenty-two that she had) were sent away from her. . . . He also whipped, or ''licked'' as they say, terribly. For the last year he was determined to make them work as much as they possibly could, because ''he was afraid the Yankees were coming''; and so he kept them in the fields from morning till night and lashed them every day. Susannah herself never had a whipping after she was a child. Her mistress used to tell her she would ''lash her,'' and scolded her, but Susannah used to say ''Whippin' never does me no good, ma'am. I'll explain and I'll do better next time. I only wants to know what you want and I'll do it. If my pride and principle won't make me do it right, lashing won't.'' . . . She was sickly, and she made all the ladies' dresses—two reasons for her being spared. ''I never axed no wagers, but my two clothes for the year. I was quite satisfy if dey did n't lick me.''[7]

On the backs of other women—those who were not spared—Towne was to see the evidence of beating.

> Loretta . . . showed me her back and arms today. In many places there were ridges as high and long as my little finger, and she said she had had

four babies killed within her by whipping, one of which had its eye cut out, another its arm broken, and others with marks of the lash. She says it was because even while "heaviest" she was required to do as much as usual for a field hand. . . . No wonder Grace, her child, is of the lowest type; no wonder she is more indifferent about her clothes and house than any one here.[8]

From Susannah, Towne learns of the experience of the Battle of Port Royal and the arrival of Union soldiers from the slaves' fearful and uncertain point of view.

The day after the "Guns at Baypoint" . . . her master went away, taking his family. He wanted Susannah to go with him . . . but she refused. He told her that if she stayed she would either be killed by the Yankees or sold to Cuba; but she said, why should they kill poor black folks who did no harm and could only be guided by white folks? After he went, his son came back once and told the negroes that they must burn the cotton; but they said, "Why for we burn de cotton? Where we get money then fo buy clo' and shoe and salt?" So instead of burning it, they guarded it every night, the women keeping watch and the men ready to defend it when the watchers gave the alarm. Some of the masters came back to persuade their negroes to go with them, and when they would not, they were shot down. One man told me he had known of thirty being shot. . . . Nevertheless, a great part of them stayed, and many of those who went came back, or are coming every day. . . . Susannah's master has never come back. He is probably afraid of his negroes. . . . Her young 'missuses' cried when they went away, and said "Oh, Zannah, the Yankees'll kill you. If you see a Yankee it'll drive you crazy." "Why, miss, ain't dey natural folks?" "Oh, no, Zannah, they don't look like us." So, when Susannah saw soldiers coming, she ran out to Marcus, her husband, and said "Oh, deys soldiers, deys come to kill us," and her hands shook with trembling. But Marcus said they would n't hurt her and ordered her to go to them to see what they wanted. When they saw her fright, they said to her "We are not going to hurt you. We only want you to get us something to eat, and we'll pay you for it." "Oh, such pretty men," she said, "and so respectful."[9]

Once the news is out about freedom, though, slaves begin to struggle toward it.

They transfer their gratitude to "Government." One woman told me, "I was servant-born, ma'am, and now 'cause de Gov'ment fightin' for me, I'll work for Gov'ment, dat I will, and welcome." Another woman, today, just from "the main," said to me that she had hard work to escape, sleeping in "de ma'sh' and hiding all day. She brought away her two little

*children, and said her master had just "licked" her eldest son almost to
death because he was suspected of wanting to join the Yankees. "They
does it to spite us, ma'am, 'cause you come here. Dey spites us now
'cause de Yankees come."[10]*

To women like Susannah and Loretta, even the uncertainties of life under
the Yankees and the ever-threatened return of the rebels are a vast improvement.
("One woman said the differences in the times were as great as if God had sent
another Moses and a great deliverance—that it was heaven upon earth and earth
in heaven now."[11])

Most of the slaves freed by the Battle of Port Royal on November 7, 1861,
were in Susannah's position, "perhaps the most helpless of their race." Cotton
ruled their lives—there were no slack times in the cotton year; "the older ones
were dulled with incessant labor, the younger had had no chance to learn anything." Rough board houses through which the winter cold leaked, with glass-
less windows and sand and lime floors, contained an open hearth where a single
pot cooked hominy and peas and salt pork. "The older people slept in bunks,
the younger on the floor."[12]

By the end of the first year, many agents from the North had given up and
returned home, but Towne had established a school for 80, had nursed innumerable patients through a small pox epidemic, and had made something of a difference in the lives of the ex-slaves. People needed clothes; Towne sold items
sent by aid societies in the North. "How they come thronging here for clothes
and go away 'too satisfied—too thank,' one woman said, at receiving some few
things. . . . They will give two or three eggs . . . for a needle and a little wisp
of tangled cotton."[13] Basic needs fulfilled, other needs can be looked to. The
"poor, down-hearted, 'confused' negroes are already in better spirits from
having a little decent clothing to put on." "The first rations of pork—'splendid
bacon,' everybody says—was dealt out the other day and there has been great
joy ever since."[14]

The inheritance from slavery of disrupted, discontinuous family life requires adjustment.

*The men and women living together on this place are not all of them
married. When Miss Walker [representative of Salmon P. Chase, Secretary of the Treasury] asks them they say, "No, not married, ma'am, but I
just tuck (took) her and brought her home." They make not the slightest
preparation for an expected infant, having always been used to thinking it
"massa's" concern whether it was kept alive or not.[15]*

Yet women sacrifice for their children: "One woman bought a great bundle of
clothes, and I said, 'Don't spend all your money.' 'All for my chiluns,' she
said. . . . 'My chiluns naked, quite naked—in rags.' "[16]

Scenes of the community—adult and children—impress Towne.

The people come, with their flat baskets on their heads, to the cornhouse, to "take allowance," and then sit down in the sand, and old and young fall to shelling the corn from the cob with a speed that was marvellous, the little babies toddling about or slung on the back of their mammies, or lugged about by the older sisters, not able to stand straight under their weight.[17]

Willingness to work is predicated on physical well-being and a share in the result of one's labor. Able women work in the fields as well as in household jobs, work harder than the men even. Instilling the work ethic in both places is the result of pay for labor:

Mr. Philbrick [Superintendent of Coffin Point, largest St. Helena plantation] says that, after telling each man that he should be paid exactly according to the quantity of cotton he put in, they all went to work with a will, and each man did his task [one-fourth acre of hoeing or planting] per day, but that two women each did two tasks a day and were to be paid accordingly.[18]

Eventually, and inevitably, the question of work and self-sufficiency is tied to land ownership. However, as with the promises of the Freedmen's Bureau after the war for "forty acres and a mule" for every ex-slave, there is difficulty during the war in making good on promises. In February of 1863, Towne writes, "Hurrah! Jubilee! Lands are to be set apart for the people so that they cannot be oppressed, or driven to work for speculators, or ejected from their homesteads."[19] A year later she is writing that the exempting was to be withdrawn, "a fearful disappointment to the people."[20]

All the time that basic needs have to be met—for food, clothing, shelter, education—and all the time the seasons change, bringing heat and cold, sowing and harvesting, the ongoing war and the threat of the rebels' return hangs like a doomsday cloud over the islands. Though the threat of rebel attack is always rumored, the real impact of the war is in the forced enlisting of the Negro men in the Union forces. Soldiers come to take the men without forewarning, lest they run away in fear. In May of 1862, Towne writes, "It is heart-rending to hear of the scenes to-day—of how some places the women and children clung and cried—in others, how the men took to the woods and were hunted out by the soldiers." The ongoing drafting of the black men is an ironic reminder of the slaves' terror of being sold. But Rina, an elderly black woman, reminds them that the latter was much worse. " 'Dey used to catch we up like fowls and sell we when dey wanted a little money for spend.' "[21]

As the war goes on, the residents of the Sea Islands gain in information, understanding, and appreciation of the larger picture of which they are a small, experimental part. In July of 1862, Edisto Island is evacuated by federal troops, and 1,600 blacks are brought to St. Helena Island with their pigs and chickens, aboard flatboats covered with tree branch camouflage for protection against rebel sharpshooters.[22] In July, too, on the Fourth, "our flag" is raised and the people process to the church, carrying branches in their hands, singing "Roll, Jordan, Roll" and "[John Greenleaf] Whittier's song":

> *Now praise and tank de Lord, he come*
> *To set de people free;*
> *Ole massa tink it day ob doom,*
> *But we ob jubilee.*[23]

In July of 1863, Colonel Robert Gould Shaw, commander of the Black 54th Massachusetts Regiment, is killed in the attack on Fort Wagner and "buried in the trench with his soldiers." Ox-loads of watermelons pour in "from all parts of the island" for the soldiers, " 'wounded for we,' they say." In September $107 is collected for a monument to Colonel Shaw, and, when the need for fresh food for the soldiers on Morris Island is announced, "the whole church responded that they would give the potatoes."[24]

On 1 January 1864, in "piercing cold," at a "grand celebration" of Emancipation Day, "the colored people of these islands" present a sword to General Saxton [Military Governor of the War Department], and Colonel Thomas Wentworth Higginson's black regiment presents one to him.[25] News of General Sherman's arrival in Savannah on 22 December 1864, after his march from Atlanta to the sea, is soon followed by the arrival of more refugees. On 8 January 1865, Towne writes:

> *Another great crowd of negroes has come from Sherman's army. They are utterly wretched in circumstances—clothes all torn to rags; in some cases children naked. . . . It is astonishing with what open-hearted charity the people here—themselves refugees from Edisto two years ago—have received these newcomers right into their houses. . . . I asked our Brister [Towne's household help] if he found any friends among the refugees from Georgia. "All friends to-night," he said.*[26]

On 14 April 1865 the United States flag is raised on Fort Sumter in Charleston Harbor by the same general who had surrendered the fort four years earlier. And on 14 April 1865, President Lincoln is assassinated. On St. Helena Island, the people at first refuse to believe that he is dead, but finally express their grief:

> *"I have lost a friend. . . . Uncle Sam, the best friend ever I had" . . . Rina says she can't sleep for thinking how sorry she is to lose "Pa Linkum." You know they call their elders in the church . . . with fear and*

awe as "Pa." . . . *One man said to me, "Lincoln died for we, Christ died for we, and me believe him de same mans."*[27]

The end of the war brings its own difficulties. Many of the "rebels" return to their former lands, penniless, some to be taken in by their former slaves. Government rations and pay after the war become even more undependable, and the military, Towne finds, "are often more pro-slavery than the rebels themselves, and only care to make the blacks work—being quite unconcerned about making the employers pay."[28] Towne believes the "Southern Relief" plan of 1868 will aid not the colored people, but the planters—"a thriftless, greedy set."[29]

The death of slavery sees the birth of segregation and other forms of discrimination on the Islands and elsewhere in the South. In 1867 "the white folks of the island who . . . are getting too uppish . . . to associate with blacks, even in church, have determined to have a white church of their own."[30] The white men do not attend the mass meeting of Republicans: "they are going to have a *white* party, they say," while, on the all-Negro platform, speeches are given to the effect that, " '[Even] if dere skins *is* white, dey may have principle.' "[31]

Females become the new second-class citizens: " 'The meeting is for men voters. . . . The womens will stay at home and cut grass,' that is, hoe the corn and cotton fields."[32] Violence against women increases, and political violence against Negroes escalates, including the shooting of the Negro Senator from South Carolina in 1868.[33] By 1877, Towne is writing of "Old slavery reviving here, and base treachery in Washington."[34] "Nobody seems to remember that the South is only half-civilized, and that the negroes are nearly as well informed and a great deal more loyal than the whites."[35]

But it is with the issue of the schools that Towne concentrates her efforts after the war, organizing a protest resolution to the Democratic legislature's having forbidden school districts to levy any school tax

> *because the people here are the taxpayers, there being on the island five thousand blacks and not fifty whites, twelve hundred and eighty black children of age to attend school, and only seven white children, and because the few white people here are as anxious for schools as the blacks, and willing to pay the tax voted at these meetings.*[36]

Towne, in her 40 years on St. Helena Island, sees generations pass before her. Progress is difficult to assign to nations, but in individuals and their sacrifices, their progeny, one can see fruits. Long after the war, Towne writes of a visit to one of the early freed slaves to arrive on the island:

> *"Oh, my baby, my beloved!* . . . *has you come to see Mom Peg? Oh, Lord, missus, I so glad.* . . . *My old hands has done dere share of work in de worl'—but, my dear missus, my ole head cold now."* . . . *[Old Aunt*

*Peg] is the mother of a princely set. She had six sons, and no overseer
ever dared to order one a whipping. . . . They are all tall and handsome
and take high rank in church and council.*[37]

Laura Towne's life and legacy and the lives and legacies of the Southern
women to whom she gave voice are aptly summed up by Edith Dabbs:

*The story of Penn School is inseparably the story of a whole island people.
School and community work were interwoven from the first day. The
teaching and Miss Towne's visiting among the sick and troubled began to
develop throughout St. Helena a sense of common denominators and community responsibility. Although at the end of the century St. Helena
seemed to all outward appearances much the same as at the beginning, it
was in fact a new world with new people.*[38]

Penn School turned to industrial education after Towne's death early in the
20th century.[39] In 1951, after the State of South Carolina took over education on
St. Helena Island, Penn School became Penn Community Services, Inc., still
assisting in community development, health services, child care, and conferences. Penn School was designated a National Historical Landmark in 1974.

We move back, again, to the years after the Civil War, to the spring of
1867. From the new home she has come to love on St. Helena Island, Laura
Mathilda Towne writes a letter to her family in the North:

*I enclose a few sprigs of jessamine. They will revive when very dead, and
I hope you can see what the flower looks like (by putting them into water)
that covers trees and hedges with gold every spring. We are just in the
midst of the rose season. . . . The school-children bring them by basins
full, and school-rooms and parlor are full of them. Pomegranate blossoms
have come too. Blackberries are the size of a thimble. . . . You, I suppose, are yet banked up in snow.*[40]

NOTES

1. Rupert Sargent Holland, ed., *Letters and Diary of Laura M. Towne* (Cambridge,
   MA: Riverside Press, 1912; reprint ed., Negro Universities Press, 1969). Towne's
   manuscripts are in the Southern Historical Collection, University of North Carolina, Chapel Hill.
2. Willie Lee Rose, *Rehearsal for Reconstruction: The Port Royal Experiment* (New
   York: Bobbs Merrill Co., Inc., 1964), with an Introduction by C. Vann Woodward; Edith Dabbs, *Sea Island Diary: A History of St. Helena Island* (Spartanburg,
   SC: The Reprint Company, 1986).
3. Rose makes extensive use of the letters and diaries of the missionaries from the
   North in her book, calling them "the single indispensable category of primary
   material." A book such as Bert James Loewenberg and Ruth Bogin's *Black*

Women in Nineteenth-Century Life: Their Words; Their Thoughts; Their Feelings (University Park and London, PA: Pennsylvania State University Press, 1976) of necessity focuses on "a variety of life experiences of some *articulate* black women" (emphasis added) Preface. What could be called "intentional autobiographies" of slave women begin with Harriet Jacobs' *Incidents in the Life of a Slave Girl* (1861; reprint ed., New York: Harcourt, Brace, Jovanovich, 1973). See William Andrews, *To Tell A Free Story: The First Century of Afro-American Autobiography* (Urbana, IL: University of Illinois Press, 1986). It is useful to contrast Towne's descriptions to those of Southern white women as described in Minrose C. Gwin's *Black and White Women of the Old South: The Peculiar Sisterhood in American Literature* (Knoxville, TN: University of Tennessee Press, 1985). Says Gwin of "white women—fictional or actual, writers or subjects," they see black women "as a color, as servants, as children, as adjuncts, as sexual competition, as dark sides of their own sexual selves—as black Other. They beat black women, nurture them, sentimentalize them, despise them—but they seldom see them as individuals with selves commensurate to their own" (p. 5). Elizabeth Ware Pearson, ed., *Letters from Port Royal: Written at the Time of the Civil War* (Boston: W. B. Clarke Company, 1906), includes the letters of many others besides Towne, but Towne is most adept at recording the language of the blacks. It must also be said that Towne and the other women "missionaries" are more alert to and sensitive to the stories of the women than are the male diarists and letter writers.

4. Holland, *Letters and Diary of Laura M. Towne*, pp. 3–4.
5. Ibid., p. 4.
6. Ibid., pp. 11, 13.
7. Ibid., pp. 28–29.
8. Ibid., p. 58.
9. Ibid., pp. 27–29.
10. Ibid., pp. 23–24.
11. Ibid., p. 57.
12. Ibid., "Introduction," p. xii.
13. Ibid., pp. 16, 19.
14. Ibid., pp. 39, 61.
15. Ibid., pp. 24–25.
16. Ibid., p. 54.
17. Ibid., p. 70.
18. Ibid., p. 31.
19. Ibid., p. 103.
20. Ibid., p. 129.
21. Ibid., pp. 46, 107.
22. Rose, *Rehearsal for Reconstruction*, p. 182.
23. Holland, *Letters and Diary of Laura M. Towne*, p. 73.
24. Ibid., pp. 115, 116.
25. Ibid, p. 122. Higginson was the author of *Army Life in a Black Regiment* (1869; reprint edition, Boston: Beacon Press, 1962); and Commander of the 1st South Carolina Volunteers, later the 33rd U.S. Colored Troops, the first black regiment in the U.S. armed forces.
26. Ibid., pp. 146–150.

27. Ibid., pp. 159, 162.
28. Ibid., p. 171.
29. Ibid., p. 187.
30. Ibid., p. 177.
31. Ibid., p. 182.
32. Ibid., p. 183.
33. Ibid., p. 199.
34. Ibid., p. 271.
35. Ibid., p. 261.
36. Ibid., p. 270.
37. Ibid., pp. 224–225.
38. Dabbs, *Sea Island Diary: A History of St. Helena Island* (Spartanburg, SC: The Reprint Company, 1986), p. 187.
39. See Elizabeth Jacoby, *Yankee Missionaries in the South: The Penn School Experiment* (Baton Rouge, LA: Louisiana State University Press, 1981).
40. Holland, *Letters and Diary of Laura M. Towne*, p. 180.

Chapter 8

HEIRS OF THE SOUTHERN PROGRESSIVE TRADITION: WOMEN IN SOUTHERN LEGISLATURES IN THE 1920s[1]

JOANNE V. HAWKS AND MARY CAROLYN ELLIS

"Women don't belong in politics." In various ways this message issued forth from Southern pulpits, political rostrums, and presses during the 19th and early 20th century. When the women's movement began in the North at mid-century, Southern gentlemen prided themselves that their women were not interested. Later when Southern women's participation in temperance and other reform movements led some women to realize a need for suffrage, they were met with objections from men and women. All sorts of antisuffrage arguments were used: notably, women were too good to vote; they were not educated enough; the franchise would destroy the home; and the Bible taught that God did not mean for women to assume such public responsibilities.

Although there were suffrage organizations in most of the Southern states, in 1920 pro-Amendment forces failed to rally the necessary votes for ratification of the 19th Amendment in most of them. Only three of the former Confederate states, Texas, Arkansas, and Tennessee, voted to ratify the amendment. Yet, despite what could at best be described as lukewarm popular acquiescence to an increasing political role for women, women began entering Southern legislatures shortly after enfranchisement. By this time, Southern Progressivism had lost much of its vitality and unity. However, as Dewey Grantham has shown in his 1983 book on the movement, reformers' efforts "to reconcile progress and tradition" continued.[2] Many of the women who entered Southern legislatures in the 1920s could aptly be described as "cultural traditionalists."[3] Their middle-class status was a common thread, and they viewed their world through that perspective. They were reform-minded, but at the same time they were staunch supporters of their society. They sought reform but not radical change. Generally, they appeared to be content with the political structure that existed in the South—the one-party, white-dominated politics of the day. They focused primarily on need for improvements in the social sphere.

By and large the pioneer women were either products of reform movements, the burgeoning service organizations of the period, or broadening professional opportunities. Several of them were supporters of the suffrage movement. Many more came out of the temperance movement, other social reform efforts, or service organizations. At least half of them were professional women, generally teachers or lawyers.

While many of them had little interest in the suffrage movement, some came to believe strongly in the cause simply because they realized that suffrage was necessary to accomplish some of the social reforms that they advocated. Sometimes their religious beliefs shaped their desire to improve society and to alleviate the misfortunes of others. Products of the Bible Belt, many adhered to the principle that as Christians they had a moral responsibility to help their neighbors. In order to help the needy they turned to state government as a source of funds and programs. They chose to pursue a gradual change in an established manner, in some part because this was the model that they had previously observed. Yet, while they were concerned with the plight of the disadvantaged, they, nonetheless, shared the biases of other Southern progressive reformers.[4]

Thirty-two women became legislators in 10 Southern states in the decade following enfranchisement. Three states—Alabama, Florida, and South Carolina—each had one. Georgia had two; North Carolina and Texas, three; Mississippi, Tennessee, and Virginia, five; and Arkansas, six.[5] The first woman to serve was Lillian Exum Clement, an attorney, who was nominated before the ratification of the 19th Amendment and elected to a seat in the North Carolina House of Representatives in 1920.[6]

As a whole, they were an impressive group of women. Among them were eight lawyers,[7] eight school teachers, four authors, two journalists, and a cosmetologist. Many of the professional women and most of the housewives were also actively involved in women's organizations. They ranged in age from 26 to 69, although most were in their 40s and 50s. About a third of the women were single at the time they served, and the remainder were married or widowed.

The early women legislators tended to fall in one of three main categories. One group of women entered the legislature to exercise their new prerogative. Another group chose politics to pursue idealistic goals. A third group had a more specific goal or personal reason for entering politics. These three groups were not mutually exclusive, and many women shared characteristics of at least two of the three.

A woman who sought office to assert her new right was Hattie Wilkins, Alabama's first woman legislator. Wilkins had been president of the local suffrage organization in Selma, Alabama. During her legislative campaign she observed that women should be involved in the decision-making process. Optimistically, she predicted that soon every county would be represented by both male and female legislators.[8]

Others who had also been active in the suffrage movement before entering the legislature included Sarah Ruth Frazier of Tennessee and Edith Wilmans and Margie Neal of Texas. Helen Moore, another Texan, explained her support of woman suffrage:

In working to secure suffrage for women I did so not only because I believed they should be enfranchised, but because I believed the broadening of the interest of women through their participation in governmental affairs would tend to . . . vindicate our sex of the age-old accusation that we are creatures of sentiment and prejudice and incapable of reasoning.[9]

Three Mississippi legislators, Nellie Somerville, Belle Kearney, and Pauline Clark, were actively involved in woman suffrage efforts. Somerville and Kearney were officers of the state and national associations. Finally, Edna Giles Fuller, Florida's first woman legislator, had been president of the Florida Suffrage Association.[10] She based her campaign for office "on a record of 20 years of constructive public service."[11]

Although Sarah Fain, Virginia's first assembly woman, acknowledged that she had not been too concerned initially about woman suffrage, she later realized that women had something important to contribute to government. Her successful work in a political campaign led a group of friends to suggest that she run for office in 1924. Years later she quoted one of her supporters as saying, "You weren't all we wanted, but you were all we could get."[12] Fain and several others were involved with the League of Women Voters, successor organization to the National American Woman Suffrage Association (NAWSA). Erle Chambers, an Arkansas attorney, was recruited by members of the League to run for office in 1922.[13]

Ironically, Tennessee's first woman legislator was the wife of a state senator, J. Parks Worley, who had led the fight against a 1919 bill to grant presidential and municipal suffrage to women. In so doing, Worley said he was representing the "women of Tennessee who were not present, but who were at home tending to their home duties." Worley considered woman suffrage contrary to "both moral and spiritual law." He believed that 90% of Tennessee's women opposed woman suffrage and the other 10% were "deluded."[14] When Worley died in office in 1921, his widow, Ann Lee Worley, not only succeeded him but sponsored legislation to remove disabilities from women to make them eligible to hold any office in the state.[15]

Erle Rutherford Chambers exemplified the women who sought political power for idealistic reasons. She used her legislative years as one phase of a lifelong crusade to improve conditions for women and children. A former teacher and law clerk, Chambers obtained a law degree in 1912 but was not allowed to practice in Arkansas. While serving as a probation officer, she worked to establish a state industrial school for girls and to convert the boys' reform school into an industrial school. She was also instrumental in the establishment of a boys' club in Little Rock. Later, as executive secretary of the Arkansas Tuberculosis Association, she successfully promoted the creation of a state sanatorium for blacks. While in the legislature, she sponsored a bill to abolish the husband's right of curtesy in his wife's estate, co-sponsored infant and maternity legislation with Frances Hunt, advocated the creation of a commission for the care of the blind, and successfully floor-managed the proposed federal Child Labor Amendment, ratified first by Arkansas.[16]

Many of the women legislators with idealistic concerns hoped to improve conditions for women, children, and mentally or physically handicapped persons. Several were also concerned about maintaining prohibition. This was a natural stance in light of the heavy involvement of many women in the Women's Christian Temperance Union (WCTU) and other efforts to restrict the sale and use of alcohol.

The legislative women with legal training often sought to improve the legal status of women. Edith Wilmans, Texas' first woman representative, entered the legislature at age 40 after raising three daughters and working in parent-teacher associations, church activities, and temperance and other reforms. Interested primarily in issues regarding women and children, she decided to study law to learn how to effect change. During her one term in office she sponsored a variety of bills, including a supplemental school appropriation, a bill to create a court of domestic relations in Dallas County, county assistance for mothers who were unable to care properly for minor children, certification that couples who intended to marry were free of venereal disease, compulsory school attendance, and an increase in the mandatory school age. Only the first measure passed while she was in office, but her concerns, like those of many of her female contemporaries, were harbingers of future legislative enactments.[17]

Other particular issues addressed by the women legislators in the 1920s included appointment of more women to state boards, especially boards of eleemosynary institutions, construction and/or improvement of conditions of institutions for the mentally and physically handicapped, provision of a 40-hour work week for women, outlawing of child labor, compulsory education, improvement of facilities and curriculum of schools, and many other issues. Many of them also, learning the ways of elective politics, sponsored or supported issues of import to their local constituents.

Many women sought legislative office not merely because they had gained the right to do so or had generally idealistic goals but because they hoped to use their position to foster passage of certain pieces of legislation or promote particular types of reform. Not all seemed as blatant as Frances Hunt of Arkansas, a cosmetologist, who was appointed to office by the governor in the spring of 1922 and elected to a full term later in the year. She was instrumental in the passage of a law to regulate the practice of cosmetology. She then retired after her second term to become the state cosmetology board's chief inspector![18]

Those who had a particular interest in education used their positions to effect educational reform. Margie Neal, elected to the Texas Senate in 1926, sought legislative office after lobbying for educational reform. In 1921 she was appointed as the first female to the Board of Regents of the State Normal School. As a regent she often travelled to Austin to lobby for changes the board wished to accomplish. Finally she concluded, "If I had a vote [in the legislature] . . . I might do more for education . . . than I am doing as a college regent sitting in the Gallery."[19] Once in office, she introduced a bill to create a State Board of Education, worked for increased funding for rural schools, creation of physical education classes, and rehabilitation of handicapped persons. A supporter of higher standards for teacher certification, she opposed a measure to grant permanent certification to persons with six years of successful teaching experience.

Occasionally women would stray off into pet issues or even extraneous remarks, as Belle Kearney was known to do. For instance, on one occasion she incorporated " 'personal reminiscences encountered during her European travels' during the debate on a dog tax bill . . . [even though] the correlation between the two could not be found."[20] Yet despite her idiosyncrasies Kearney was also interested in serious legislation. As her biographer noted, "Although only four bills introduced by [Kearney] . . . actually became law, the twenty [she] introduced . . . presented a valid attempt at reform of governmental operations, management of eleemosynary institutions and temperance enforcement."[21]

The entrance of women into formerly all-male preserves evoked a mixed reaction from the legislature and the general public. Belle Kearney and Nellie Somerville made notable entrances into the Mississippi legislature in 1924. Kearney, a rather flamboyant figure, entered the senate attired in a black crepe dress. As she went to her seat, her colleagues stood and applauded. Later they presented her with a bouquet of red roses, which she acknowledged "with a bow and a gesture of appreciation that brought up visions of Queen Bess and Queen Anne."[22] Her colleague, Nellie Somerville, also caused a stir when she entered wearing a hat, thus breaking Rule 10 of the House of Representatives.[23]

When Margie Neal entered the Texas Senate on January 11, 1927, the gentleman senators "smiled indulgently." She asked her colleagues to lend assistance "while she got 'into the harness.' " Despite initial skepticism, by February her fellow senators were calling her " 'our lady senator.' "[24] Similarly, when Edna Giles Fuller was introduced to the Florida House of Representatives by the Speaker, she said, " 'There may be some trepidation among members of the House as to a woman serving in its ranks, but I urge you not to feel this way about me.' "[25]

While their colleagues looked more or less favorably on them, the press sometimes took a different approach. Often they focused on the physical appearance and attire of "lady legislators," as noted in the account of Belle Kearney's entrance. The *Austin American,* in a column headlined "Here's What The Lady Wore When She Began Work," discussed the appearance of Edith Wilmans the first time she or any other woman was seated in the lower house of the Texas legislature:

> *"She had on a gold and grey turban.*
> *"She wore a grey sport coat—somebody said it was astrakan.*
> *"Her dress was a creation of brown satin.*
> *"She wore brown shoes and hose, and—*
> *"She did not have the proverbial bouquet."*[26]

The Virginia press commented on the "special significance" of the election of Sarah Fain and Helen T. Henderson to the Virginia House of Delegates in 1923. It was noted that "they were the first female participants in the oldest legislature in America, and they sat in halls 'made famous by the membership of giants like Thomas Jefferson and Patrick Henry.' " The *Richmond Times Dispatch* commented that, "were he alive, Sir George Yeardley, the Virginia governor who had convened the assembly of 1619, would probably be distressed at the inclusion of women in the legislature." Yet, the article continued, " 'who cares for Governor Yeardley? Virginia is 300 years wiser now than it was in his day. That is why Mrs. Fain and Mrs. Henderson will sit in the next House of Delegates.' " The Norfolk *Virginian-Pilot* noted that Fain and Henderson would probably be " 'only the first in a long procession of women to hold public office in Virginia,' " but as the first " 'the spotlight will play upon them as it will play on none of their confreres.' " When the women arrived in Richmond in January 1924, it was reported that they

> *immediately found themselves in the limelight. Their presence in the Capitol was a novelty, and the two women drew attention from apprehensive colleagues, eager reporters, and curious Richmonders. Few freshmen representatives made a stir in official circles, but the two first-term women were treated as legislative debutantes.*[27]

Margie Neal faced critical comments from the press when she voted against a measure she had sponsored because of the amendment. Several newspapers related that the lady senator had become so overwhelmed by the involved parliamentary procedures that she had voted against her own bill. Neal's biographer, noted that she was amazed at the press' reaction:

> *After reading the newspapers, Senator Neal rose to a point of personal privilege and explained that she had voted against the amended bill because the amendment mutilated her bill so thoroughly that she no longer considered it her own. She acknowledged a certain unfamiliarity with parliamentary technicalities, and requested the continued patience and forbearance of her colleagues. She stated emphatically, however, that she desired no quarter from the gentlemen merely because she was a woman.*

The manner in which she spoke drew the spontaneous applause of fellow senators, and possibly went far toward making her acceptance by the Senate a reality.[28]

As might be expected, some of the women were more active and effective than others. Their personal styles varied, with some much more vocal and forward in their approach to their office. Many received accolades at the time or assessments later which focused on their ladylike approach to their position and their general effectiveness. Oveta Culp Hobby's remarks about Margie Neal mirrored comments made at one time or another about several of the women:

In the Senate Miss Margie was a unique figure: First, simply because she was a woman; and second, because she was so unlike those driving, militant, admirable women—but not always enchanting women—that we were left to expect after the suffragettes had made their march in the United States. Miss Margie felt as free to be feminine as a Senator as she had as a private citizen of Carthage [Texas].[29]

Reflections on the career of Mary Ellis, the only woman legislator elected in South Carolina in the 1920s, referred to her "serenity" and "winning smile" and the "quiet, dignified but forceful manner" with which she served out her senatorial term.[30] Sarah Fain of Virginia also received complimentary comments on her "superb record" and effectiveness.[31]

Nellie Somerville and Belle Kearney of Mississippi were praised for their dignity. Tongue-in-cheek remarks in the *Jackson Daily News* contrasted them with their male colleagues in the following manner:

Neither of them has, up to this moment, ripped and reared and pitched and shouted that she yields to no other lady in her love for this gr-r-rand and gle-or-ious old commonwealth. . . . We don't suppose the lady senator from Madison or the lady representative from Washington will ever amount to much in public life. They have all the earmarks of rational human beings, even when they are making speeches.[32]

Most of the early women were short-term legislators. Few served more than four years.[33] From the information available, several observations can be made. Four women did not begin their legislative service until they were 60 years old or more, a probable factor in their decision not to seek reelection. Somerville and Kearney each retired after one four-year term when both were in their mid-60s. Vinnie Caldwell of Virginia served only one two-year term. Her colleague, Sallie Booker, a veteran of 20 years as a school teacher, was elected at the age of 69. She retired at the conclusion of her second two-year term.[34] Three women, Pauline Clark of Mississippi, Mary Ellis of South Carolina, and

Edna Giles Fuller of Florida were defeated in reelection bids. Helen T. Henderson of Virginia died before her term expired.[35]

Several decided to pursue other goals. Ellen Woodward, elected to the Mississippi legislature in 1925 to complete the term of her deceased husband, felt that she could not support her son adequately on her salary as a legislator. After several years of experience with the Mississippi Board of Development, she received the first of several federal appointments in the Roosevelt administration.[36] Margie Neal of Texas received a New Deal appointment before the completion of her second term.[37] Edith Wilmans of Texas ran for governor in 1924, and Sarah Fain of Virginia ran for Congress in 1930.[38] Neither was elected. Wilmans, later described as a "perennial candidate," ran for governor again in 1926, for the legislature in 1935, and for Congress in 1948 and 1951, all without success.[39] Fain served in several New Deal agencies after her Congressional defeat. She was the organizer and first director of the United States Information Service.[40]

Some of the others may have left to pursue other careers. Bessie Kempton, of Georgia, became editor and publisher of the *Fulton County Times* after eight years in office.[41] Marion Griffin, the first woman lawyer in Tennessee, returned to Memphis to practice law.[42] Helen Moore, of Texas, a diligent clubwoman and philanthropist, remained active in public service for many years after leaving the legislature.[43]

None of the women appeared to approach legislative service as a career. Some, like Moore, seemed to view it as one stage in a varied career of public service. A few may even have sought office as a novelty, although most seemed to have undertaken their responsibilities seriously. Shortly after the ratification of the suffrage amendment in 1920 the *Florida Times-Union* (Jacksonville) ran the following comment:

> *Yesterday the Tennessee legislature ratified the Anthony amendment giving women the right to vote but the sun did not stop or hurry in its course. The waters continued to flow towards the sea and the breeze fanned the people of Jacksonville as was their custom. Nature did not celebrate the event even with a thunderstorm. We do not look for any seismic disturbances in the political field. The number of persons qualified for participation in the election will be increased by about one-fourth and that is about all. We look neither for the millenium nor for the destruction of the world.[44]*

Ten years later, at the end of a decade when women had begun to serve in the legislatures of 10 Southern states, similar observations might have been made. Neither Armageddon nor the millennium had occurred. Legislative chambers still stood, and proceedings droned on much as they always had. Although many of their male colleagues praised the women publicly, too much emphasis probably should not be placed on this. Many of the flowery statements may have been motivated more by Southern chivalry than by the legislators' true feelings. Supporters and critics of women in public office continued to hold their conflicting opinions, although critics were probably a little relieved and supporters somewhat disappointed with what the pioneers had accomplished.

Yet, despite the lack of dazzling accomplishments, a breakthrough had been made. All of the states continued to elect women to office, generally in increasing though modest numbers. The old cliché, "Women don't belong in politics," was finally laid to rest. Some diehards might continue to begrudge them their place, but the women were there to stay. Their accomplishments in future years is another story for another time, but later women might well look back at the pioneers who haltingly or steadfastly or in an occasional blaze of glory had marked the trail for them. A remark made about Margie Neal could well serve as a tribute to all: "Although identified with many public interests, 'the woman herself remains a woman to the last, still linked with herself and with humanity.' "[45] The lady legislators of the 1920s by being there had made their mark.

NOTES

1. The research for the paper was supported by a grant from the National Endowment for the Humanities.
2. Dewey W. Grantham, *Southern Progressivism: The Reconciliation of Progress and Tradition* (Knoxville: University of Tennessee Press, 1983), p. 422.
3. Ibid., p. 418.
4. Ibid, pp. xvii–xviii.
5. The following is a list of women elected to Southern legislatures in the 1920s and details of their service:

Name	State	House	Year elected	Years served
Lillian Clement	NC	HR	1920	1921–23
Ann Worley	TN	SEN	1921*	1921–22
Viola Napier	GA	HR	1922	1923–24
Bessie Kempton	GA	HR	1922	1923–29
Frances Hunt	AR	HR	1922	1923–26
Erle Chambers	AR	HR	1922	1923–25
Hattie Wilkins	AL	HR	1922	1923–24
Edith Wilmans	TX	HR	1922	1923–25
Marion Griffin	TN	HR	1922	1923–24
Nellie Somerville	MS	HR	1923	1924–27
Belle Kearney	MS	SEN	1923	1924–27
Helen T. Henderson	VA	HD	1923	1924–25
Sarah Lee Fain	VA	HD	1923	1924–29
Julia McGehee Alexander	NC	HR	1924	1925–27
Anne M. Davis	TN	HR	1924	1925–26
Elizabeth (Lizzie) Lea Miller	TN	HR	1924	1925–26
Elizabeth H. Thompson	AR	HR	1924	1925–26

Name	State	House	Year elected	Years served
Ellen Sullivan Woodward	MS	HR	1925*	1925–27
Sallie Cook Booker	VA	HD	1925	1926–29
Florence McGraw McRaven	AR	HR	1926	1927–30
Carrie Lee McLean	NC	HR	1926	1927–29
Sarah Ruth Frazier	TN	HR	1926	1927–28
Margie Elizabeth Neal	TX	SEN	1926	1927–35
Mary B. Wigstrand	AR	HR	1926	1927–28
Pauline Alston Clark	MS	HR	1927	1928–31
Mildred Jeffries Nail	MS	HR	1927	1928–31
Vinnie Caldwell	VA	HD	1927	1928–29
Helen Ruth Henderson	VA	HD	1927	1928–30
Edna Giles Fuller	FL	HR	1928	1929–32
Maude R. Brown	AR	HR	1928	1929–30
Mary Gordon Ellis	SC	SEN	1928	1929–32
Helen Edmunds Moore	TX	HR	1928	1929–37

* Succeeded husband who died in office.

6. Representatives in the General Assembly, *North Carolina Handbook,* 1921, p. 457.
7. Several of the women who had studied law were not allowed to practice because of their state's refusal to license women for the practice of law.
8. Joanne Varner Hawks, "A Select Few: Alabama's Women Legislators, 1922–1983," *The Alabama Review,* 38(1985):177–178, quoting unidentified newspaper clipping, "Beautiful Reception Honoring Mrs. Wilkins."
9. Helen Moore to Mrs. Jane Y. McCallum, March 6, 1929; letter in McCallum Papers, State Library of Texas, Austin.
10. Their activities have been described in the following theses: Mary Louise Meredith, "The Mississippi Women's Rights Movement, 1889–1923: The Leadership Role of Nellie Nugent Somerville in Suffrage Reform" (Master's thesis, Delta State University, 1974) and Nancy Carol Tipton, " 'It Is My Duty': The Public Career of Belle Kearney" (Master's thesis, The University of Mississippi, 1975). See also Clarksdale *Press Register,* March 14, 1944.
11. Allen Morris, "Florida's Women Candidates," *The Florida Historical Quarterly* 63(1985):414.
12. *The Richmond News-Leader,* December 6, 1952 and July 20, 1962.
13. *Arkansas Democrat,* January 10, 1941.
14. A. Elizabeth Taylor, *The Woman Suffrage Movement in Tennessee* (New York: Bookman Associates, 1957), pp. 101–102.
15. "Women Who Have Served in the General Assembly of Tennessee, January 1921– January 1985," an unpublished compendium prepared by the Office of Legal Services, Nashville, Tennessee, March, 1985.
16. *Arkansas Democrat,* January 10, 1941.
17. Mary Beth Rogers, ed., *Texas Women, A Celebration of History,* p. 203; Elizabeth W. Fernea and Marilyn P. Duncan, eds., Texas Women in Politics (Austin: Foundation for Women's Resources, 1981), pp. 6–9; "Mrs. Wilmans Again Running for Congress," *Dallas Morning News,* July 8, 1951; "Last Rites Slated for Mrs. Wilmans," *Dallas Times Herald,* March 22, 1966; Sue Hall, "The 1925 All

Woman Supreme Court, Texas,'' Women in Texas History Files at Texas Woman's University, Denton, Texas.

18. Frances Rowena Mathews Jones Hunt, Biographical Memoranda, Arkansas History Commission, Little Rock.

19. *The Longview Morning Journal*, November 20, 1977.

20. Tipton, " 'It Is My Duty': The Public Career of Belle Kearney,'' pp. 123–126, quoting Jackson's *Clarion Ledger*, March 28, 1924.

21. Ibid., p. 127.

22. Ibid., pp. 120–121, quoting *Woman Voter*, January 11, 1924; *Jackson Daily News*, January 9, 1924; and Jackson's *Clarion Ledger*, January 9, 1924.

23. Ibid., pp. 120, 122, citing an interview with Somerville's daughter, Lucy Somerville Howorth, and Jackson's *Clarion Ledger*, January 9, 1924.

24. Walter Lawrence Harris, "The Life of Margie Neal" (Master's thesis, University of Texas, 1955), pp. 99–100.

25. Morris, "Florida's First Women Candidates," p. 415, quoting *The Florida Times-Union* (Jacksonville), April 4, 1929.

26. *Austin American*, January 10, 1923.

27. These comments were included in a feature article by Sandra Gioia Treadway, "Sarah Lee Fain, Norfolk's First Woman Legislator," *Virginia Cavalcade*, 30 (1981):129. Treadway quoted several contemporary comments by the Virginia press.

28. Walter L. Harris, "Margie E. Neal: First Woman Senator in Texas," *East Texas Historical Journal*, 9(1973):42.

29. Ibid., p. 41, quoting remarks by Oveta Culp Hobby at a Margie E. Neal Appreciation Day Program in 1952.

30. Eleanor Winn Foxworth, "She Entered the Senate to Work for Education," *The State* (Columbia), April 22, 1970.

31. "First Virginia Assembly Woman Dies in California," *The Richmond News-Leader*, July 20, 1962.

32. Tipton, " 'It Is My Duty': The Public Career of Belle Kearney," p. 126, quoting *Jackson Daily News*, March 2, 1924.

33. Only Bessie Kempton (Georgia), Helen Moore (Texas), and Margie Neal (Texas) served as long as eight years.

34. *The Richmond News-Leader*, January 21, 1942; *Times Dispatch* (Richmond), December 21, 1944.

35. Mary Ellis, who gained her seat by defeating an incumbent, lost to him in the next election (*The State* [Columbia], April 22, 1970, p. 16). Fuller was defeated in 1932 along with a number of other incumbents (Morris, "Florida's First Women Candidates," p. 416). Allen Morris, Clerk of the Florida House of Representatives since 1966, said an extensive search turned up no reasons for her defeat other than the general dissatisfaction with incumbents in the "greatest turnover in the history of the Florida house." Helen Henderson died July 12, 1925. Her daughter, Helen Ruth Henderson, was elected to the seat in 1928 and served one term (*Times Dispatch* [Richmond], February 23, 1982).

36. Joanne V. Hawks, M. Carolyn Ellis, and J. Byron Morris, "Women in the Mississippi Legislature (1924–1981)," *Journal of Mississippi History*, 43(1981):275–276.

37. Harris, "Margie E. Neal: First Woman Senator in Texas," p. 46.

38. Wilmans had received an appointment by Governor Pat Neff to the Texas Supreme Court in 1924 but was denied a seat because of inadequate legal experience. Sue Hall, "The 1925 All Woman Supreme Court, Texas," p. 21.
39. Rogers, *Texas Women, A Celebration of History*, p. 203.
40. Treadway, "Sarah Lee Fain, Norfolk's First Woman Legislator," p. 132; Radford Mobley, "Mrs. Fain, First Woman Solon Gives Aid to Homesteaders, "*The Richmond News-Leader*, April 16, 1935; Nancy King, "Mrs. Fain, Ex-Solon Visits Here," *The Richmond News-Leader*, December 6, 1952.
41. Peggy Childs, "Women in the Georgia Legislature" (unpublished paper, August 1983), p. 2.
42. Marion Griffin received a law degree from the University of Michigan in 1906. After passing the bar examination, she was informed by the Tennessee State Supreme Court that Tennessee law did not allow women to practice. She appealed to the state legislature which passed a law allowing women to practice. After one term in the legislature (1923–1924), she practiced law in Memphis until 1949. "Women Who Have Served in the General Assembly of Tennessee."
43. *The Galveston Daily News*, September 23, 1968; *The Press* (Houston), April 19, 1935; *The Houston Post*, October 28, 1936.
44. Morris, "Florida's First Women Candidates," p. 407, quoting *The Florida Times-Union* (Jacksonville), August 19, 1920.
45. *Who's Who of the Womanhood of Texas*, Vol. I, sponsored, edited, and compiled by the Texas Federation of Women's Clubs, 1923–1924.

Chapter 9

THE BLACK DOMESTIC IN THE SOUTH: HER LEGACY AS MOTHER AND MOTHER SURROGATE

SUSAN TUCKER

"Nearly every traveler in the American South reported the ubiquity of the black child nurse," David Katzman noted in his book *Seven Days a Week: Women and Domestic Service in Industrializing America*.[1] In this statement, Katzman was particularly noting the travel literature from 1870 to 1920, but his remark holds true in countless other works depicting Southern life throughout the 19th and early 20th centuries. The black child nurse was, indeed, long linked with many facets of the South in the popular imagination. She is the robust mammy of the plantation. Or she is the woman drawn in lithographs, mother surrogate to white children, sitting with them on wrought iron benches in parks where other blacks were denied access. More obscurely but still powerfully depicted, she is also a mother to her own children, predecessor of the black matriarch, sometimes blamed by society for the disruption of the black family. Alternately, she is the woman to whom books are dedicated, the woman who labors at menial jobs so that her children will not have to do the same.

Both as a mother surrogate and mother, however, she has been largely ignored in scholarly works exploring the lives of Southern women. Her work has not seemed important enough to have been documented.[2] And yet, it is primarily through her that Southern white and black women engaged in common and sometimes shared gender-related tasks, particularly in childrearing.

It is the purpose here, therefore, to examine what we do know of the lives and work of black domestics who labored from roughly 1880 to 1965. I am interested particularly in the labor of domestics who were primarily caretakers of children, in the ways in which the work of these domestics did or did not join

Southern white and black women, and in the meaning of her "ubiquity" as a legacy to the larger Southern community—white and black, male and female in the 20th century. An interdisciplinary approach is utilized, drawing upon the image of the child nurse in literature and the portrait we can draw from historical analyses and from interviews with domestics and employers of domestics. These latter were conducted in extensive open-ended interviews with approximately 100 women born between 1880 and 1960 in the Gulf South area—Louisiana, Mississippi, Alabama, and Florida.[3]

Her role, as I have noted, is two-fold in that she is both mother and mother surrogate. But it is two-fold once over again because she is also both a literary persona and a historical persona. It is the literary persona, however, that is most visible. For example, in the 19th century, she was portrayed in such roles as Nanny in *The Recollections of a Southern Matron* by Caroline Howard Gillman, Mammy in *Uncle Tom's Cabin* by Harriet Beecher Stowe, Aunt Phillis in *Aunt Phillis's Cabin* by Mary Eastman, and Mammy Krenda in *Red Rock* by Thomas Nelson Page.[4] All of these works show her as a devoted mother surrogate to white children, a powerful figure within the white family but a powerless one in the external world. As Stephen Vincent Benét wrote in *John Brown's Body,* she was both "matriarch and slave."[5]

Mammy Krenda is a particularly striking example of this paradoxical role for she is the epitome of the film version of the household worker with settings in the late part of the 19th and early 20th centuries. She is described as an "old Mammy" and she wears "a white apron, with a tall bandana turban around her head." The white child, Blair, and Blair's mother both answer to her, and she is described when leaving a white party as both curtseying and carrying "her head as high as a princess."[6]

Twentieth-century works such as Julia Peterkin's *Green Thursday,* William Faulkner's *The Sound and the Fury,* Katherine Ann Porter's *The Leaning Tower and Other Stories,* Lillian Smith's *Strange Fruit,* Carson McCuller's *The Member of the Wedding,* Harper Lee's *To Kill a Mockingbird,* Shirley Ann Grau's *The Keeper of the House,* and many other recent works continue to present household workers who mother white families.[7] In these works, however, she has evolved into a character of more complexity and individuality. She is no longer linked in false kinship with the white family and most often not called "Mammy," "Aunt," or "Nanny." And we see that she lives her life in two communities—both white and black.

Yet, her strength as a mothering character is still pronounced. Since white adults could not act toward her as they had once in childhood, they internalized, idealized, and exaggerated the conditions under which they had known her. Thus, they did not renounce the stereotypical mammy completely. Instead, they made her into something of a superwoman.

The domestic as this superwoman is an image that has remained popular until the present. Such an image allows readers the picture of a foster mother who loves and administers to white children no matter what the circumstances.[8]

Her strength reflects a rationalization about how she could labor under harsh societal and economic conditions. But the effect of her strength is one in which readers themselves feel strong.

One of the most memorable of these 20th-century strong domestics in white Southern literature is Carson McCuller's Berenice, from *The Member of the Wedding*. Berenice brings such examples as perseverance and victory over life's limits. Because Berenice has not been defeated by cultural attitudes, nor an unhappy though plentiful love life, she helps Frankie, the young *motherless* white girl, understand and accept herself. Berenice speaks of the need to work within life's limits. She explains her own disappointments in terms of historical and social forces. No white woman known to the girl Frankie could have told of life so directly or so vividly.[9]

Countless other literary domestics bring to white women and white children stories of life's wisdom. In *To Kill a Mockingbird,* Calpurnia's story of learning to read—having an education denied to the other blacks in the book—may be contrasted with the frivolous tea party of the children's aunt. It is with Calpurnia that the children learn of life's more important messages.[10] And in Ellen Gilchrist's *The Annunciation,* it is the black domestic who first believes the white protagonist can be anything other than a drinking society lady.[11]

The historical domestic served, of course, as the basis of such strong literary domestics. The complex psychology of oppression worked in such a way that black women saw themselves and were seen as stronger than white women. In going into the white home, black domestics saw the problems of white women; they saw particularly another form of oppression in the passivity demanded of white women. They saw specifically that Southern white women, even those in positions of power, attempted to conceal their strength. Thus, the sheltered white lady could not teach or encourage others in life. Lillian Hellman wrote of her long time housekeeper, Helen, saying that the latter did not think white people "capable of dealing with trouble."[12] It seems likely that other white and black women held, and continue to hold, similar thoughts, thus choosing black women as heroines, as women who can "deal with trouble."

It is in this image of strength, however, that the depiction of household workers by black authors departs most radically from that of whites. Black authors, instead, show the burden of such an image, show the physical and emotional injury born of the oppression of blacks, show specific injuries done the black domestic and her family. In *From Mammies to Militants: Domestics in Black American Literature,* Trudier Harris divides maids as portrayed in works by black authors into three categories: "Thus true southern maids epitomize mammyism; transitional or moderate figures wear masks evoking the true southern maid; and militants wear southern masks only to bring about violence or never wear them—instead confronting exploitation directly."[13] In her analysis, the "southern maid" neglects her own family almost entirely to serve the white family and has no sense of the resultant damage.

The "transitional" maid, on the other hand, realizes the problems of laboring as both mother and mother surrogate in the poor world of blacks and the rich world of whites. Ann Petry's book *The Street* is one of the books in which Harris locates a "transitional maid." Although the setting of this novel is in the North, Lutie's fatigue is not different from what actual Southern domestics surely felt. The predominant mood is one of despair constantly building. Lutie is also aware of the contrast between affluent white life and her own poverty. In an early episode, Lutie is standing on the subway looking at an advertisement for a modern kitchen. "A miracle of a kitchen, it is just like that kitchen in Connecticut that had changed her whole life—that kitchen, all tricks and white enamel."[14] It is precisely because Lutie wants a life similar to the one she has known in the white household that she takes on attitudes that will ultimately be her downfall.

Lutie, however, entered domestic service because she had no other choice. Countless other actual black women found no other choice throughout America for all but the last two decades. Thus, forced by economic necessity, black domestics moved daily between the white and black communities. Herein, they became the interpreters, go-betweens, messengers of sorts. They explained, directly or indirectly, black life to whites and white life to blacks.

It is therefore logical that in literature the domestic has been chosen to explain and reflect upon life, particularly on the ways of Southern segregation. In choosing the domestic to play this central role, authors have provided images of the black working mother there in life, but denied historical documentation. The child nurse who also happens to be a mother and who lived in reality is, after all, not so clearly located in written sources. Labor statistics, for example, do not even give her work a consistent name or job title. In the decennial censuses covering the period 1890 to 1960, she was classed variously with servants, nurses (not trained), housekeepers, or private household workers.[15] The various biographical, sociological, and historical studies that do exist lump her into the category with other domestics because no specific sources on her work alone can be found.[16]

We do know, however, that throughout the 19th century and the first five decades of the 20th century, Southern black women had little other choice of employment but domestic work and that many of these workers were mothers. As late as 1960, one half of all working black women in the urban South were domestic workers.[17] Among the 48 domestic workers I interviewed, all but one had children, all but two had worked in the years their children were young, and all had worked at both housekeeping and childminding.

Who was the Southern black domestic who worked primarily with children, then? From the interviews I conducted with domestics and their employers, I would say that she was often a woman who had worked most of her life caring for children, either her own or someone else's. Most of the women I spoke with also had strong bonds with their extended families and neighbors. They told stories of the white families for whom they labored and of their own families and neighbors. Through stories of their connections with both these groups—white and black—a picture of the working conditions and work of the black child nurse can be seen.

It is the image of the mother working for her own children that predominated in all my interviews. One of the most poignant stories told to me was of a black woman's journey to work one very cold morning. She left her own neighborhood at 6:30 a.m.; left her three children asleep in the living room with her mother; left grits on the stove for their breakfast; left the house, smelling of the gas space heater but being damp and cold. She left this two-room house, catching one bus and when she stood, "waiting for the second bus," she was so cold her fingers "wouldn't move." She continued: "I started to go back because I had waited so long. But I decided to walk on to Miz Jernigan's. I walked and walked. On the way it started to snow. So, that's why the bus hadn't come. The coldest day in New Orleans history. I stood there, turned around to go back. I thought of my little children, I went on." She then described her fingers—blue from cold—and the warm spacious house of her employers. When she got there, "They said, 'Hurry up. Mister Charles has been waiting for his coffee!' They didn't even offer to let me warm up."

Most other women "went on" for their children as well. They often described their goals, in terms exclusively centered on their children. They also described how these goals made them continue work. Conscientious mothers, they found domestic work better suited for a flexible schedule demanded by their role as mothers. They compared domestic work with defense work during the 1940s "where you could never bring the children to work." And they noted that in other forms of work, having a sick child, you could not make up "days" later. Also in domestic work, black women could "keep their job going," during emergencies, and particularly following childbirth, by having a sister, mother, friend, or even an older child take over the job in their absence. They called this "keeping the job going," and this was the only form of pregnancy leave described to me. All of these choices were based on a male-dominated segregated labor force, but they also were formed by conscious decisions by the workers within this labor force to be caring mothers.

Black children, who daily saw their mothers depart, knew something about such choices. And from their mother's work, they learned about the segregated world that forced such choices. They learned that white children called their mothers by their first names, not considering them equal to white mothers. To visit their mothers' workplace meant coming in the back door, sitting in the kitchen, and possibly polishing silver, or performing some other tasks. If they played with the white children their mothers cared for, this often meant games where they, as blacks, were chosen last, or were cast as losers.

From such encounters, and from their mothers' desires, black girl children often chose different work for themselves. In one of the first interviews, a woman who had been born of a white man and a black woman spoke. Her mother had been a baby nurse, one who went from house to house for periods of two weeks to two months helping with newborns and their mothers. The speaker, daughter to this baby nurse, told a particularly telling story of the desire of her mother. She was said to have made her father and his brothers swear on her deathbed that her child "would never have to nurse no babies until she nursed her own." Although the daughter did not speculate upon the meaning of this promise, it seems clear that her mother wanted for her a life in which she could be a mother to her own children at least before having to go into the homes of whites. Her daughter could avoid the sexual harassment that did sometime accompany the job.

Other domestics also described conscious steps of not duplicating older traditions of the ties between domestics and whites. They spoke of not borrowing money from whites, as "Mama had to do." And many spoke of "not marrying yourself to a job." They also spoke of hiding goals of higher education for their children from their employers. They spoke of "old ways" where "if you worked for a family, your daughter was expected to, too" and of conscious steps to break this pattern.

In the memories of white women, the domestic worker is seen as the same caring woman, but in a more idealized way as a superwoman similar to her counterpart in literature. "Her even-handed care, easy going ways, and folk remedies" are remembered frequently. And she is often contrasted with the white mother. An often heard sentence was, "I was closer to her than I was to my own mother."

The biological mothers of the white women I spoke with were upper-middle class, for the most part, and were seen as distant, involved in community and church work in a way that made the domestic clearly in charge of the children. Many of the white mothers who were not upper-middle class worked themselves as secretaries and shopkeepers—and again, their work outside the home made them seem distant. However, such distance was not viewed negatively by any of the white children or white mothers I interviewed. Instead these white children remembered having much more independence than their friends whose mothers stayed home. And the white mothers remembered a lifestyle greatly enhanced by the help of black women.

At the same time, black domestics were seen as much closer physically to the white children, and this too was seen as desirable. One woman who now works as a psychiatrist told me that she found white children raised by black women to have an easier acceptance of their bodies, to be more sensual and caring people. Another white woman told how she always felt comforted as a teenager in that the black community she knew through the family maid, unlike the white community, did not send away unwed mothers in shame.

It is in such memories that we find one way that a shared gender affected the bonds between white and black women as they were perceived by white women. As in literature, black domestics inspired white women by their strength and perseverance. Particularly, many working white women told me of how the memory of black domestics aided them in their dual roles as mothers and workers.

These and other individual influences, of course, are difficult to pull together in an analysis of how shared gender affected white and black women. In addition, I found only two remembrances among 52 black women in which black women were similarly influenced by white women. David Katzman in his book *Seven Days a Week* noted that between the white mistress and black servant from the period of 1870 to 1920 the ''shared roles of motherhood were denied.'' He cites an example of a working mother who could not even speak to her children when they passed the white home, her work place.[18]

Although Katzman's example is an extreme one, strong social constraints seemed to have prohibited any true reciprocity between white women employers and black domestics. There was, for example, no discussion between white and black women about pregnancy leave or the continued care of white and black children together as a solution to a working black woman's care of her own children. Although black women did mention bringing their children to work on school holidays and in emergencies, not one person told me of establishing such arrangements on a full-time basis. Indeed, as integration became a possibility, white employers seemed to have resisted even these temporary arrangements involving the care of a black domestic's children in white homes. One black woman, remembering a job in the early 1960s, told of bringing her son to her employers' one day after school. The next day, the employers wanted to be assured that this was only a one-time arrangement. White women were also not noted for asking about child-care arrangements. All whites, said one black woman, ''assume you have a mother, or an older daughter, to keep your child, so it's all right to leave your kids.'' Stories of white employers not believing the children of domestics were sick, but hearing this as an excuse not to work, were also common. Stories, too, of white women who did not inquire of a domestic's family—even when that domestic went on extended trips with the family—were not uncommon. And work on Christmas morning and other holidays for black mothers was not considered by white employers as unfair. Indeed, work on these days was seen as particularly important to the job.

Black women felt intensely the irony of the fact that to care for their own children, they had to work with white children, while white women led lives centered around shopping for clothes, playing cards, and planning parties. ''You were taking good care of their children, and yours were probably just running wild,'' said one black woman. White women were seen as frivolous even in their more altruistic pursuits, such as their community work, which was often oriented toward helping the less privileged in far-away places while ignoring the less privileged in the immediate environment.

And so, any bonds based on shared gender appear to have been one sided. White women saw in black domestics shared work in a job that is generally done alone, generally relegated to the women in the family. And they also saw that without the black woman and her low wages their lifestyles would be radically different. They saw, but did not choose to admit, that their lifestyles were most often ones in which they exploited the same women for whom they felt such affection.

And so, white women chose, in all but one or two rare cases among my interviews, not to question the hard lives of black women, not to question what their affection for these other women meant. White women who paid above a certain wage, for example, were frowned upon by other whites. And even those who gave away items to black women in the paternalistic way of compensating low pay were told, "Don't give them your best things." Racial etiquette also deemed it unacceptable to discuss race with blacks. Because race governed so much of what kind of life one led, white women who daily saw the same black woman year after year often knew little of her troubles. Moreover, they feared that discussing such intimacies might make black domestics "uppity."

Black domestics, wearing the masks learned in slavery—and often mothers whose jobs were crucial to their families' survival—conformed to this code of silence as well. And so, shared gender roles did not enable these two—white and black women—to form a bond that worked towards more than continuing the role of black domestics as laborers at a subsistence level.

Again, though, it is important to come back to the literary persona of the black child nurse. In her we can relocate the bonds that at times existed and can look more clearly at the legacy found in the memory of the domestic child nurse. In Katherine Anne Porter's "The Last Leaf," the role of Nannie as a mother surrogate is reiterated in the ending. We are told she could always win arguments with one of the adult sons of the white family by claiming she had nursed him at her breast.[19] Thus, he acknowledges her surrogate motherhood and the memory of his own mother—for and with whom Nannie had labored since girlhood—and by extension, brings us back to the author's purpose in showing her as an equal participant in his early life. In this latter acknowledgment, readers within the segregated society are asked to look more closely at the relationship between whites and blacks.

In nonfiction works, such acknowledgments often begin in recollections of black child nurses, noting how they are forgotten and misplaced people in the memories of white adults. Lillian Smith and Adrienne Rich are two white women writers who have written in this way of domestics who were known to them in childhood. Lillian Smith wrote extensively of the mother role in Southern culture, comparing the black caretaker to the ineffectual white mother who conformed to Southern expectations of docile women. She presents the black nurse as the kind, comforting, and strong parent—as opposed to the white mother whom she found lacking in courage, strength, and warmth. Smith wrote of how her own education in racism and that of so many other white children occurs first through the repression of feelings for black domestics.[20] Similarly, Adrienne Rich speaks of the black domestic who nurtured and cared for her as a child. She speaks of how "there is little yet known, unearthed of the time when we [black and white women] were mothers and daughters."[21]

Paralleling these thoughts of whites are thoughts concerning a different displacement of the black domestic in the memories of black adults. In black culture, the domestic who mothered white children has most often been blamed for an alliance with whites and this blame has largely overshadowed her very real contributions. As the daughter of a domestic told me: "There's always been a tendency to look down on maids. . . . But I wonder. . . . It seems that what these women did, their very survival and our very survival, may just have defied some male white view of life, so that no one believes it." Or as Mildred, the domestic in Alice Childress's *Like One of the Family . . . Conversations from a Domestic's Life* says: "Domestic workers have done an awful lot of good things in this country besides clean up people's houses."[22]

That domestics left such marks upon America, and particularly the American South, deserves further attention. Certainly, the black female child nurse left a legacy to the history of Southern women. Through her coming and going between white and black cultures she left a body of memories through which we can begin to sort out many of the intersections of race, class, and gender in our society.

NOTES

1. David Katzman, *Seven Days a Week: Women and Domestic Service in Industrializing America* (New York: Oxford University Press, 1978), p. 187.
2. Only in very recent times have studies on domestic workers begun to appear. Among these are Robert Hamburger's *A Stranger in the House* (New York: Macmillan, 1978), a book of oral histories of Northern domestic workers; a chapter in Bettina Aptheker's book, *Woman's Legacy: Essays on Race, Sex, Class in American History* (Amherst, MA: University of Massachusetts Press, 1982), an exploration of domestic work within a Marxist framework; Elizabeth Clark-Lewis's " 'This Work Had A' End': The Transition From Live-In to Day Work," (Memphis, TN: Memphis State University, The Center for Research on Women, 1985), a working paper discussing live-in versus live-out work among domestic workers in the Washington, D. C., area from 1900 to 1920; Judith Rollin's book *Between Women: Domestics and Their Employers* (Philadelphia: Temple University Press, 1985), a study of the roles and attitudes of domestics and employers in the Boston area in the 1980s; Linda Martin's and Kerry Segrave's *The Servant Problem: Domestic Workers in North America* (Jefferson, NC: McFarland, 1985), a study of domestic workers nationwide from 1940 to the present; Daniel Sutherland's *Americans and Their Servants: Domestic Service in the United States from 1800 to 1920* (Baton Rouge, LA: Louisiana State University Press, 1981), a historical study; Trudier Harris's *From Mammies to Militants: Domestics in Black American Literature* (Philadelphia: Temple University Press, 1982), a book analyzing the evolution of the literary domestic in Afro-American literature; and a number of publications of the Department of Labor and the National Committee on Household Employment. Most helpful and thorough is David Katzman's *Seven Days a Week,* which contains a chapter on Southern domestics during the period 1870 to 1920. Although it deals primarily with 19th-century black and white women, Minrose Gwin's *Black and White Women of the Old South: The Peculiar Sisterhood in American Literature* (Knoxville, TN: University of Tennessee Press, 1985) is also helpful in looking at bonds documented in literature between earlier black and white Southern women, bonds almost exclusively centered on the domestic sphere.
3. The interviews were conducted between 1979 and 1985. Some of the interviews

conducted on this project will be published in a book under contract to Louisiana State University Press.

4. Caroline Howard Gilman, *The Recollections of a Southern Matron* (New York: Harper and Row, 1938); Harriet Beecher Stowe, *Uncle Tom's Cabin; or Life Among the Lonely* (Boston: Houghton, Osgood & Company, 1888); Mary H. Eastman, *Aunt Phillis's Cabin; or Southern Life as It Is* (1852; reprint ed., Gregg Press, 1968); Thomas Nelson Page, *Red Rock: A Chronicle of Reconstruction* (1898; reprint ed., Ridgewood, NJ: Gregg Press, 1967).

5. Stephen Vincent Benét, *John Brown's Body* (New York: Brandt and Brandt, 1928), see especially p. 138.

6. Page, *Red Rock, A Chronicle of Reconstruction*, p. 23.

7. Julia Peterkin, *Green Thursday; Stories* (New York: Knopf, 1928); William Faulkner, *The Sound and The Fury* (New York: Random House, 1929); Katherine Ann Porter, *The Leaning Tower and Other Stories* (New York: Harcourt Brace & Company, 1934); Lillian Smith, *Strange Fruit* (Harcourt Brace & World, 1944); Carson McCullers, *The Members of the Wedding* (New York: Bantam Books, 1946); Harper Lee, *To Kill a Mockingbird* (Philadelphia: Lippincott, 1960); Shirley Ann Grau, *The Keepers of the House* (New York: Knopf, 1964).

8. The idea of the black domestic as a foster mother image similar to earth mothers or mythical mothering characters is explored by Catherine Juanita Starke in *Black Portraiture in American Fiction: Stock Characters, Archetypes and Individuals* (New York: Bantam Books, 1971), pp. 125–135, and by Richard King in *A Southern Renaissance: The Cultural Awakening of the American South, 1930–1955* (New York: Oxford University Press, 1980), pp. 37, 190, 191.

9. McCullers, *The Member of the Wedding*, pp. 95–96, 113–114.

10. Lee, *To Kill a Mockingbird*, pp. 127–138.

11. Ellen Gilchrist, *The Annunciation* (Boston: Little, Brown & Company, 1983).

12. Lillian Hellman, *An Unfinished Woman* (Boston: Little, Brown & Company, 1960), p. 245.

13. Harris, *From Mammies to Militants*, p. 23.

14. Ann Petry, *The Street* (Boston: Houghton Mifflin Company, 1946), pp. 28–30, 51.

15. See U.S. Bureau of the Census, Decennial Census for the states of Alabama, Mississippi, Georgia, Louisiana, South Carolina, 1890–1960.

16. Such studies include those listed in Note 2, as well as earlier studies as "Negroes in Domestic Service in the United States," by Elizabeth Ross Haynes, *Journal of Negro History* 8(1923):384–442; "The Vanishing Servant and the Contemporary Status System of the American South," by C. Arnold Anderson and Mary Jean Bowman, *American Journal of Sociology* 54(1953):215–230; and "Negro Women of Gainesville" by Ruth Reed, Phelps-Stokes Fellowship Studies, No. 6, *Bulletin of the University of Georgia*, XXII (December 1921).

17. See U.S. Bureau of Census, Decennial Census for the states of Alabama, Mississippi, Georgia, Louisiana, South Carolina, 1890–1960.

18. Katzman, *Seven Days a Week*, pp. 201–202.

19. Porter, "The Last Leaf," in *The Leaning Tower and Other Stories*, pp. 64–65.

20. Lillian Smith, *The Killers of the Dream* (New York: Norton, 1961), pp. 28–29.

21. Adrienne Rich, *Of Woman Born: Motherhood as Experience and Institution* (New York: Norton, 1976), pp. 253–254.

22. Alice Childress, *Like one of the Family . . . Conversations from a Domestic's Life* (New York: Independence, 1956), pp. 36–37.

Chapter 10

SOCIALIZATION FOR CHANGE: THE CULTURAL HERITAGE OF THE WHITE SOUTHERN WOMAN[1]

SARAH BRABANT

INTRODUCTION

Several years ago, my youngest daughter asked, "Mom, what's life really all about?" I replied that first and foremost one has to survive. Second, one must survive with as much dignity as possible. Finally, one must accept responsibility for others, especially for those to whom one has given life. I was surprised at how quickly the answer came. As I thought about it later, however, I realized the answer was not formulated by me, but was rather a paradigm for action acquired through my socialization. I knew I had been socialized overtly to become a Southern lady. At a more covert level, I had been socialized to accept and adapt to a changing social environment. This chapter describes and examines the covert level of socialization for the Southern female.

BACKGROUND

My childhood was probably fairly typical for an upper-middle-class Southern female in the 1930s. I was reared primarily by a black nurse who protected me from any harm and loved me unconditionally. My early school years consisted of school with additional lessons in dancing, speech, and piano. My parents were indulgent and I was rarely punished. I did not need to be. My mother's flared nostrils and piercing glance were enough to warn me I was in trouble. King[2] refers to "the Southern woman's all-powerful silent reproach" as "freezing." The word *freezing* is not familiar to me, but the behavior King describes, "pained hauteur and courageous endurance topped off with flaring nostrils and a stiffening just this side of rigor mortis," certainly is. That look was warning enough. I stopped whatever I was doing.

King[3] writes that the precipitation for the reproach was being "trashy." The word I was familiar with was *tacky*. King never asked what trashy meant; neither did I ask what tacky meant. I just knew I had better stop doing whatever I was doing. I never asked what happened to people who persisted in being tacky. I never wanted to know!

My high school years could best be described as moonlight and magnolias. There was school, of course, and lessons in golf and tennis, but getting my card filled at proms was of paramount importance. My parents wanted me to have a good time as long as I wasn't tacky. Somehow, without being told explicitly, I understood that "going too far" with a boy was the ultimate tackiness. I was cautiously correct.

I attended college, several colleges, made my debut in Atlanta, and married "in the presence of a fashionable assemblage of relatives and friends,"[4] all in proper order. I expected my life to continue on an orderly course. It did not.

At the age of 30, I had three children. I could make perfect cup custard and delicious teacakes and I could do beautiful hand sewing. But my husband would or could not hold a job and my father was dead. The world for which I had been reared, or so I thought at the time, no longer existed for me. The role of the Junior League matron was no longer a viable one. Whatever opportunities my children would have were up to me to provide.

I returned to college and, after matriculating part time for three years and full time for one year, received a bachelor's degree in sociology from Memphis State University. I had hoped to go into social work, but a woman with small children was *persona non grata* in the 1960s. A new master's program in sociology was beginning, and the department was anxious for students, even an older woman. I completed my master's degree and was offered an instructorship. The chair of the department, the late Charles H. Newton, encouraged me to continue my education.

Two years later, my divorce being final, I petitioned the courts for permission to remove my children from the state, packed up the family heirlooms, and went to Athens, Georgia, to work on my doctorate at the University of Georgia. Three years later, degree in hand, I accepted a position at the University of Southwestern Louisiana.

I am often asked how, after leading such a sheltered and protected life, I managed, single and with three small children, to pursue three degrees and begin a new life. How could a woman, raised to be a Southern lady, become a professional career woman in mid-life?

Certainly one factor was my not fully comprehending what I had undertaken until I had gone too far to turn back. But I contend that the most important factor was my socialization, the very same socialization that prepared me to be a Southern lady. Beneath the icing of the traditional Southern culture lay a body of norms, values, and beliefs organized in such a way that the Southern female of my era was prepared not only to live within the confines of traditional Southern society, but also to survive change, even rapid catastrophic change. I was taught to make cup custard; I was taught to avoid tackiness at all cost. Although not cognizant of it at the time, I was also taught how to adapt to change.

The concept of tackiness is, I believe, critical to the socialization of the Southern woman with respect to both the traditional way of life and also the adaptation to change. Abbott[5] refers to "outward and sometimes inward forms of courtesy [that] are scrupulously observed." Tackiness, however, includes not only a failure to act appropriately but also a lack of sensitivity and insight into the response of others. The Southern lady was constantly alert to what was going on around her and the implications of those events for her and for her family. Glaring, that is, freezing, signaled the child that some behavior was not appropriate. Why? Because it was not. One did not question why, but one did learn to become attentive to what was going on around one. Verbal admonitions were not uncommon, but they too carried the same message. Certain behavior was not permissible. Why? Because it wasn't.

Freezing and verbal admonitions were only two ways by which the Southern female was socialized. Another way was through stories. McKern[6] writes about the two separate histories she learned as a child: one in school, one at home after supper. I too grew up hearing the same stories repeated over and over. They were told at family dinners, on the porch on long summer evenings, and in front of the fireplace in the winter. I have my doubts about the accuracy of these stories—their validity does not matter. The glares, the verbal admonitions, the stories conveyed a common message. Certain behaviors were inexcusable; other behaviors were essential.

I argue that on the subconscious level the glares, the verbal admonitions, and the stories communicated a more profound theme. One survives; one survives with as much dignity as possible; one is responsible for others. The obvious message prepared the Southern female to live in the traditional society; the more profound theme prepared her to cope with change. The remainder of this article describes my personal experiences and compares them with those described by others who have written about the Southern woman and her coping strategies.

SURVIVAL

McKern[7] writes about the stories she heard as a child:

It was a long time before I realized that these men and women had done nothing more remarkable, really, than survive in a world that made survival a tricky bit of business, especially for women.

Over and over I heard the story of my great-great-grandmother, who in 1865, walked into Columbus (Georgia) from the family plantation to request an officer to protect her daughters from the marauding enlisted men camped on her lawn. This same woman never laced her own shoes before the Civil War, or the War Between the States, as I was taught to say. After the war, she supervised the planting and picking of cotton while her husband's health and, I suspect, his mind as well slowly deteriorated. There were also stories about my great-grand-father, who lost two fortunes and made three, of my father, who turned grief from his child's death into a crusade against cancer. The theme was always the same. One fought until one won or died. There were no other choices. One came home "bearing one's shield or on it."

Admonitions reinforced these stories. I was staying with my father's mother, who lived next door, while my parents were away. I must have been about nine. During recess at school I got into an argument with a playmate. She tore my dress and matters went from bad to worse. She was a good six inches taller than I, or seems to be in my memory, and retreat seemed the best option. I ran home, only to be confronted by "Bam," as we called my grandmother. I explained the situation to her and told her I could not return to school since my friend had vowed to continue the fight at second recess. Bam was not impressed with my argument. She agreed defeat seemed inevitable, but retreat was un-thinkable. I was a Callaway and Callaways didn't run. I returned to school and was thrashed soundly as I had predicted. That evening Bam took me and my foe to the fair. My adversary remains to this day one of my dearest friends.

The survival theme was also reinforced in books. Abbott[8] writes about the significance of *Gone With the Wind*[9] in her life, particularly with regard to sur-vival models. Mitchell's story did not influence me, for I was in my teens before I saw the movie, an adult before I read the book. The books my friends and I read over and over, just as had our mothers before us, were the Little Colonel series by Annie Fellows Johnston. A noted author onced commented that Southern women were reared on the warm milk of Annie Fellows Johnston. I doubt if the author examined the series too closely. The books may appear to be warm milk on the surface, but underneath one finds the recurrent theme of sur-vival, dignity, and responsibility for others. With respect to survival, there was the Little Colonel's mother who refused to turn to her father for help, despite the threat of poverty,[10] Phil Tremont's determination to rebuild his life,[11] and, of course, Mary Ware, whose credo was that of the Vicar of Wakefield: "Let us be inflexible, and fortune will at last change in our favor!"[12]

The book that so influenced Abbott,[13] *Gone With the Wind*,[14] is based on a collection of stories Mitchell heard as a child growing up in Georgia. Her rendi-tion of these stories supports the argument proposed in the present article. Through the characters Scarlett O'Hara, Melanie Hamilton, Rhett Butler, and Ashley Wilkes, Mitchell describes Southern life during and following the Civil War.

Following the fall of Atlanta, Scarlett flees home to Tara only to find her mother dead, her father insane, and the cotton fields desolate. Describing Scar-lett's reaction, Mitchell writes:

Of a sudden, the oft-told family tales to which she had listened since ba-
byhood, listened half-bored, impatient and but partly comprehending
were crystal clear.

. . . .

All [the family members described in the stories] had suffered crushing
misfortunes and had not been crushed. . . . Malign fate had broken their
necks, perhaps, but never their hearts. They had not whined, they had
fought. And when they died, they died spent but unquenched.

Thus, through stories, admonitions, and books, the covert theme was
transmitted to the Southern female. Survival is an active, not a passive, process.
Death may be inevitable, but one dies fighting.

SURVIVAL WITH DIGNITY

Survival was not enough. The Southern female was taught not only to
survive, but to do so with dignity. Again, the message was transmitted through
looks, admonitions, stories, and books. Scarlett, the central character in *Gone
With the Wind* faces the prospect of losing Tara for lack of funds. She decides to
go to Atlanta to seek money from Rhett Butler. Mitchell[16] describes Ashley
Wilkes's thoughts as he watches Scarlett prepare for her trip.

He knew that she took life as it came, opposed her tough-fibered mind to
whatever obstacles there might be, fought on with a determination that
would not recognize defeat, and kept on fighting even when she saw that
defeat was inevitable.

As he stands watching, he realizes

that he had never known such gallantry as the gallantry of Scarlett
O'Hara going forth to conquer the world in her Mother's velvet curtains
and the tail feathers of a rooster.

This same theme is emphasized again and again in the Little Colonel
series. There is the gentle dignity, despite poverty and fear for her husband's
life, maintained by the Little Colonel's mother before her reconciliation with the
Little Colonel's grandfather;[17] there are the Wares, beset with poverty and illness, yet still determined to live as graciously as possible in the Arizona
desert;[18] and there is the story of Ida Shane, disowned by her family because of
her drunken husband, alone and penniless, yet determined to keep her child
beautifully dressed until her own illness rendered this impossible.[19]

A story often repeated in my family was one about my grandmother, Bam.
Faced with a family scandal, she put on her hat and gloves and walked downtown, daring anyone to intimate by glance or whisper that anything was not as it

should be. The theme was reinforced for me quite strongly in the late 1960s. My divorce was an ugly one and numerous court hearings were necessary. My attorney was a young man recommended to me by my husband's attorney, an associate of my husband's cousin. I was naive in those days and failed to see the lack of ethics in such a procedure. All I knew was that my husband was usually accompanied by two or more attorneys and that my attorney seemed more concerned with not antagonizing them than with representing me. One hearing was particularly trying.

Early in the morning before the hearing, my cousin called from LaGrange to tell us my mother's house had burned. The back sitting room had burst into flame in the early morning hours. The smoke was still too acrid to permit entry into the house to see if anything might be salvaged. The source of the fire was unknown, but arson was suspected. My mother sat by the phone a few minutes, a look of despair on her face. Then turning to me she said, "I'll fly home this afternoon. Meantime, get dressed. We have a court appointment at 10." I forget what that particular hearing was about. I sat in the courtroom in a daze. There seemed to be no hope. My attorney was no match for the staff of one of the leading law firms in Memphis. Mother's house, all she owned was ruined. Her beloved heirlooms were probably destroyed. There seemed to be no end to our misfortunes. Suddenly I was awakened from my reverie by the tapping of my mother's gloved hand on my knee. With nostrils flared and eyes flashing she whispered: "Will you be so kind as to remember who you are and sit up straight!" I sat up straight for the remainder of the hearing.

Some years later, my mother died after a long and valiant fight with cancer. She refused all drugs during her illness. She told me she had never done anything tacky in her life and she certainly wasn't going to take the risk of doing so while drugged. She died at home in her own bed without drugs, just as she wanted. As I sat by her bed that last afternoon and watched her die, I thought of that day in court. Cancer killed her; it never robbed her of her dignity. I sat up straight.

RESPONSIBILITY FOR OTHERS

Clinton[20] refers to the importance of honor and virtue for the Southern woman of plantation days. Abbott[21] describes the piety, or at least the appearance of piety, in the women of her childhood. I suggest that these attributes are part of the overt definition of not being tacky. At the profound level, the message is responsibility for others.

Mitchell[22] illustrates this in one of the most poignant scenes in her book. Scarlett finds a row of radishes in back of an old slave cabin. Assaulted by hunger, she eats one. Her empty stomach rebels and she vomits. Hunger gnawing at her empty stomach, she cries out:

> As God is my witness, as God is my witness, the Yankees aren't going to

lick me. I'm going to live through this, and when it's over, I'm never going to be hungry again. No, nor any of my folks. If I have to steal or kill—as God is my witness, I'm never going to be hungry again.

Scarlett often complained about having to care for her sisters, her father, the Wilkes, and the former slaves who remained at Tara. They were an unwanted burden, but she never questioned that they were her burden to bear.

Responsibility for others is also a recurrent theme in the Little Colonel books. Miss Allison's dedication to those in need,[23] the Ware's concern for Phil,[24] Mary Ware's work with the poor,[25] and other stories illustrate concern for others again and again.

In my own family a mixture of two blessings from the *Episcopal Book of Common Prayer* was a constant reminder: "Lord, bless this food to our use and us to thy service and help us to be ever mindful of the needs of others." My father's life was a particular exemplification of this prayer for he was dedicated to the sick and the poor. Stories told about other family members, however, emphasized that although my father's dedication to the needs of others went far beyond cultural expectations, responsibility for others was the norm not the exception. There were stories about how my grandmother and great-aunt made soup in large vats at St. Paul's Methodist Church in Columbus for the ill during the flu epidemic of 1918. There were also stories of earlier ancestors who taught without pay following the Civil War in order to keep schools open.

One of the most touching stories regarding concern for one's own children was about my maternal grandmother. My mother's brother died from a sudden and overwhelming infection shortly before Christmas. He was only seven at the time, and his Santa Claus gifts were already purchased and in the house. The other children were small, and although saddened by their brother's death, were soon caught up in the joy of the season. Mother told me that it was a happy Christmas with all traditions followed. The day after Christmas my grandmother sent all her children to visit various relatives, stripped the house of all decorations, and began to mourn the death of her child. My mother told me she was grown with children of her own before she understood what her mother had done. When she asked my grandmother how she managed to postpone her grieving, she replied: "You were little children. I had no right to deprive you of one of your childhood Christmases." Often when the care and responsibility of my own children seemed overwhelming to me as a single parent and graduate student, I would think of the story of my grandmother, set aside my books and my concerns, and play with my children.

SUMMARY

The ability of the Southern woman to adapt to change has been well documented. Researchers Scott,[26] Spruill,[27] and Clinton,[28] demonstrate that this attribute was a noted characteristic of Southern women from colonial days up to the Civil War. Gay[29] provides additional evidence with respect to Southern women during the war. The novelists Johnston and Mitchell suggest that this attribute continued to be characteristic of Southern women in the years immediately following.

McKern and Abbott focus on Southern women in the 20th century. Abbott described the way in which women of her mother's generation demeaned men as a means of survival.[30] McKern describes the modern Southern woman as a "skilled survivor" and illustrates how such women are able to capitalize on disaster by turning a crisis into personal advantage.[31]

The present article has examined this ability of the Southern woman to adapt to change and suggests ways in which and by which the Southern woman was subtly socialized to do so. Through admonitions, stories, and example, the traditions of the South were handed down from generation to generation. Hospitality, graciousness, and the ever-avoidance of tackiness were all part of this tradition. However, these concerns were only the surface forms of a more profound scheme of action that lay at the very core of the Southern way of life. First, one has to take active means to survive. Second, one does so with as much dignity as possible. Maybe all one can do is sit up straight, but that, at least, one must do. Finally, one is responsible for others, particularly those to whom one has given life. Abbott[32] writes that she, like many other Southern women, left home because "the glorious Southland was not what [she] had taken it to be." I have no illusions about the South as utopia. I do believe, however, that the socialization I received as a Southern woman not only prepared me for change but also enabled me to render meaning to the flux of events.

NOTES

1. This article is a revision of a lecture prepared for the Lyceum "Change" series, Augusta College, Augusta, Georgia, 1980, and presented at Augusta College on January 15, 1980.
2. Florence King, *Southern Ladies and Gentlemen* (New York: Bantam Books, Inc., 1976), p. 3.
3. Ibid.
4. "Miss Sarah Redd Callaway, Mr. Brabant wed in LaGrange," *Columbus Enquirer*, October 14, 1953, p. 8.
5. Shirley Abbott, *Womenfolks: Growing Up Down South* (New York: Ticknor and Fields, 1983), p. 210.
6. Sharon McKern, *Redneck Mothers, Good Ol' Girls and Other Southern Belles* (New York: The Viking Press, 1979), pp. xii–xiii.
7. Ibid., xii.
8. Abbott, *Womenfolks*.
9. Margaret Mitchell, *Gone With the Wind* (New York: The Macmillan Company, 1936).
10. Annie Fellows Johnston, *The Little Colonel Stories* (Boston: L. C. Page and Company, 1895), pp. 40–41.

11. Annie Fellows Johnston, *The Little Colonel in Arizona* (Boston: L. C. Page and Company, 1904), pp. 307–308.
12. Annie Fellows Johnston, *The Little Colonel's Knight Comes Riding* (Boston: L. C. Page and Company, 1907), pp. 176–177.
13. Abbott, *Womenfolks.*
14. Mitchell, *Gone With the Wind.*
15. Ibid., pp. 420–421.
16. Ibid., pp. 550–551.
17. Johnston, *The Little Colonel Stories,* pp. 40–41.
18. Johnston, *The Little Colonel in Arizona,* pp. 64–65.
19. Johnston, *The Little Colonel's Knight Comes Riding,* pp. 176–177.
20. Catherine Clinton, *The Plantation Mistress* (New York: Pantheon Books, 1982).
21. Abbott, *Womenfolks.*
22. Mitchell, *Gone With the Wind,* p. 428.
23. Annie Fellows Johnston, *The Little Colonel's Christmas Vacation* (Boston: L. C. Page and Company, 1905), pp. 240–253.
24. Johnson, *The Little Colonel in Arizona,* pp. 306–307.
25. Annie Fellows Johnston, *Mary Ware's Promised Land* (Boston: L. C. Page and Company, 1912), pp. 244–265.
26. Anne Firor Scott, *The Southern Lady: From Pedestal to Politics, 1830–1930* (Chicago: The University of Chicago Press, 1970).
27. Julia Cherry Spruill, *Women's Life and Work in the Southern Colonies* (New York: W. W. Norton and Co., Inc., 1972).
28. Clinton, *The Plantation Mistress.*
29. Mary A. H. Gay, *Life in Dixie during the War* (Atlanta: Constitution Job Office, 1892).
30. Abbott, *Womenfolks,* p. 169.
31. McKern, *Redneck Mothers,* p. 6.
32. Abbott, *Womenfolks,* p. 182.

Chapter 11

THE CODE OF THE NEW SOUTHERN BELLE: GENERATING TYPIFICATIONS TO STRUCTURE SOCIAL INTERACTION

JOHN LYNXWILER AND MICHELE WILSON

The term *Southern woman* conjures up a specific cultural image. Southern womanhood is essentially white and relatively well to do. From journalistic satire[1] to scholarly writings[2] a consistent, dominant image of the Southern woman emerges. Southern by "the Grace of God," she is a lady in her innocence, including the absence of knowledge of vulgar topics and language. She is modest in her concerns, dress, and demeanor. Her timidity, never marred by assertiveness or anger, is complemented by her submissiveness to her parents, husband, spiritual counselor, and God. All of these protect her from the harsh realities of money, the world of work, and rapists. She, of course, matches or rewards this protectiveness with self-denial and a compassionate concern for others.

This lady may be the dominant cultural image of white, Southern womanhood, but it is not the only image. There are Hee Haw Honeys, redneck women, woman rednecks, Honky-Tonk women, poor trash, and pitiable eccentrics among others.[3] One of the best known of these alternate types is the Southern belle. Immortalized in popular fiction and Hollywood cinema, the Southern belle, as a stereotype, dates back to the antebellum South. Her popular mystique is organized around youth, physical attractiveness, sensuality, and a command of social proprieties. There is a tendency to view the Southern belle as the larval form of the Southern lady.[4] However, in everyday interactions our cultural stereotypes of females are reified as distinct stages rather than evolutionary patterns.

As with other female stereotypes in our society, cultural images of Southern women generally are considered more childlike and of less value than their male counterparts. Some critics have argued that female stereotypes have little grounding in reality: that the squealing, mindless girl and the lady with her chaste morality and groveling deference are merely parodies, with little validity. However, cultural stereotypes do have an impact on our lives. They function as controls in the sense that individuals internalize them, monitor their own behavior, and restrict their presentations in a manner approaching the ideal.[5] In turn, others react to us in ways that encourage mutual acceptance of the stereotype as a norm.

Along with their restrictive nature, stereotypes have other functions. They contribute to role expectations which serve as guides for behavior. As guides to appropriate behaviors, personalities, and attitudes, one can see the expectations positively, and call the result role performance. Another "purpose" is indicated by a focus on role-taking as an essential element of interaction. What one does and says is given meaning, is understood, in and through frames of reference that stereotypes provide. It follows that one can affect the course of interaction by presentations of self which direct others to typify us as one kind of person rather than another.

This chapter examines issues related to the utility of female stereotypes. Specifically, we are interested in how women appropriate a particular social type—the New Southern Belle—to structure interactional encounters for themselves and others. We use the term *New Southern Belle* to avoid reader confusion with such fictional characters as Scarlett O'Hara, Hollywood's version of the *femme fatale*. As with most stereotypes, true Southern belles were something of a rarity in the old South; however, they are approaching commonplace in modern times. In fact, the increasing popularity of the stereotype was the impetus for our research. By using the term New Southern Belle, we are able to build from the historic image familiar to many while recognizing that the social type has been adjusted to accommodate the modern settings of the new South.

Also, we prefer the term typification because it combines both the cultural images of stereotypes and the behavioral processes associated with role performances.[6] In this sense, a typification is a stereotype in action.[7] Our analysis is organized around the essential elements of this typification process as displayed in the code of the New Southern Belle (NSB).

THE TYPIFICATION PROCESS

Simply put, the process of typification is the social construction of reality.[8] Metaphorically, we may liken the process to a jigsaw puzzle. As each piece is fitted together, the finished product gains clarity. Hence, we interpret the location of a particular puzzle piece by reference to the other pieces and, more importantly, to the emerging picture. Likewise, during interaction we seek to "fit" each constituent element of the encounter into an emerging understanding that gives meaning to the total situation. The elements gain meaning by and through their relationship with each other. Each constituent element of the social encounter is organized into a unified whole. All subsequent information is framed within the parameters of this interpretation. The process is similar to the whole-part relationship of a Gestalt configuration in which

> *there prevails the particular relationship of Gestalt-coherence defined as the determining and conditioning of the constituents upon each other [with respect to the meaning of each constituent]. In thoroughgoing reciprocity the constituents assign to, and derive from, one another the functional significance [meaning] which gives to each one its qualification in a concrete case. In this sense, the constituents may be said to exist through each other; each retaining its qualified existence only if and as long as the others have theirs.*[9]

By grouping the constituent bits of information found in the interaction, the total act gains meaning as a "typified" instance of familiar behavior. In this manner, each participant and his or her actions acquire an ordered, stable appearance.

Typifying another as a social type creates a frame for understanding how his or her behavior and the situation is to be interpreted.[10] Similar to the jigsaw puzzle, knowledge of the final product serves as a reference for fitting particular pieces together. Thus, understanding and interpretation are reflexively dependent on each other and constitute the cognitive aspects of typification.[11] But to leave our discussion at this point would be to fail to consider fully the dynamics of the process. For unlike jigsaw puzzles, social encounters are not solitary activities but joint adventures, and the maintenance of this "Gestalt-like" reality is a moral matter complete with ritualized occasions for its display and acceptance.[12]

The typification process explains how interactants formulate meaning, but the particular meaning arrived at is dependent on the social type that is displayed and honored during the course of the encounter. Analytically, we may reduce each social type to a set of cultural items or specifics that endure through time. However, in real life, the specifics of a social type are, at best, only tacitly known by participants, and the tenuous quality of most interactions makes direct reference problematic. Thus, recognition of other as a social type is a continuous, ongoing process. A code is the term we use to refer to the process of grouping the constituent elements of interaction into a coherent social type. When individuals invoke a code, they "fit together" the contextual features of the encounter to create a stabilized interpretation.

The act of honoring a code in social interaction gives direction to the typification process. Through verbal references to a code specific, our attention is drawn to a social type which, in turn, elicits our understanding of the type along with other aspects of the code. This understanding constitutes the frame for attributing motives and interpreting another's actions as instances of typical-behavior-for-that-social-type. In this way, the code, when reproduced during interaction, structures the subsequent behavior and interpretations of participants.

D. Lawrence Wieder's research on convicts in a halfway house provides insight into how the code operates to maintain order.[13] Wieder examined the convicts' code by breaking it down into a set of specifics or maxims. He learned that inmates knew staff personnel were aware of the code and would honor it under normal conditions. Wieder then demonstrated how members of the halfway house used the code, through its "telling," as a device to formulate meaning and structure the environment of staff personnel. By employing code words and phrases, the inmate could "remind" staff personnel of his typification as a convict and, thereby, structure the encounter's meaning for both participants. Thus, telling the code accomplished work. Its invocation and acceptance helped formulate situational meaning while maintaining a sense of business as usual.

Our work focuses on the New Southern Belle (NSB) and the code that accompanies this social type. After explicating the specifics of the code, we examine how women "tell the code" to typify themselves as a unique social type and formulate, for others, the situational meaning of the encounter.

METHODOLOGY

To identify essential aspects of the New Southern Belle, we relied on two sources of information. First, we conducted unstructured interviews with 20 women—some were NSBs, some had been NSBs, and a few were contemptuous of the NSB. Because males are critical to the behavior of an NSB, we interviewed 10 males—each had dated NSBs. Our interview respondents were Southerners from the middle to upper-middle classes. Their ages ranged from 19 to 45.

During the course of our interviews, respondents often spoke in code specifics. However, when queried for specifics, they could only provide a general understanding. Most referred to the New Southern Belle as being a "lady." We found several parallels between the two social types, but the anomalies indicated that the New Southern Belle was, at best, a variation of the lady as a social type (if not a distinct type). This being the case, we began isolating aspects of the New Southern Belle to explicate code specifics. Relying on a grounded theory approach, we continually worked to revise our understanding of the NSB throughout the interviewing process.[14]

The second source of data involved participant observation over a six-month period. During this period, we frequented places where NSBs spend much of their leisure activities (e.g., restaurants, social events, nightclubs, etc.). In these settings we scheduled some of our interviews. However, the majority of time was spent unobtrusively observing NSBs interacting with others. Our field notes combined with interview materials provided the data from which we developed and analyzed the code of the New Southern Belle.

THE CODE OF THE NEW SOUTHERN BELLE

The focus of our study was to isolate those features which distinguish the NSB as a social type from other cultural images of Southern women. Ultimately, our goal in this effort was an examination the New Southern Belle's code. We do not argue that our scheme is exhaustive; however, we do maintain that, together, the following specifics represent the major components of the code.

Never Forget Your Status Lest Others Forget Theirs

Status consciousness permeates the life of the NSB. It directs her decisions about where to go, what to do, and with whom. It also dictates how she will interact with those of higher and lower status. In short, NSBs are masters of place in the social structure. This attention to status indicators is a form of boundary maintenance and includes, among other things, material goods, knowledge of social rituals, deference and demeanor ceremonies, and membership in organizations, sororities, and clubs. It is not that friendly association with those of lower status is intrinsically illegitimate; rather attention to these symbolic locators indicates what kind of person one is, and consistent failure to honor them may be taken as evidence that one does not possess a legitimate claim to the status.

As is true of in-groups everywhere, interaction is limited to members, and membership demands loyalty. Loyalty to the social type reifies its value to self and others and provides boundary maintenance. Hence, one who plays with the wrong company is as much in danger of falling out of favor as is one who pretends to be an NSB is in danger of being detected and rejected.

Honor the "Natural" Distinctions Between Men and Women

Reliance on traditional sex roles is one of the ways in which Southern women of most types differ from the women of other parts of the country.[15] The NSB does this in a more obvious way than other women from her region. Not only are men to be adored, they are to be deferred to in decision-making and conversation. The role-taking ability of the NSB is well honed. She, more than any other group of women, recognizes that men have power, that they control the system of rewards in society. Rather than opting for achievement on her own, she achieves through affiliations with men.[16]

The ability to achieve is dependent on being male oriented. There is a quid pro quo, not just in deference but in ego building and face-saving for males. She takes an interest in sports, tells him how great he is, and intercedes or explains for him when he has committed a faux pas. Since she assumes that males operate on the basis of their hormones, she dresses to please him and sharpens to a razor's edge her skills in coquetry. Sexuality based on traditional sex role distinctions is paramount to understanding the NSB.[17]

In return, she expects that traditional rituals will be followed. There are door opening ceremonies which must be honored. Both opening and lifting must

be done by men if they are present. Often these expectations become demands
—communicated behaviorally.

Don't Be a Slut

The NSB emphasizes chaste sexuality. As the pedestal is narrow for any
"lady" and thus she may lose her status through violations of a stringent set of
restrictions, so too is the path narrow for the NSB. However, for the NSB, these
are not merely prescriptions but proscriptions as well. In this instance, the NSB
is expected to be a tease or a flirt, to promise sexual accessibility, and to be
physically provocative. Nonetheless, she never crosses that line of being loose
or a slut although she may have to "put out" for her fiancé or steady partner.

Her reputation as a "good girl" is maintained through chastity, that is, not
being available to one and all, rather than virginity. As a scarce resource to be
saved for that special relationship, it is the promise which is important. In daily
interaction with men, coy sexuality is advertised through dress and demeanor.

Remain Loyal to the Southern Tradition

That Southerners of all kinds are likely to identify themselves as Southerners and to have loyalties to their state and community has been documented.[18] Localism of this sort provides an unusual geography lesson for outsiders who soon learn that Deep South introductions include the home community, specifically the town of birth. This orientation is reinforced by those who
play the part of significant other or reference group: they are likely to be family
members or be from one's hometown. The specifically local orientation is complemented by a Southern emphasis on tradition.

For the NSB, this is not merely the keeping alive of memories about "The
War," it is concern with the heritage of one's own family. The NSB is not just
aware of and knowledgeable about a long family line—her line is particularly
old and gracious. As one observer noted, all NSBs have pretensions to aristocracy; not one of them had a great-great-granddaddy who was a private in The
War or was a sharecropper. Of particular importance is the lineage and folk
wisdom of the parental generation. In fact, NSBs frequently resolve dilemmas
with "Daddy says . . . ."

You Can Never Be Too Rich or Too Thin

An NSB may be wealthy but all NSBs have pretensions of being so and,
thus, live above their means. This is not an assured characteristic—rather it
involves conspicous consumption. The NSB has charge cards, shops at all of the
right stores, and wears the "in" name brands. The joke—"What four words
does an NSB never hear? 'Good evening K-Mart shoppers' "— is true of this
kind of woman. Even her makeup is name brand and her hairdresser is someone
known by all. Much of her leisure activities center around conspicuous consumption: going shopping is a form of recreation, where one bought what is a
topic of conversation, and a slavish attention to fads is demanded.

These "tribal" indicators are all important means of marking one's place in the status hierarchy. The markers are not exhibited by default, rather they are consciously pursued. One result is to see the presence of these as a means of differentiating those who belong from those who don't. Those who pretend to or aspire to belong but have not attained the appropriate allotments are treated with disdain. Those who do not have the appropriate dress, demeanor, rituals, and material goods are ignored. Those who, in turn, disdain the package of indicators are treated with awe.

Pretty Is as Pretty Does

The NSB craves confirmation of her appearance from others, especially males. She becomes particularly anxious if not told how well she looks. In large part, this is done through dress, makeup, and presentation of self.

The NSB is quick to compliment the dress, hairdo, and children of others at the beginning of a conversation. As a form of manners, it paves the way for further chit-chat while allowing her to present herself as a caring person. However, just as there is never a free lunch, this behavior demands reciprocation. Hence, the NSB is quick to feel slighted should others fail to return the compliment.

As we have become aware, one's self-concept is dependent on the expressed opinions of others. Perhaps this behavior explains why so many Southern women are considered charming and self-assured. They do in fact expend energy in being nice to others, but as in the case of the NSB, the behavior is undertaken primarily for its boomerang effect.

THE CODE AS EXPLANATION FOR BEHAVIOR

The code of the NSB may be employed as a traditional sociological explanation for the behavior of its adherents. As such, the code defines boundaries of acceptability and provides motives for the NSB's behavior.

Compliance to *Pretty Is as Pretty Does* would direct the woman to look her best in all situations. For example, while giving a lecture on human sexuality to a group of students at a local Baptist college at 8:00 a.m., one of the authors was struck by the fact that the young women in the class must get up quite early in order to be so complete at that hour. As a Northerner raised as a Baptist, this observer was curious about the heavy makeup and sexy or cute little girl dress of these young Southern women. In her background, they would have been considered "painted" and on their way to harlotdom. This turned into an occasion to discuss the parallels between a prostitute's come-on and that of a young woman on the marriage market. Only the instructor and the one middle-aged student present saw the connection, although all of the female students did admit that preparation for class included a concerted effort to "look good" for men.

In some respects, each code specific involves behavioral prescriptions. *Pretty Is as Pretty Does,* as illustrated above, motivates the NSB to attend to her appearance and manners in all situations. *Never Forget Your Status Lest Others Forget Theirs* requires strict attention to the proprieties of sociability. Additionally, this dictate will influence where and with whom the NSB travels. Restaurants, lounges, and even social organizations are frequented because they are "in" or reflect the proper places to be seen (while others are shunned).

Attention to status markers is so entrenched in some NSBs that it interferes with other aspects of their lives. For example, on remarking she "could not" go to a recent music concert, we probed one of our respondents, Melanie Louise,[19] for reasons. Her reply was significant:

> *I mean, I could have gone. Like my legs weren't broken [laughs], and I like the band. But, like they aren't real popular anymore. And, besides the only person who asked me was Frank. And, he's a sweet guy; a real sweet guy. But, he doesn't know any of my friends, and like, he doesn't even belong to a fraternity or anything, you know?*

By the same token, the maxim *Remain Loyal to the Southern Tradition* would require that the NSB locate many of her opinions within a context that supports Southern traditionalism. It is sometimes interesting to note the extent to which an NSB will go to force her opinions into such a framework. Charolette, a very intelligent NSB of about 25, found herself in a discussion over racial discrimination, which she was outspokenly against. As the conversation turned to examples of Southern racism and their relationship to symbolic elements in the Southern culture, Charolette increasingly had less to say. When asked point blank for her opinion, she abandoned her normally intellectual perspective by stating that her "Daddy" says a true understanding of the South requires a true Southern birthright.

This identification with Southern tradition is functional for the NSB. As a social type, the NSB is not directly attached to culturally recognized support structures. That is, many social types are anchored within an institutional base which provides legitimation for the incumbent (e.g., a police officer gains legitimacy by his/her connection to the state apparatus). The NSB gains much of her status through association with the antebellum myths and the oral tradition of the South. Thus, it is only natural that NSBs be staunch defenders of Southern heritage. Perpetuating popular images of Southern tradition strengthens the legitimacy of the NSB as a valued status to appropriate if you are a female—and to possess if you are a male.

REACTIONS TO CODE BREAKING

On several occasions we feigned ignorance of the code to engage an NSB in code telling activities (e.g., failure to recognize the code specific *Honor the Natural Distinctions Between Men and Women*). The reaction of NSBs was interesting and patterned. First, the NSB would repeat her remark with more emphasis, perhaps to "remind" the violator. This often included a seemingly sincere attempt to supplement our ignorance through suggestions. Failing this, she would alter her comments for a more direct reference to the code. These comments usually included an evaluation of our presented self. When these efforts proved unsuccessful, the NSB would either engage in a lengthy, sometimes hostile, explanation regarding her status or terminate the conversation. It was during these code breaking activities that we were able to piece together much of our typology of code specifics.

Additionally, we discovered that adherence to the code carried moral overtones. That is, although there is no tight membership to enforce group norms and uphold values, sanctioning practices occur when others fail to honor the code. Sometimes a nonverbal sanction will suffice as when a look of coquetry becomes the glare of a cockatrice in the blink of an eye.

In general, the code is enforced through the application of a name or label to the code breaker. Negative labels are reinforced through gossip and retrospective interpretation of the deviant's identity. Some of these labels include "slut," "trash," "prick tease," "redneck," and "feminist." Once applied, labeling is documented to others through recounting the violative (i.e., code breaking) behavior to others.

Women who present themselves as NSBs are constrained to honor the code. Failure to do so can, and usually does, lead to stigmatization. However, by complying to the code, women are motivated to adopt particular behaviors. In this sense, code adherence as well as code breaking provides role clarification.

The preceding discussion appears to conform to the accepted notions of role behavior.[20] That is, role requirements constrain the incumbent's behavior while shaping other's expectations. In this sense, efforts to account for behavior and to attribute motive are dependent on audience approval. However, the code, as we are using it, draws attention to the dynamic qualities that are part of the "code telling" process. It is to this aspect of the NSB's code that we now turn.

TELLING THE CODE TO FORMULATE MEANING FOR OTHERS

Bestowal of a social type on another organizes interaction because it automatically closes the door to other, equally plausible, interpretations. Further, telling the code draws attention away from situational explanations by making the explanation a reasonable account for *any* NSB. That is, it provides readymade motives and explanations for another's actions. It contextualizes behavior by bringing past knowledge and future expectations together so that others can locate a person's behavior as commonplace or typical-for-that-social-type.

For example, a comment such as "You know I'm not that kind of girl" made in response to introductory sexual advances by a male could be interpreted as a rejection of the suitor as undesirable. However, if the male frames the remark in reference to the code specific *Don't Be a Slut,* the response no longer refers to a quality of the suitor, but rather, to a quality of the NSB as one who is faithful to her man. Once formulated, the remark can be understood as typical of *any* NSB attached to another male, or, alternatively, this particular NSB's remark would hold for *any* suitor who approached her. Simply put, situational meaning becomes trans-situational by formulating it within the code of the NSB. In so doing, the male saves face by contextualizing the remark as an aspect of the NSB's code.

As such, code telling functions to organize another's experience of self. We can see how the code is used by others to transform a particular person into a social type, such that their behavior appears to be the result of compliance to a normative order. As Goffman notes, a linguistic display (i.e., code telling) is "attributed to a figure animated, not the animator."[21]

Through negotiation, an interactional device (in this case, the code specific) elicits a common stock of knowledge relevant to the occasion that, in turn, provides a sense of order. A normative order did constrain behavior and account for its occurrence. However, and more importantly, this normative order was generated within the interaction itself. Hence, order is not imposed but created. Another example will help illustrate this point.

There is no code specific which states "An NSB should keep her date waiting when he arrives." When her date admonishes her for making him wait, a code specific can be invoked to render her action acceptable. For example, the NSB could reply that she was "talking to Daddy" or "trying to look perfect for her date." Both comments can be located within code specifics: the former, *Remain Loyal to Southern Tradition;* the latter, *Honor the Natural Distinctions Between Men and Women.*

In this way, an equivocal act is made clear by reference to the code. Thus, telling the code is a mechanism used to define the situation for others. It places or identifies an act within the context of the code which, in turn, constitutes a pattern for interpretation. It also formulates future expectations for the listener.

When an NSB compliments another on his or her appearance, she is not only being sociable but also calling for reciprocity and validation of her appearance (i.e., *Pretty Is as Pretty Does*). Male respondents recalled instances when they had experienced "social amnesia" and failed to adhere to this code specific. Their dates usually feigned hurt or acted slighted. When the male finally ran out of "What's the matter?" queries, the female would reference the code specific (e.g., "You think I'm ugly"). At this point, they reported total recall of their obligation to compliment their date. In this fashion, role relationships were established for the encounter. Several males revealed to us that they learned to pro-offer compliments automatically and without genuine feeling. For these individuals, the exchange located a more persisting role relationship and formulated future expectations between the participants.

It is important to restate the fact that the code is not found outside the scene but embedded within it. Code telling is a continuous part of the interaction and has an impact on how the interaction will be defined in the future. As a device to formulate meaning, it states "My immediate behavior is guided by, and an extension of, this social type." Telling the code to another organizes the constituent elements of behavior into a unified whole that is already familiar; hence, the elements of behavior themselves become recognizable as common-place.[22]

CONCLUSIONS

As a social type, the New Southern Belle is highly valued by aspirants. But audience recognition is not automatic. In the first place, the NSB is a trans-situational status. It is not donned for particular occasions (e.g., work) and audiences (e.g., co-workers) only to be discarded or exchanged in other situations. Rather, it is somewhat akin to a master status, permeating all encounters with each an occasion for its portrayal and evaluation.

Because her audience is not selective but comprised of those with whom she is interacting at the time, there is very little backstage region to the NSB's performance. Further, there is no direct linkage to an institutional support structure that can be brandished to others for role validation. Hence, the status of the NSB must be carefully monitored and continually won anew to be maintained. Ever present is the threat that her claim will be challenged by others or discredited through behavior incongruent with the code. Thus, like Alice, the NSB must ever run faster just to stay in the same place.

Her means for maintaining the NSB status involves the embracement of the social type. The code of the NSB accompanies this stereotype and defines the boundaries of acceptable behavior. Code adherence provides motives for the woman not as an individual but as a social type.[23] Telling the code is an interactional device that identifies the meaning of an act by placing it in the context of a pattern.[24]

The woman's behavior becomes an instance of the NSB as a social type complete with motives, expectations, and understandings appropriate for the type. In this manner, it defines the immediate relationship for participants. It also formulates for other the qualities of a persisting role relationship. In short, code telling does the work of organizing another's experience of self. Most importantly, this process unfolds within the interaction. That is, participants actually generate the social type during verbal exchanges and thereby bring meaning to the interaction.

Cultural stereotypes are not simply mass media images and classifications which reduce individuals to the lowest common denominator.[25] They are appropriated and reified by individuals in the unfolding of their occurrence.[26] In the case of the NSB, we find that a stereotype which restricts female mobility and inhibits gender equality has positive consequences for many females.

The South, long the bastion of anti-ERA sentiments, is replete with traditional stereotypes that function to maintain gender stratification. While the

South's emphasis on fundamentalist religion and traditional values are oft cited as primary causes for the prevalence of gender inequality, we found that, for some women, traditional roles are actively sought and nurtured. More importantly, our study indicates that recent, and for the most part, unsuccessful efforts to obtain gender equality through legislation may be partly explained through the utility of these seemingly restrictive stereotypes. While beyond the scope of this work, future research should examine how other typifications of Southern females are used to structure experiences for both the incumbent and their audience. At that point, we can begin evaluating the positive and negative aspects of traditional female roles and their implications for gender equality in the South and across the country.

NOTES

1. Florence King, *Southern Ladies and Gentlemen* (New York: Bantam, 1975).
2. Anne Firor Scott, *The Southern Lady: From Pedestal to Politics 1830–1930* (Chicago: The University of Chicago Press, 1972).
3. Julian P. Roebuck and Mark Hickson, III, *The Southern Redneck: A Phenomenological Class Study* (New York: Praeger Publishers, 1982).
4. John Shelton Reed, *Southerners: The Social Psychology of Sectionalism* (Chapel Hill: The University of North Carolina Press, 1983).
5. Edwin M. Schur, *Labeling Women Deviant: Gender, Stigma and Social Control* (Philadelphia: Temple University Press, 1984).
6. John P. Hewitt and Randall Stokes, "Disclaimers," *American Sociological Review* 40(1975):1–11.
7. Alfred Schutz, *Collected Papers,* volume 2 (The Hague: Martinus Nijhoff, 1964).
8. Peter L. Berger and Thomas Luckmann, *The Social Construction of Reality* (New York: Anchor Books, 1967).
9. A. Gurwitsch, *The Field of Consciousness* (Duquesne University Press, 1964), pp. 134–135.
10. Erving Goffman, *Frame Analysis* (New York: Harper Colophon Books, 1974).
11. Howard Schwartz and Jerry Jacobs, *Qualitative Sociology: A Method to the Madness* (New York: The Free Press, 1979).
12. Erving Goffman, *Interactional Ritual* (New York: Anchor Books, 1967).
13. D. Lawrence Wieder, *Language and Social Reality: The Case of Telling the Convict Code* (Mouton: The Hague Press, 1975).
14. Barney Glaser and Anslem Strauss, *The Discovery of Grounded Theory* (Chicago: Aldine Publishers, 1967).
15. John Shelton Reed, *Southern Folk, Plain & Fancy: Native White Social Types* (University of Georgia Press, 1987).
16. See Raymond D. Gastil, *Cultural Regions of the United States* (Seattle, WA: University of Washington Press, 1975); Hodding Carter, *Southern Legacy* (Baton Rouge, LA: Louisiana State University Press, 1950); Rosemary Daniell, *Fatal Flowers* (New York: Holt, Rinehart and Winston, 1980).
17. See Daniell, *Fatal Flowers,* and King, *Southern Ladies and Gentlemen.*
18. Reed, *Southerners: The Social Psychology of Sectionalism.*
19. All names have been changed to protect the identity of the respondents.

20. Morris Rosenberg and Ralph H. Turner, eds., *Social Psychology: Sociological Perspectives* (New York: Basic Books, 1981).
21. Goffman, *Frame Analysis,* p. 547.
22. Wieder, *Language and Social Reality.*
23. C. Wright Mills, "Situated Actions and Vocabularies of Motives," in *Symbolic Interaction,* 3rd ed., Jerome Manis and Bernard Meltzer, eds. (New York: Basic Books, 1978), pp. 301–307.
24. Wieder, *Language and Social Reality.*
25. Herbert J. Gans, *Popular Culture and High Culture* (New York: Basic Books, 1974).
26. B. J. Skrypnek and M. Snyder, "On the Self-Perpetuating Nature of Stereotypes About Women and Men," *Journal of Experimental Social Psychology* 18(1982):277–291.

Chapter 12
LADIES: SOUTH BY NORTHWEST

JACQUELINE BOLES AND MAXINE P. ATKINSON

Women are moving from the private to the public sphere. No longer confined to the home, women work in traditionally male jobs, assume management positions, and assert themselves in the political life of this country. Still, not all women have chosen the executive suite, and many express their ambivalence, if not hostility, to this new role for women. Nontraditional women often express a nostalgia for that paragon of female virtue and rectitude—the lady.

Except for black and native American women, the lady was the role model for most American white women throughout the 19th century.[1] The lady made the long trek from the East across the Oregon Trail to western territories. Yet, her most congenial home was the South where she reigned supreme even after the Civil War when the way of life that supported her disappeared. Though most white women of the 19th and 20th centuries attempted to emulate the lady, the deprivation of the frontier made this impractical.[2] Frontier women, through necessity, often rejected the traditional role model in favor of a more egalitarian "pioneering" one.[3]

Though there is little research on regional variations in gender role attitudes and values,[4] available findings indicate that Southern women are the most conservative and Western women the least.[5] These regional variations in gender role attitudes and values are reflected in the traditional and conservative ideology of the South[6] as contrasted with the more liberal and egalitarian ideology of the West.[7] Regional differences in gender role ideology, as well as other values and attitudes, have been attributed to differences in the cultural values of the first inhabitants,[8] the interweave of geography and the economy,[9] and a "consciousness of kind" that develops under circumstances unique to each region.[10] The viability of the lady as role model in understanding regional differences in gender role attitudes and behaviors has not been examined.[11]

127

This study examines the salience of the lady as a role model in two regions of the country. If women still want to be ladies, then the continuation of a conservative gender role ideology manifested in resistance to the Equal Rights Amendment, legalized abortions, and other "women's issues" on the part of traditional women is understandable. Using a constructed type method,[12] we developed a model for the ideal lady, emphasizing the Southern variant of that ideal. We then contrasted the lady with the ideal pioneer woman and traced the effects of these conflicting models on frontier women. Finally, based on our constructed type of the ideal lady, a sample of Southern and Western women responded to a questionnaire examining the extent of their agreement with the temperamental and behavioral qualities of the lady and the extent to which they themselves exemplify those qualities.

THE LADY: A CONSTRUCTED TYPE

The constructed type has been employed by Simmel, Weber, Becker, Redfield, and others.[13] A constructed typology identifies recurring patterns and abstracts and simplifies these elements in order to make (systematic) comparisons.[14] We derived our constructed type from novels, diaries, memoirs, and historical documents.[15]

As with most histories, the history of the lady began (at least for Western civilization) with Greece and the wives of the citizens of the Greek city-states.[16] The assumed attributes of the lady have evolved over the centuries; however, the defining characteristic is gentility, which is achieved by "doing nothing at all."[17]

Over the centuries ladies in Western civilization gradually began to assert themselves and step out of the male shadows in which they lived. This movement of ladies into the public sphere gathered momentum in the 17th century, but those who left the safety of home and hearth for the public sphere risked antagonizing men and thereby jeopardizing their social and financial positions.

The lady alone of all classes of society had succeeded in breaking her tabu, while leaving her economic base untouched, in altering her social relations in several fundamental directions . . . but since her economic position was unchanged, since men were still officially in control and what she enjoyed was won by favour, it was necessary that all changes in her position should be wrought by the connivance of men. . . . She had to be careful to cultivate her powers but not give offense to men.[18]

The identification of the lady with gentility was exaggerated by the industrial revolution. As increasing numbers of poor women sought jobs in factories, it became doubly important for the wives of middle-class men to appear delicate, useless appendages. "Gentility came to be associated with inactivity."[19] Moreover, gentility connoted higher moral responsibility, sensitivity, and compassion.[20] In the United States, the popular magazine *Gody's Lady's Book* published articles by Catherine Beecher and others who emphasized the special cultural and social responsibilities of women. This "cult of domesticity" extolled the home as the sphere of influence for women whose primary responsibility it was to create retreats of domestic peace and tranquility because they, like Christ, were "humble in their purity and innocence."[21]

Gentility comprised a variety of temperamental and behavioral traits. Perhaps the best single description of the lady is by Lord Acton[22] writing on "The Perfect Ideal of an English Wife":

> *I believe this lady a perfect ideal of an English wife and mother, kind, considerate, self-sacrificing and sensible, so pure-hearted as to be utterly ignorant of and averse to any sensual indulgence, but so unselfishly attached to the man she loves as to be willing to give up her own wishes and feelings for his sake.*

The Southern Lady

The image of the lady held currency all over the United States, but it found a special niche in the South. This agrarian society, made possible by slavery, provided a strong ideological base that elevated the ladies of the manor to secular sainthood: "According to the social theory of the Old South, the lady's equilibrium was that of a Gothic Saint in her niche."[23] The ideas about women's special sphere circulated in journals, sermons, novels, and speeches, and "That well-born Southern woman, at least, attempted to live up to the cultural norms is clearly evident in their diaries and other writings."[24]

Anne Firor Scott wrote the definitive historical treatment of the Southern lady.[25] The lady's life was one of devotion to God, husband, and children whose training was her major responsibility. As a wife she was submissive, obedient, self-denying, innocent, and dependent. But even the home, her primary sphere of influence, was subject to the will of her husband. "The clear demarcation of women's sphere as separate and subsidiary was a necessary part of a social analysis which gave white males total authority over all others."[26] Though possessed of fine (and refined) sensibilities, the lady required control, protection, and guidance from men, and she was dutifully passed on from father to husband to son.

Her education consisted primarily of training in correct behavior, for intelligence in a woman was more distressing than pleasing to a man. She must be well read to be an engaging conversationalist, but this reading should be limited to the Bible, classical literature, and history. By temperament she was calm, pious, enduring, tactful, tender, amiable, sweet, and prudent.[27] Another historian describes the Southern lady as a "beautiful, innocent, incapable, devoted, and obedient wife, the exemplar of all virtues and the forgiver of all vices."[28]

Despite the ideal of incapability, Southern ladies were by no means inactive. Their diaries contain vivid accounts of their day-to-day existence on the plantations. Isolated from kin and neighbors, they had the responsibility for the health and well-being of slaves, children, and sharecroppers.[29] Regardless of the responsibilities these women bore, they played the part of the Southern lady because to do otherwise would have "reflected on their husbands' ability to compete with other men for the prizes of life."[30] The lady, in the South as elsewhere, symbolized the success achieved by her husband.

Temperamental and Behavioral Characteristics of the Lady

From the survey of historical documents written by and about Southern ladies, we identified 20 temperamental descriptors that typify this ideal woman: simple, good, passive, delicate, innocent, submissive, mannerly, economical, humble, sacrificing, sympathetic, kind, weak, generous, pious, shallow, nonintellectual, hospitable, rich, and calm.

Further, Southern ladies were expected to engage in activities centered in the home and connected with their responsibilities as wives and mothers.[31] To be amusing the lady should read history and the classics and play a musical instrument. She should entertain her husband's friends, family, and business acquaintances. She must maintain frequent contact with her family and his family, and she must teach her children the family history and traditions. She should manage her household, and in her free time she might write in her diary.

Except for her duty to manage her household, her responsibilities correspond to the image of the lady as genteel, passive, pious, and obedient, dedicated to providing unflagging service and devotion to her husband and children. For middle- and upper-class Northern and Southern women, the realization of the role demands of the lady was obtainable, but for their sisters on the frontier, the illusion of uselessness and passivity was difficult, if not impossible, to sustain. In the following section the conflict between the ideal image of the lady and the actual life of frontier women is discussed with a view toward explicating the ambivalence felt by pioneer women toward the world they imagined and the life they actually lived.

The Woman of the Moving Frontier

Most 19th-century women lived with a continuing contradiction between myth and reality:

> The concept of women's special nature appeared very early in American history. Beneath the surface of the rhetoric over the finer sensibilities which developed in the 19th century, woman often found herself in conflict. Part of the difficulty was that the myth, at least for most of the country, conflicted with reality. While Americans were officially adopting the belief that women were made of fabric not suited for the more mundane tasks of life, the vast majority of Americans were still living on farms where women worked, and, in fact, pulled their fair share of the load so that the family farm would not collapse.[32]

Nowhere was this contradiction greater than on the Western frontier. The great Western migration forced women, many of whom were from the South, to leave their homes and take up shelters in Conestoga wagons, log and sod houses, and even teepees. The image of the lady and the cult of domesticity traveled with these women as their letters, diaries, and memoirs attest.[33] These first-generation pioneer women certainly perceived the contradiction between what they had been taught and the grim realities of their experience on the frontier.

The reactions of frontier women to their deprivations varied greatly, according to social-class background, age, health of self and family, and region from which they came.[34] While many women succumbed to loneliness, physical and psychological deprivation, and ill-health, others became prototypical pioneer women who not only survived but flourished. The image of the ideal frontier woman began to take shape from the experiences of these women who braved a hostile environment in order to wring subsistence from the soil.

Those pioneer women who survived soon learned that they could not hope to be the passive partner that was a requisite of the lady role. One pioneer bride described her understanding of that responsibility:

I already had ideas of my own about the husband being the head of the family. I had taken the precaution to sound him on "obey" in the marriage pact and found he did not approve of the term. Approval or no approval that word "obey" would have to be left out. I had served my time in tutelage to my parents as all children are supposed to. I was a woman now and capable of being the other half of the head of the family. His word and my word would have equal strength.[35]

One cannot imagine a Southern belle on the eve of her marriage making such a statement.

Descriptions by and about pioneer women portray their temperaments as distinctly different from those attributed to the lady. From our vantage point today, the pioneer woman was androgynous, and she appeared rather masculine to many observers of the time: "One contemporary writer said that 'We admit they were masculine, if you term that masculine which prompted them to defend, aye, die for their husbands and their children.' "[36]

Frontier women described themselves as self-sufficient, hardy, tough, resourceful, courageous, taciturn, adventuresome, fatalistic, and brave.[37] Rebecca Boone, wife of Daniel, was described by her contemporaries as "self-sufficient, hardy, tough, resourceful, and courageous."[38]

The frontier women also had many responsibilities beyond those of the Southern lady. She worked beside her husband in the field often longer than he did. One Texas folk song aptly describes her work status: "Texas is heaven for men and dogs; but it is hell for women and oxen."[39] Women also took care of their families, the sick, the injured, and the poor. They defended themselves and their children against Indians and outlaws. One such woman was described as "hefty, grotesque, and mean with a pistol."[40]

Even though these frontier women assumed many stereotypically masculine traits, they, because of their "special [i.e., feminine] nature," took responsibility for civilizing the West. They consciously set out to capture the teaching profession so that they could use that position to bring civilization, culture, and religion to the frontier.[41] They organized clubs and civic and religious associations to further their goals. Western women played a stronger community leadership role than did their sisters in the North and the South because they took "civilizing" as a calling.

Thus, the historical images of Western and Southern women differ substantially. Because a Western woman's life paralleled a man's, Western women were seen as almost the equal of men. The Western woman was tough, strong, and courageous. Conversely, the Southern lady was idolized for her assumed weakness and innocence. Her own work went unrecognized, and she was praised not because of it but rather for her ability to remain untouched by it. The ideal image of the lady was inconsistent with the realities of life for Southern women, but the contradictions were much more apparent for Western women.

Still, the lady was presented as a role model for all women, and Western women, in particular, experienced considerable anxiety about their inability to live up to that image. Their dedication to civilizing (some said "feminizing") the West was, in part, a response to their own defeminization.

The industrialization of the South and the West now, in contemporary times, provides similar economic life conditions for women in both regions. They differ primarily on the basis of their cultural heritage. In the South the lady as role model has continued validity for upper-class women.[42] Do Western women emulate the lady now that the frontier has been settled? In the following section we respond to that question and offer a comparison of contemporary women from these two regions.

THE LADY: SOUTH BY NORTHWEST

In a previous article we explored the viability of the lady as a role model for a sample of Southern women.[43] Using a constructed type method we developed a set of behavioral and temperamental characteristics typical of the lady (see Tables 1 and 2). Using the reputational approach, we identified 56 respondents who were upper-middle- and upper-class females and who were members of garden, genealogical, and debutante clubs.[44] These women responded to a questionnaire that included (1) demographic information; (2) a list of 20 temperamental traits arranged in a semantic differential format; and (3) a list of behavioral traits defined as characteristic of the lady. Our respondents were asked to identify from those lists the temperamental and behavioral characteristics representative of the lady. Additionally, they identified those traits that they themselves possessed and the activities that they pursued. This strategy enabled us to

TABLE 1 Characteristics: Ideal and Actual*

Constructed Type	Ideal Behaviors				Actual Behaviors			
	Important		Not Important		Performed		Not Performed	
	South	Northwest	South	Northwest	South	Northwest	South	Northwest
Entertaining to help husband professionally	X			X			X	X
Teaching children family traditions	X	X				X	X	
Writing letters to her own family	X	X				X	X	
Entertaining her own family	X			X		X	X	
Entertaining her husband's family	X			X			X	X
Writing letters to her husband's family	X	X					X	X
Reading history	X			X			X	X
Reading classics	X			X			X	X
Managing household	X	X				X		
Keeping in touch with husband's family by phone	X	X				X	X	
Keeping a diary			X	X			X	X
Playing a musical instrument			X	X			X	X
Keeping in touch with her own family by phone	X	X				X	X	

* Behaviors judged to be important or performed were divided on the basis of 55% or more agreement among respondents.

TABLE 2 Temperamental Characteristics or Role: Semantic Differential Constructed Type, Contemporary Ideal Role, and Contemporary Actual Role

Constructed Type*	Contemporary Ideal Role** Strong Agreement 70%+ South	Contemporary Ideal Role** Strong Agreement 70%+ Northwest	Contemporary Ideal Role** Agreement 52–70% South	Contemporary Ideal Role** Agreement 52–70% Northwest	Contemporary Actual Role** Strong Agreement 70%+ South	Contemporary Actual Role** Strong Agreement 70%+ Northwest	Contemporary Actual Role** Agreement 52–70% South	Contemporary Actual Role** Agreement 52–70% Northwest	Difference Ideal and Actual South	Difference Ideal and Actual Northwest
Simple	X						X			***
Good	X	X				X	O		***	***
Passive		O	X				X			***
Delicate			O	X			X			
Rich	O		X				O		***	
Innocent							O			
Submissive	X					X	X	O		
Mannerly	X	X				X	O		***	
Economical	X			X			O	X		
Humble	X			O			X	O		
Sacrificing		X	X			X	O			
Nonintellectual	O	O					O			
Sympathetic		X	X			X	O			
Kind	X	X				X	X		***	
Weak		O	O			O	O			
Generous	X	X				X	X		***	
Pious			X	X			X	X		
Shallow			O	O			X	O		
Hospitable	X	X				X	X		***	
Calm	X	X				X	O		***	

* The Semantic Differential Scales were Simple-Complex, Bad-Good, Active-Passive, Rugged-Delicate, Rich-Poor, Innocent-Experienced, Aggressive-Submissive, Unruly-Mannerly, Economical-Extravagant, Assertive-Humble, Selfish-Sacrificing, Intellectual-Nonintellectual, Critical-Sympathetic, Kind-Cruel, Weak-Strong, Selfish-Generous, Pious-Profane, Deep-Shallow, Hospitable-Rude, Agitated-Calm.

** X signifies agreement with the constructed type; O signifies agreement with the opposite of the constructed type.

*** $p > .05$ as judged by Chi Square.

134

identify (1) the differences between their current conception of the ideal and the historical ideal and (2) the differences between the ideal and their own behaviors and temperaments.

The Pacific Northwest was the last part of the frontier settled; trappers began to move into that country in the 1840s, and settlers followed around a decade later.[45] Our second sample of women were natives of this region. Using a reputational approach similar to the one utilized in our study of Southern women, we identified 26 Northwest women who were similar in social class to those from the South. These women lived in a medium-sized Northwestern city and participated in the same types of community groups as did the women from the South. The Northwestern women responded to the same questionnaire used for Southern women. The addition of a sample of Northwestern women allowed us to compare the responses of women from two historically dissimilar regions of the United States.

FINDINGS

Table 1 indicates that our Southern respondents agreed with the historical ideal behavior of the lady, including entertaining to help her husband, teaching children the family traditions, entertaining both sides of the family, writing letters to her husband's family, reading the classics and history, managing her household, and keeping in touch with her husband's family by telephone. The only ideal behaviors that they did not accept were keeping a diary and playing a musical instrument.

Of the 13 behavioral dimensions on the ideal behavior scale, the women of the Northwest concurred with only 6: teaching children family traditions, writing letters to both sides of the family, managing their households, and keeping in touch with both sides of the family by telephone. They did not see keeping a diary, entertaining to help their husbands professionally, entertaining both sides of the family, reading history and the classics, or playing a musical instrument as important aspects of the lady role. Thus, the Southern women were significantly more in agreement with the ideal role behaviors of the lady (84%) than were the Northwestern women (46%). Also, several of the women in our Southern sample wrote vivid descriptions of the behavioral attributes of the lady which, we believe, indicate the depth of their feelings on this subject:

> *[F]amilies and their homes are their chief concerns, and they generally have a "live in" maid or helper, children's nurse, and cook. They belong to clubs, and give afternoon teas, but their main attention is given to family matters.*

and

> *A true Southern lady never complains, she meets adversity with dignity and grace, she never discusses money or the cost of anything, she is infi-*

nitely polite to servants or those less fortunate, she puts everyone at ease. She never belittles, ridicules, or criticizes; she greets friends and relatives alike with a hug and a kiss, male or female; she uses no profanity; she always stands for older people when she is young through middle age; she has excellent table manners, often carves with excellence; she keeps her ailments, allergies, idiosyncracies to herself; she eats with pleasure anything served no matter what; she believes in putting herself out for company and family; she is very polite to her husband and children; and it is always clearly understood that her husband is the head of the family.

Contemporary Southern women also agreed with the historical ideal temperamental characteristics (see Table 2). At least 70% thought that the lady ought to be simple, good, submissive, mannerly, humble, kind, economical, generous, hospitable, and calm. At least 50% believed that the lady must be passive, innocent, sacrificing, sympathetic, and pious. Our respondents did not consider the following descriptors applicable to the Southern lady: delicate, rich, nonintellectual, weak, and shallow. Thus, contemporary Southern women were in strong agreement with the ideal image of the lady as presented in historical and literary accounts.

While the Southern women agreed with 75% of the historical ideal temperamental traits of the lady, the Northwestern women concurred with only 55%. Although these women from the West agreed with fewer items than their sisters from the South, they did support the historical ideal. There are, however, a few interesting points of disagreement between the two groups of women.

Southern women thought the ideal lady was rugged, while Western women asserted that she should be delicate, the ideal trait. Southern women also thought the lady should be poor, but those from the Northwest are neutral on that point. Also, the Northwestern women are more strongly in accord with the model ideal in some respects than are the Southern women. For example, all 26 Northwestern respondents believed that the lady should be hospitable compared with only 84% of the Southern women. This finding seems especially surprising given the Southern tradition of hospitality. One area of disagreement does seem congruent with historical stereotypes: the Southern women identified passivity as an ideal quality while Northwestern women thought the lady should be active.

Also included in our analysis is the extent to which women in both regions believe that they themselves live up to the ideal image. The Southern women appear to be more self-critical than their Northwestern counterparts, for the only behaviors that they fully perform are managing their households and keeping in touch with their husband's family by telephone (see Table 1).

By their own estimation, however, Northwestern women do a superior job of meeting role expectations. Of the six behaviors they said the lady should perform, they performed five. The only ideal behavior they fail to perform is writing letters to their husband's family. They also identified one behavior that they do perform but do not consider a necessary activity for the lady: entertaining one's own family.

Additionally, the Northwestern women believe they possess more ladylike temperamental traits than do the women from the South. Seventy percent or more of the Northwestern women felt that they were good, mannerly, nonintellectual, sympathetic, kind, generous, hospitable, and calm. Also, over 50% saw themselves as economical, sacrificing, and pious. The Northwestern women differed from the ideal on only three descriptors: strong, assertive, and deep, terms that they had rejected as typical of the lady. In a word, the Northwestern women in our sample felt that they play the lady role quite well. But this was not so for the Southern women: their responses indicated feelings of inadequacy— of falling far short of the ideal. For example, there was not one temperamental trait that 70% or more of our sample thought they had achieved (see Table 2). However, over 50% did think they had acquired some traits of the lady: simplicity, passivity, delicateness, submissiveness, humility, weakness, piousness, shallowness, and hospitality. Yet, these Southern women are not as good, rich, innocent, mannerly, economical, sacrificing, nonintellectual, sympathetic, kind, weak, and calm as they believed they should be. Moreover, while the 3 descriptors that the Western women did not achieve were those that they rejected as typical of the lady, of the 11 descriptors not acquired by the Southerners, they rejected only one (nonintellectual) as not representative of the lady.

In terms of both behavior and temperament, Southern women are more apt to agree with the ideal than are the Western women but they fail in the commission of them. Southern women generally see themselves as failing whereas Westerners view themselves as succeeding. Does this finding mean that, contrary to what might be our expectations based on the histories of these two regions, Western women are more ladylike than their Southern female cousins, the descendants of Melanie Wilkes and all the other Southern belles and ladies who once graced the plantations of the Old South?

DISCUSSION

Our findings both point to the continued viability of the lady-role model and suggest important differences between upper-middle- and upper-class Western and Southern women, the latter not surprising, given the historical differences between the two regions. During the frontier years Western women felt considerable ambivalence about their femininity because the roles they were forced to adopt led them to acquire stereotypically male behaviors and temperamental traits. Conversely, Southern women were rewarded for femininity, and the complex activities that upper-status Southern women actually performed were unrecognized and unrewarded.

Our findings suggest that today it is the Southern woman who feels ambivalent, torn between her desire to emulate the true Southern lady and her feelings of personal inadequacy for being unable to do so. After all, the ideal role model did not really exist but was a fiction created to sustain an agrarian economy based on slave labor. Our sample of Southern women feel they have fallen short of the mark despite their best intentions.

The South is a region undergoing rapid social change. As part of the Sun Belt, the South is host to many "Yankees," some of whom try to assimilate the "Southern way of life" by, among other things, reading *Southern Living* to see how it's done.[46] Also, Southern nouveau riche are moving into positions of power formerly held by the "old families." As the positions of the wives and daughters of the old families are threatened with displacement, they may become increasingly concerned with preserving the authentic Southern way of life including the role of the Southern lady. Many of our Southern respondents reacted to this perceived threat with written comments that accompanied their questionnaires. One typical response was, "A great deal of stress is laid on who you are and how mannerly you are. Money does not matter as much as family and behavior."

In one of his recent books John Shelton Reed developed a typology of Southerners.[47] The "fire eaters" were high on consciousness and held a traditional value orientation. The women in our Southern sample are, most probably, fire eaters with both traditional Southern values and a strong regional consciousness. If Southern women are fire eaters, then they will espouse traditional gender role values and political conservatism to a greater extent than will women in other regions of the country.

Southern women, in contrast to Western women, are ideally more committed to preserving what they see as a special traditional way of life. However, as was historically true, the ideal definitions of the lady are impossible to attain. Western women set more realistic goals and, consequently, are much more likely to feel that they can successfully live up to the role they define — indeed they believe that they have exceeded the ideal images! The lessons that Margaret Mitchell tried to teach in *Gone With the Wind* have not been learned.[48] The role of the Southern lady was dysfunctional then and remains so, even by the admission of the women who aspire to the role.

Southern women find their traditional lifestyle threatened both from within and without. They react to this threat by attempting to mold themselves after the lady, a fictional creation of a bygone era.

NOTES

1. Emily J. Putnam, *The Lady: Studies of Certain Significant Phases in Her History* (Chicago: University of Chicago Press, 1910).
2. Glenda Riley, *Frontierswoman: The Iowa Experience* (Ames, IA: The Iowa University Press, 1981); Joanna Stratton, *Pioneer Woman: Voices from the Kansas Frontier* (New York: Simon and Schuster, 1981).
3. The term *pioneer* has been used to label women who are in nontraditional occupations. For a review of the literature on "pioneer" in this sense, see Leonard Chusmir, "Characteristics and Predictive Dimensions of Women Who Make Nontraditional Vocational Choices," *Personnel and Guidance Journal* 62(1983):43–47.
4. Andrew Cherlin and Pamela B. Walters, "Trends in United States Men's and Women's Sex Role Attitudes, 1972–1978, " *American Sociological Review* 46(1981):453–460.

5. Karen M. Mason, John L. Czajk, and Sara Arber, ''Change in U.S. Women's Sex Role Attitudes, 1964–1974,'' *American Sociological Review* 41(1976):573–596; Nan E Johnson and C. Channon Stokes, ''Southern Traditionalism and Sex Role Ideology: A Research Note'' (Paper presented at the meeting of the Southern Sociological Society, Atlanta, 1979).

6. Harold Grasmick, ''Social Change and the Wallace Movement in the South'' (Ph.D. diss., University of North Carolina, 1973); John Shelton Reed, *Southerners: The Social Psychology of Sectionalism* (Chapel Hill, NC: The University of North Carolina Press, 1983).

7. Raymond Gastil, *Cultural Regions of the United States* (Seattle, WA: University of Washington Press, 1975).

8. Ibid.

9. Stephan Birdsall and John Florin, *Regional Landscapes of the United States and Canada* (New York: John Wiley, 1978).

10. Howard Odum, *Southern Regions of the United States* (Chapel Hill, NC: The University of North Carolina Press, 1964); John Shelton Reed, *One South: An Ethnic Approach to Regional Culture* (Chapel Hill, NC: The University of North Carolina Press, 1982).

11. Sheila M. Rothman, *Women's Proper Place: A History of Changing Ideals and Practices, 1870 to the Present* (New York: Basic Books, 1978); Maxine Atkinson and Jacqueline Boles, ''The Southern Lady; Yesterday and Today,'' *Southern Studies,* 24(1985):398–406; Vern Bullough, *The Subordinate Sex: A History of Attitudes Toward Women* (Urbana, IL: University of Illinois Press, 1976).

12. John C. McKinney, *Constructive Typology and Social Theory* (New York: Meredith, 1966).

13. Georg Simmel, *The Sociology of Georg Simmel,* trans. and ed. Kurt H. Wolff (Glencoe, IL: The Free Press, 1950); Max Weber, *Theory and Social and Economic Organization,* trans. A. M. Henderson and Talcott Parsons (Glencoe, IL: The Free Press, 1947); Howard Becker, *Through Values to Social Interpretation* (Durham, NC: Duke University Press, 1950); Robert Redfield, ''The Folk Society,'' *American Journal of Sociology* 52(1947):293–308.

14. McKinney, *Constructive Typology.*

15. For example, see novels such as Ellen Glasgow, *Virginia* (Garden City, NY: Doubleday, Page, 1913); Harnett P. Kane, *Bride of Fortune* (Garden City, NY: Doubleday, 1948). See also diaries such as Ben Ames Williams, ed., *A Diary from Dixie by Mary Boykin Chestnut* (Boston: Houghton Mifflin, 1949); Elizabeth C. Wallace, *Glencoe Diary* (Chesapeake, VA: Norfolk County Historical Society, 1968). See also published letters, for example, William W. Hassler, ed., *The General and His Lady: The Civil War Letters of William Dorsey Pender to Fanny Pender* (Chapel Hill, NC: The University of North Carolina Press, 1965); Hunter D. Farrish, ed., *The Journal and Letters of Phillip Vichers Fithian, 1773–1774, A Plantation Tour of the Old Dominion* (Charlottesville, VA: The University of Virginia Press, 1957).

16. Putnam, *The Lady.*

17. Ibid., p. xxxviii.

18. Ibid., p. 225.

19. Bullough, *The Subordinate Sex,* p. 284.

20. Bullough, *The Subordinate Sex;* Rothman, *Women's Proper Place;* Julie R. Jeffrey,

Frontier Women: The Trans-Mississippi West, 1840–1880 (New York: Hill and Wang, 1979).

21. Jeffrey, *Frontier Women*, p. 7.
22. William Acton, *The Functions and Disorders of the Reproductive Organs in Childhood, Adult, Age, and Advanced Life, Considered in Their Physiological, Social and Moral Relations*, 6th ed. (London: J. A. Churchill, 1876), p. 432.
23. Putnam, *The Lady*, p. 282.
24. Jeffrey, *Frontier Women*, p. 7.
25. Anne Firor Scott, *The Southern Lady: From Pedestal to Politics, 1830–1930* (Chicago: University of Chicago Press, 1970).
26. Jeffrey, *Frontier Women*, pp. 7–8.
27. Scott, *The Southern Lady*.
28. Hodding Carter, *Southern Legacy* (Baton Rouge, LA: Louisiana State University Press, 1950), p. 69.
29. Glasgow, *Virginia;* Josephine Habersham, *Ebb Tide,* ed. Spencer Bidwell King (Athens, GA: University of Georgia Press, 1958); Wallace, *Glencoe Diary.*
30. Putnam, *The Lady*, p. 320.
31. To make our assessment of behavioral traits current, we added ''keeping in touch with husband's family by telephone.'' Obviously the documents used to develop our constructed type did not refer to telephone usage.
32. Bullough, *The Subordinate Sex*, p. 312.
33. Jeffrey, *Frontier Women;* Ann P. Malone, *Women on the Texas Frontier: A Cross-Cultural Perspective* (El Paso, TX: Texas Western Press, 1983); Stratton, *Pioneer Woman;* Riley, *Frontierswoman.*
34. Malone, *Women on the Texas Frontier.*
35. Stratton, *Pioneer Woman*, p. 58. Reprinted by permission of Simon and Schuster, Copyright © 1981 by Joanna L. Stratton.
36. Jeffrey, *Frontier Women*, p. 19.
37. Jeffrey, *Frontier Women;* Malone, *Women on the Texas Frontier;* Riley, *Frontierswoman;* Stratton, *Pioneer Woman;* Barbara Stoeltze, ''A Helpmate for Man Indeed,'' in *Women and Folklore,* Claire R. Farrar, ed. (Austin, TX: University of Texas Press, 1975), pp. 25–41.
38. Jeffrey, *Frontier Women*, p. 38.
39. Malone, *Women on the Texas Frontier*, p. 14.
40. Mody C. Boatright, *Folk Laughter on the American Frontier* (Gloucester, MA: P. Smith, 1971), p. 44.
41. Jeffrey, *Frontier Women.*
42. Atkinson and Boles, *The Southern Lady.*
43. Ibid.
44. Our purposive sample was constructed to include women who might be expected both to be knowledgeable about the traits of the lady as well as to model themselves on that. For that reason our respondents were upper-middle-class women who belonged to a few prestigious women's groups oriented around family traditions and ''feminine'' concerns.
45. Gastil, *Cultural Regions of the United States.*
46. Reed, *Southerners: The Social Psychology of Sectionalism.*
47. Ibid.
48. Margaret Mitchell, *Gone With the Wind* (New York: Macmillan, 1936).

Chapter 13

MAGNOLIAS AND MICROCHIPS: REGIONAL SUBCULTURAL CONSTRUCTIONS OF FEMININITY[1]

SUSAN MIDDLETON-KEIRN

INTRODUCTION

This article addresses two specific questions: First, do women who are both *in* the South, geographically, and *of* the South, socially and culturally, differ from women living in other U.S. regions?[2] In other words, are contemporary Southern women distinct among American women and, if so, in what specific ways? Second, in what distinctive ways do the regional traditions of the American South embody and express gender roles? More than two decades ago the Southern author Lillian Smith wrote that the time had come for women to risk the "great and daring creative act" of discovering and articulating their own identity.[3] Today in the continuing clash between the old and the new conceptions of their "appropriate" roles, women from all walks of life and all regions are confronted with choices, decisions, and images of what it means to be "feminine." If this is true in the contemporary United States as a whole, it is especially true of the South where many regional traditions express characteristics of idealized, stylized gender roles.

The Southern Lady

The idea of the lady was part of the larger American and even Anglo-American culture of the 19th century, but in the South this image took "deep root and had far-reaching social consequences. The social role of women was unusually confining there, and the sanctions used to enforce obedience peculiarly effective. One result was that Southern women became in time a distinct

type among American women, and another was that their efforts to free themselves were more complex than those of women elsewhere.''[4]

The Plain Folk

In order to begin to answer the broad questions posed about Southern
women, it is essential to remember that the ladies of the Southern plantation
tradition described by Scott were by no means representative of the great mass
of the female populace. In fact, the relatively idle Southern lady was rare even
among the privileged few of the plantation tradition. Most Southern women
have always worked hard, and the great mass of the populace can be better
understood by examining what one writer calls the ''plain folk of the old
South.''[5] The reality of the plain folk tradition is aptly summarized in the remarks of an unidentified woman textile worker who, at the beginning of the
Great Depression, put it this way:

> *"It is nothing new for married women to work. . . . They have always*
> *worked. . . . Some girls think that as long as a mother takes in washings,*
> *keeps ten or twelve boarders or perhaps takes in sewing, she isn't*
> *working. But I can say that either one of the three is as hard work as*
> *women can do. . . ."*[6]

However, a genuine paucity of data on the plain folk tradition, and particularly on the women who are an integral part of that tradition, hampers our
understanding of both past and present objective and ideological conditions
under which the majority of Southern women live. Both Bruce[7] and Hill[8] have
stressed the neglect of plain folk in the literature and have noted the heuristic
value of a plain folk model in understanding the mainstream South. ''The traditions of the descendants of these people, many of them still rural or living in
small towns, provide a key to the understanding of the modern South.''[9]
Anthropologists have only recently come to view an effort to understand and
explore the South and its traditions as a respectable intellectual endeavor. This
effort and its extant literature have been well summarized by Hill,[10] and more
recently by Dillman,[11] who points out the particular definitional and methodological complexities involved in studying Southern women. Because of their
excellent efforts, I will turn directly to my field research.

This article takes a comparative approach and describes some of the results of my recent anthropological field research. It represents one of the first
empirical efforts to delineate regional or subcultural differences in contemporary
gender role ideology. The comparative research described here introduces some
of the women of the contemporary plain folk tradition whose daily lives are both
in the South, geographically, and *of* the South, socially and culturally. Then,
later, comparative field research data from the lives of Western women provide
a perspective that enhances our understanding of cultural continuity and persistence in the South.

PROJECT DESIGN AND FOCUS

The field work described below began while I was a professor of anthropology at a Southern university. As I came to know my neighbors, my students, and many of my colleagues who were Southerners, I realized that here was a way of life different from any I had known previously. Having studied cultures abroad using the methods of anthropology, I knew their utility in helping an outsider understand the world view of insiders, that is, those whose behavior is generated and guided by an abstract set of specific values and ideals. " 'If it is our serious purpose to understand the thoughts of a people the whole analysis of experience must be based on their concepts, not ours.' "[12] This emic approach is also referred to as "ethnoscience," "ethnosemantics," and "the New Ethnography."

In order to frame hypotheses that are as objective and free of cultural or regional bias as possible, anthropologists typically develop their hypotheses through a kind of total immersion in the field—becoming so familiar with the minute details of the situation that they can begin to recognize patterns inherent in the data. It is important to recognize those patterns inherent in the data *after* immersion (instead of imposing one's own set of categories on the situation initially). Hence the focus of the research and the design of the interview schedule occurred after I had already been living and working in the South for an extended period.

Methods

Participant observation and open-ended interview schedules provided the ideal methods for determining how the women viewed their own lives. While obtaining this emic perspective, I taught at a Southern university for five years. This extended period of residence permitted an immersion not only in the lives of respondents, but also in the lives of friends, colleagues, neighbors, and students who, unlike me, were Southerners. Such immersion provided an opportunity to build the ongoing rapport so necessary in anthropological field work and yielded sometimes intimate glimpses not usually afforded to researchers, who rarely have the chance to live and work in one setting for such an unbroken and extended period.

Having accepted another professorship in the West and having taught there for two years, I received a research grant that enabled me to capitalize on the opportunity, afforded by my career move, to gather comparative data. I used the same open-ended interview schedules as those for the respondents in the South; and furthermore, my extended period of residence in the West afforded me the same opportunities for immersion that were available in the first phase of the research.

Respondent Sets

Respondent sets and subsets, summarized in Figure 1, were obtained

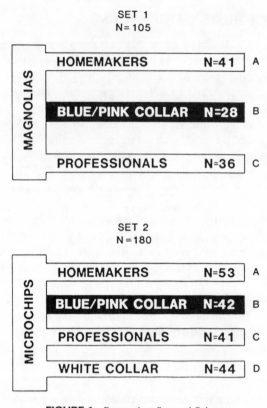

FIGURE 1   Respondent Sets and Subsets

through quota sampling.[13] As Figure 1 indicates, this article focuses exclusively on blue-collar and pink-collar women in the South and in the West.

As part of a larger project, begun in 1980, that examined gender roles and gender role ideology in the contemporary South, a total respondent set of 105 women participated in an open-ended interview schedule that focused on two spheres of their lives: first, the domestic sphere, including their relationships with the men in their lives; and second, the sphere of the economic market-place.[14] Begun in 1983, the current phase of the ongoing project on contemporary American gender role ideology involves 180 Western women. These women, living in the Central Valley of California,[15] also participated in an open-ended interview schedule focusing on the same two aspects.

The Southern respondent set was divided into three subsets: full-time homemakers, blue-collar and pink-collar workers, and professionals; the Western, into four subsets: homemakers, blue-collar and pink-collar workers, white-collar workers, and professionals. The label ''pink-collar workers,'' used extensively by Howe,[16] refers to those women whose jobs are low-paying, traditionally female ones such as clerical, sales, and service jobs.

Women interviewed in each region were predominantly white; were residents of towns or cities with populations of 100,000 or less; and had lived in those areas for most of their lives.

The Central Valley of California emphasizes agricultural pursuits in its regional economy, as do the Alabama counties in which the first phase of the research was conducted. Both regions show a concentration of women nonagricultural workers in services and retail trades.[17]

For the most part these blue-collar and pink-collar women—in both the Southern and Western subsets—were employed at types of jobs consistent with the national pattern, that is, those lowly ranked (devalued, some would say) jobs that are the salaried derivatives of homemaking and mothering: cafeteria assistants, hospital housekeepers, food and cocktail waitresses, fast food workers, dishwashers, line workers in canning plants, day-care employees, clothing and furnishings sales and order clerks, school bus drivers.

Magnolias: The Southern Respondents[18]   Almost all the 105 Southern women lived in the predominantly rural northern and north-central Alabama counties where they had been born and where, for the most part, they had attended high school. All identified themselves as Southerners, and the researcher treated this self-identification as the key factor determining membership in the respondent set.[19] Further traditional Southerners as defined by Dillman[20] possess sufficient genealogical depth to have been enculturated with an emphasis on the ideals of antebellum days in the South. While some of the women in my Southern respondent set meet this strict criterion, not all do. With only a few exceptions those who have post-secondary education attended colleges and universities in Alabama. They are white Southern women—women who have historically served as symbol and victim of a white male-dominated subculture.[21]

The set of 105 Southern women includes three subsets: 41 full-time homemakers; 36 professional workers; and 28 blue-collar and pink-collar workers whose lives are the focus of this article.[22]

Microchips: The Western Respondents[23]   The Western respondent set of 180 women includes four subsets: the 42 blue-collar and pink-collar workers who are the focal point here; 53 full-time homemakers; 44 white-collar workers; and 41 professional women.

The 42 Western blue/pink-collar respondents compare quite closely in demographic characteristics to their Southern counterparts. The Western women on average are 34 years of age, have completed a high school education, and have 2.4 children with 13 years being the average age of their children. Slightly over half (57%) of the Western blue-collar women were married (24 of 42), while 9 were single and 9 were divorced at the time of their interviews. A lower percentage of blue/pink-collar women in the Western respondent subset were married than were those in the Southern respondent subset (78% vs. 57%).

These women and those in the Southern subset were employed in the same kinds of jobs. Several of the women in the Western respondent subset who were drivers of lunch trucks described themselves as ''mobile hostesses'' and pointed out that only women held such jobs in the firms for which they worked. Men who did similar work were called "vendors" and paid more than mobile wait-resses. Of the 42 blue/pink-collar women interviewed only 6 held traditionally male jobs.[24]

DISCUSSION OF FINDINGS

The contradiction between the continuing responsibility of women for most, if not all, housework, and their increasing labor-force participation is clearly reflected in the lives of the 28 blue-collar and pink-collar Southern women who comprised this respondent subset. In contrast to the Western re-spondents the cultural image of "woman as homemaker" shows striking persis-tence among the Southern women workers. "A woman should have her own job as long as she's still a good wife and mother," they say in these or similar words. The overwhelming majority of the Southern women in this subset agreed that women workers must be both good wife and mother (unpaid worker) and wage earner.

Breadwinning and Homemaking: Double Duty

Magnolias Sixty-three percent of working white women (age 16 and over) in the South are married and live with their husbands, and more than half of Southern married women in the labor force have children under the age of 18.[25] In fact these women with children under 18 are slightly more likely to be working than women with children over 18.[26] The irony is that those women more likely to be working are also those with the heaviest domestic workload. Families with growing children are more dependent on the woman's income for economic survival. Those women who work full time contribute almost 40% of their families' incomes.[27]

Nadine Sanders,[28] a waitress at the Blue Devil Café in a small Alabama town, is typical. Married seven years, Nadine, 25, and her husband, Lee, a coal miner, have two children and were high school sweethearts who married right after graduation. Nadine says that her husband doesn't mind her working and that he's glad to have the extra income. Nadine's day begins around 6:00 when she arises to prepare breakfast for her two children and Lee. She wakes the children around 6:30 and dresses them for the day-care center. After Lee leaves, she dresses and prepares for work at the Blue Devil Café where she begins her duties at 9:00, having already dropped the children off at the day-care center on her way. She begins taking orders and serving tables. She says:

> *I'm on my feet all day and that's the worst part about this job. My hus-band gets off at three o'clock so he goes by and picks up the kids. I don't get home until around 5:30. I go in and make supper. Then we spend some*

time together watching TV, put the kids to bed around nine, and usually
go to bed around eleven.

In Nadine's opinion professional woman are people she admires: "They've
worked hard to get where they are and I hope someday to be a professional
woman." Someday, when the children are older, she hopes to go back to school
and become a nurse.

While Nadine takes orders at the Blue Devil Café, Marilyn Tate, 25, is
opening the cash register at a department store in a nearby city where she is a
sales clerk. Marilyn says that she wouldn't work if the money wasn't needed,
and her husband, who owns an auto parts store, agrees. She describes the conflict between responsibility for children and her job:

> *Some mornings when I have the morning shift, I can't take the kids to*
> *school or pick them up. Or my husband has to take care of them at night if*
> *I'm working. I feel it's the woman's responsibility to take care of the*
> *children. When I have to work late, I can't go home and see my husband*
> *and children. And I don't have time to cook and clean.*

Here is how Marilyn describes a "night off": "I cook, clean, entertain the
children, check their homework, and get them into bed by eight. I relax for a
while and then I go to bed by ten."

Most respondents agreed it is the woman's responsibility to care for house
and children. However, a small minority agreed with Beverly Allen, 22, who
has been married for four years and has worked in the family business since her
marriage. Even though Beverly and her husband, Sam, a grocery produce manager, have no children yet, there are still the household chores to do. Beverly
complained:

> *Sam and I go to work together in the morning and usually get off at about*
> *the same time. He complains that I don't have lunch (I mean a nice meal)*
> *ready when we get home. My house is usually a mess. I'm tired when I get*
> *off work, and don't want to fix a meal and clean—but I have to. I'd rather*
> *sit around like Sam does when he gets off work.*

When asked the appropriate role of women today, Marilyn Tate reflected
the opinion of most respondents when she said, "Women today are in their
rightful places—many are pressing for equal rights, which I feel is not
needed." She added later that had she had a choice, she would have "gone to
college with my girlfriend, got married afterwards, and had children later." She
and her husband married because of an unplanned pregnancy, and because, as
she remarks, "It was convenient. I wanted to get away from home—but I do
love my husband."

Jill Brown, 26, lives in the same small city as the Tates. Jill has been divorced for nearly three years. Jill's mother cares for her young daughter, Kathy, while Jill works as a teller in a local bank. Jill began working at her present job following her divorce. She says:

> I wanted to work while I was married, but my husband was the type of man that thinks the wife's place is in the home. Maybe my husband not wanting me to work had something to do with our getting a divorce. I'd just rather be out working than home playing the good little housewife.

On the subject of remarriage, Jill comments, "I hope sometime in the future to be married again, but not now. I'm enjoying my freedom and being my own person." Later in discussing woman's appropriate role in today's society, Jill explains how she feels:

> The role of the woman is to help her husband and give him all the support she can. I guess I'm not a women's libber. I'm sort of old fashioned. I like helping my husband, but like I said earlier, I think there should be some room for the woman to try to do something for herself.

As for her current job becoming a career, Jill's feeling was similar to that of just over half the other women in the subset, namely, that "the money isn't enough to make me want to make a career of it, but I'll stay here until something better comes along." Each of the remaining respondents felt (as did Marilyn Tate, whom we met earlier in this section) that she would not work outside the home if it weren't a matter of economic necessity. Women, like Jill Brown, who were hoping for a better-paying job to come their way, were those who expressed the belief that "women today are given the chance to extend themselves—there's a way to be anything you choose to be." Interestingly, several women who worked as secretaries noted that in their workplaces men held what the respondents refer to as "the more prominent and the dominant positions," as well as those that pay the most. As one succinctly observes, "There are no male secretaries here." Nevertheless, these same respondents still believed that they "were heading in the right direction" in their jobs and that they could be anything they choose. The overwhelming majority report working for money and not for advancement, job satisfaction, power, contribution to society, or fun.

Microchips Overall the Western women feel it is their duty to provide emotional and financial support to their husband and children in any way possible, including responsibility for all or most of the domestic chores as well as their job. In other words, they too do double duty by juggling the care of husband and children as well as the demands of a job. At the same time the women clearly express their desire for "someone to take care of them." This seeming inconsistency may well reflect the fact that in the 1980s the American *ideal* family remains that of the male-breadwinner/female-homemaker type, while the *reality* of the 1980s is a new type described as a husband-primary-earner/wife-secondary-earner family. In the early 1950s, 56 out of 100 American husband-wife families were (officially) supported by the husband's earnings alone. By the early 1970s, that figure had dropped to 31 out of 100 husband-wife families.[29] And in the early 1980s only 24 husband-wife families out of 100 were supported solely by the husband's earnings.[30]

Miriam Green doesn't need statistics to tell her things have changed or that double duty is a real challenge. Miriam, 32, completed high school and two years of business college and has been married for three years to her present husband (her third). She has four children and works full time as a driver of a Canteen Foods truck from which she sells food to workers at job sites. Miriam is also responsible for cleaning the truck, stocking and unstocking it, and taking inventory. Miriam's typical day starts at 4:30 in the morning when she arises in order to leave for work by 5:20. Miriam describes her schedule:

> *I start work at 5:30 by loading my truck, then I come back home at 6:30 to take my youngest to nursery school. Back at work I get the truck and arrive at the first stop at 6:45. It's 12:30 before I am back at the plant to unload my truck, and then I'm off work at 1:30. I return home and on Mondays take my dance lesson at 2:30. I enjoy Hawaiian and tap dancing. Tuesdays are my late day at work because I have to take inventory and I get off at 2:30. Wednesday's like every other day; I pick up the youngest from nursery school at 4:30. Friday after work I go to the bank, do the grocery shopping, and pay bills.*

Since her youngest child is a 5-year-old boy and her eldest, a boy of 16, Miriam has more help with her domestic chores at home than many of the other respondents. The boys do their share of the chores along with their two sisters. Miriam pointed out:

> *My 16-year-old boy takes care of his room, cleans the bathroom daily, mows the lawn and takes the trash out once a week from the compactor. Both girls alternate weekly doing dishes and dusting and vacuuming. Each girl takes care of her own room. The baby picks up his toys and also papers in the yard. My husband is a slob and does nothing. I do laundry —the kids fold their own and put it away so on Saturday and Sunday we only have to pick up. Everyone gets their own breakfast and lunch except the youngest—I give him something off the truck for breakfast. When it comes to cooking dinner my husband does 60%, I do 40%—he likes to cook and eat. Evenings, I practice dancing, play the organ, or do bills. I'm in bed by 8 p.m. while the kids watch TV, fight, or do homework. They're in bed by 10, and the next day it starts all over again.*

After Miriam's description of the double-duty juggling act that includes squeezing in a full-time job outside the home, a continuing primary responsibility for the domestic sphere (home, children, and husband), and perhaps a little relaxation, it is easy to understand why one-third of the respondents (14 of 42) expressed admiration for the lives of full-time homemakers and described them in such terms as "lucky" or "completely happy." Another 12% of the respondents (5 of 42) expressed the wish, dream, or desire to be exclusively housewives, while 19% (8 of 42) said, referring to full-time homemakers, "I couldn't be one." Several of these respondents said, "A housewife's job is boring, boring, boring," and one woman volunteered the opinion that "more women would be career women, if our society was geared to showing young women it's a possibility for them. For example, a son is sent to college, a daughter is supposed to find a nice man to marry." In sum, 45% of the women felt full-time homemakers were "lucky" or wished they could be a full-time homemaker themselves. Referring to homemakers Miriam Green remarked:

> I'm sorry there are none left. In this day and age I don't think there are any. I think housewives went out in the '50s and that's sad. I would like to be one—have your home, things cut and dry and easy-going. . . . Nowadays women can't afford to stay home due to economics. . . . If I stayed home, I would have everything done early and then do nothing all day with everyone else working.

Like the overwhelming majority (35 of 42) of the Western blue-collar and pink-collar respondents, Sylvia McDonald, 40, who completed the eighth grade, works first and foremost for money. As she said:

> I work for money and the money gives me most everything else I need. My husband resented me working at first and claimed I didn't need to work, but as our material possessions began to accumulate, he gradually accepted my position as a working woman. Most of my income is actually earned for the purpose of getting the "American Standard Package" [material possessions]. Today my husband, family, and friends are all proud of me and my gains, and I'm quite proud of myself. I feel like the cigarette commercial, "You've come a long way, baby."

Sylvia's job as a checker and sorter at a local cannery is seasonal and provides her with the winter off, so she has plenty of time to attend to her household duties. Her daughter, and only child, is 22 and no longer lives at home, so Sylvia doesn't feel as pressured by the demands of double duty that were regularly mentioned by the other blue-collar women.

Job satisfaction provides another important reason for Sylvia to be employed, as it does for 13 other women in this Western subset. Sylvia listed fun as a third reason for working, and this reason was mentioned by 12 other women also. While the great majority of the women work for money, job satisfaction also was important for one-third of the respondents and nearly one-third said they worked for fun, too.[31] Like the majority of the blue/pink-collar respondents, Sylvia says she doesn't know of any males doing her type of work.

While many Western respondents were explicitly aware of the sex-segregated nature of their work, these same women clearly saw no contradiction between this occupational segregation by sex and their own expressed ideal of each woman doing "whatever she wishes" or, as they also put it, "going as far as her abilities will take her." For example, several cocktail waitresses pointed out, when asked about working conditions and co-workers, that they had no male counterparts. But they also stated vehemently that a woman had no appropriate role in society and that she should do or be whatever she wants—"women today have a lot of choices." Since the interview schedule specifically asked "What is your opinion of a woman's appropriate role in society?" the respondent initially had to reject the basic premise built into the question, that is, that there is in fact an appropriate role for a woman, and then further state (as the great majority did—64% or 27 of 42 Western respondents) an egalitarian ideal of each woman freely choosing her own occupation and lifestyle. Five respondents (12%) felt that woman's appropriate role is in the home as a full-time helpmate and five others felt a woman should combine a job outside the home with husband and family.

In contrast, the Southern respondents stressed with striking consistency that a woman's appropriate role in society means marriage and children. The women very rarely rejected the basic premise that there is an appropriate role for women. In fact only two Southern respondents (7%) stated an egalitarian ideal of women freely choosing occupation and lifestyle. This contrasts sharply with the 27 Western respondents (64%) who stated such an ideal. It is also interesting to note that only four of the Southern women (14%) offered job satisfaction as a reason for working. Even fewer, only two (7%), mentioned fun, contrasting sharply with 13 of the Western women (31%).

Femininity and Feminism

Magnolias Two respondents link themselves with feminism in the specific sense of "equal pay for equal work," but they quickly note that feminists are "rebels, people who don't want to be treated as women." Respondents clearly state that they themselves "want to be [viewed as] feminine, and not [as] lib types [i.e., feminists]." Twenty-four of the 28 blue/pink-collar women offered a sex-stereotypic response in defining femininity. "To me femininity is being small, pretty, shy, non-aggressive, and doing what my husband says."[32] All but two of the women considered themselves feminine by these criteria, and mentioned the paramount importance of respect and "how you carry yourself" as components in defining femininity.

The cultural images of "woman as homemaker" and "lady" are powerful. Just how pervasive is illustrated by a problem that cropped up early in the field testing of the interview schedule. In its original form, the interview schedule had asked in an early item for respondents' ideas of femininity and much later for respondents' ideas of feminism. It also sought the labels respondents applied to themselves, for example, "feminine" or "feminist" (or both). However, in practice, whether the question asked was about feminism or femininity—it didn't matter—the responses given contained the same sex-stereotypic constellation of qualities: soft, gentle, motherly, dainty, quiet, ladylike, sweet, and so on. Clearly for the respondents, feminism was not a discrete or contrasting category representing a different set of ideas. Their responses reflected the social reality of their lives, namely, that feminism was not a significant or meaningful category. What they knew and what they considered important was that sex-stereotypic constellation of feminine qualities by which they defined themselves. In their view, it was these very qualities that set them apart from men and at the same time made them attractive to men. For most of the Southern respondents a woman's place and her demeanor were not matters for examination, discussion, or change—they simply *were*.

When asked in the subsequently modified interview schedules, therefore, the question on femininity was followed immediately by a general question on the women's movement (thus eliminating the term *feminism* completely). This latter open-ended item facilitated each respondent's revealing her own definition of the woman's movement (rather than the researcher imposing or suggesting one). Further, each respondent was permitted to identify herself with, or set herself apart from, its goals as she understood them. Only two Southern respondents labeled themselves "feminist" (a term they introduced and used to mean pro-ERA). Both of them also indicated that they did not consider themselves feminine by the traditionally employed criteria. Only one respondent indicated her awareness that feminists do not necessarily fit the popularly accepted portrayal. This portrayal reflects the negative labeling of feminists[33] by the linking of "women's lib" with "aggressive, pushy women." This lone respondent stresses that she "realizes ERA is not that way." Only two of the women workers clearly stated their support for the ERA in response to the women's movement query, and both women, who mentioned ERA specifically, limited their response to the "equal pay for equal work" issue.

Femininity involves a presentation of self that is not threatening to the dominant group (males) and at the same time a presentation of self that attempts to manipulate that dominant group. Femininity, according to all but one of the respondents in this subset, is "being seen and not heard"; being soft, gentle, pretty, dainty, and frilly; and being passive, less aggressive—"not trying to take over in a man's world." According to this constellation of qualities, all but two of the respondents considered themselves feminine.

Central to their definition of femininity was the element of respect and "carrying yourself with respect." For the respondents, "the way you carry yourself as a woman" included having doors opened for you, having chairs held, being allowed to go first, not being "overbearing," not "trying to take control," and having "the conversation kept decent." In fact chivalrous criteria such as these were volunteered in 89% of the responses. Femininity also means marriage as an ultimate goal. Two of the three divorced respondents mentioned that they felt like "failures" because of their divorces and wanted "someone to take care of them." Marriage, for the majority of the blue/pink-collar respondents continues to be an essential component of their definition of woman's place. As they say, "Everyone gets married if they have the chance to. All women get married except those poor women that nobody wants."

Microchips In their definitions of femininity the great majority (35 of 42) of Western blue/pink-collar respondents used two basic traditional criteria: grooming (appearance) and behavior.[34] Specifically, they referred to make-up, hair, or appearance and quality of clothing as aspects of grooming. Behavioral attributes of femininity included not "being bossy," not reprimanding one's husband, not "speaking loudly," not "swearing," and "being gracious." All but six of the women responding considered themselves feminine by these criteria. In addition it is important to note that only four of the women pointed out behavioral attributes revolving around the ideal of chivalry such as having men open doors for them, lighting their cigarettes. As one of these four women said, "I may be capable of doing something, but pretend I can't, for example, lifting."

There was, however, much less unanimity concerning the definition of a feminist. Twelve women were not sure, could not respond, or asked, "Isn't that the same thing as femininity?"[35] Another 10 women explained a feminist by saying she's a "rebel, unhappy to be a woman, or trying to take men's roles." Equality of rights, opportunities, or choices was the definition of feminist offered by 17 women, or 40% of the respondent set. However, the number of women (7) who considered themselves to be feminists was much smaller—only 17%. This reluctance of women to label themselves as feminists (even if they support many of the overall goals of feminism) has been previously reported.[36] Such reluctance stems from the assignment of deviance, that is, to be feminist is to be deviant. Therefore, within the ideology of the women respondents, what is good is to be traditional (to conform) and what is not good is to be feminist.[37]

Head of Household

Magnolias The hegemony of the cultural image of "woman as home-maker" is reinforced and complemented by the image of "man as head of household." While women working outside the home has become widely recognized as a financial necessity, Southern respondents were adamant that women should do so while remaining good wives and mothers. They should contribute to the household's income—yes, but at the same time "do it where they can still let men be men." Of the respondents, 89% (25 women) cited the male as head of household, while none claimed that title for herself. Furthermore, joint decision-making was rare—with only two women (7%) claiming they shared that responsibility. One woman, not at all atypical, stressed, "My husband is boss! He makes all the decisions for me and my children—it's him that tells the children what they can and can't do. It's not a matter of whether I like it, that's just the way it is."

Microchips   By contrast, of the Western women responding to the specific query, "Who is head of your household?" nearly half (19 of 42) viewed themselves as the head of the household, and this included seven of the respondents who were married and living with their spouses.[38] These seven women explained that they made all the major decisions and handled the money for the entire household. One woman confided that, "I try to let my husband be [head of household], but I'm truly the dominant one." Another respondent explained that after her departure for work, her husband cares for their twin sons, aged two years. Furthermore she volunteered proudly, "He's a househusband."

Ten of the respondents (nearly 24%) indicated that they shared the task of head of household, mutually discussing major decisions and family budgeting, while another 13 women (31%) designated the male as head of household.[39] Interestingly, one of these latter 13 women designated her boyfriend, with whom she had lived for six months, as head of household.

Whose Job Is Most Important?

Magnolias   In order to extract an emic perspective on the husband-primary-earner/wife-secondary-earner families already mentioned, it is essential to see how the women responded to the query, "Whose job is most important?" The Southern women respondents felt overwhelmingly that his job was more important. Using two rationales they rated his job more important, "because it's supposed to be that way" (32%) or "because he earns more" (57%). Only three of the women claimed, "My job is most important." None of the women expressed the idea that the jobs were equally important.

Microchips   Thirty-one percent of the respondents (13 of 42) viewed their own job most important in their household, while 32% (14 of 42) felt their spouse's job was most important, and 22% thought the jobs were equally important.[40] Of the women who felt their husband's job was most important, they said, nearly without exception (12 of 14 responses), that his job was most important because "he earns more." As might be expected, those Western women who viewed their own job as the most important in their household were female heads of household (5 respondents) or single women living independently (8 respondents). Only two respondents gave a sex-stereotypic response, pointing out that their husband's job was most important because "that's the way it's suppose to be."

MAGNOLIAS AND MICROCHIPS: SUMMARY OF FINDINGS

Having compared and contrasted the two regional respondent subsets of blue-collar and pink-collar women workers, a summary of the constellation of sex-stereotypic images and ideas of the Southern respondents is essential. The lives of the blue/pink-collar women who are both *in* and *of* the South reflect the continuity and persistence of attitudes such as the following: husbands should be the head of their households; femininity is essential; it is important for men to show proper respect for women by opening doors for them and allowing them to go first; no woman's life is complete until she marries and has children; unless it is absolutely necessary, women with young children should restrict their interests and activities to the home; most women who participate in the women's movement are unhappy misfits; equal political and social rights are not needed or have already been achieved by women. These attitudes are not unique to the South. What is striking, however, is the tenacity and consistency of the constellation of sex-stereotypic images and ideas.

Table 1 provides a summary overview of the Southern and the Western

TABLE 1   Summary: Blue- and Pink-Collar Women

	South (N = 28)		West (N = 42)	
A. Breadwinning and Homemaking	%	n	%	n
1. Wish to be a full-time housewife	50	14	12	5
2. "I couldn't be a full-time housewife"	4	1	19	8
3. Would continue job if not an economic necessity	50	14	85	36
4. Why work? (more than one reason sometimes given)				
a. money	86	24	83	35
b. job satisfaction	14	4	33	14
c. fun	7	2	31	13
5. Women's appropriate roles?				
a. housewife/job and family	93	26	24	10
b. egalitarian choice	7	2	64	27
c. NR	0	0	12	5
B. Femininity and Feminism				
1. Feminine (self-rated on traditional criteria)—yes	93	26	69	29
a. mentioned chivalrous criteria	89	25	9	4
2. Feminist (self-labeled)	7	2	17	7
C. Head of Household?				
1. Male	89	25	31	13
2. "I am"	0	0	45	19
3. Joint	7	2	24	10
4. NR	4	1	0	0
D. Whose Job Most Important?				
1. His—"supposed to be that way"	32	9	5	2
2. His—"he earns more"	57	16	28	12
3. Mine	11	3	31	13
4. Both equal	0	0	22	9
5. NR	0	0	14	6

respondent subsets on nine topics covered by the interviews. As can be noted from the Breadwinning and Homemaking section of the table (A-1) many more Southern blue/pink-collar women workers volunteered during an interview segment dealing with their aspirations that they wished they were housewives. When discussing career women, working women, and housewives, 50% of the Southern respondent set expressed this wish, while only 12% of the Western respondents specifically did so. In fact, 19% of the Western respondents stated (as shown in Item A-2), "I couldn't be a full-time housewife," as compared with only 4% of the Southern women. Those women who would continue their job if it were not an economic necessity are more numerous in the West than in the South (85% as opposed to 50%) as shown in Item A-3 of Table 1.

One of the most interesting differences between the two respondent subsets occurs in the Femininity and Feminism section of Table 1 (Item B). In defining femininity the Southern women mentioned what I have termed chivalrous criteria in 89% of cases, while the Western women did so in only 9% of cases. These chivalrous criteria include "being allowed to go first," "having chairs and doors held," "having language kept decent," "having cigarettes lit." The cultural hegemony of the male as head of household idea has been shown in an earlier paper[41] for the Southern women; however, it is striking to note (Item C-1) that only 31% of Western women expressed this idea when asked about their own lives compared to 89% of Southern women who cited the male as head of household.

Another striking contrast is reflected in Item D where 22% of the Western respondents view their job and their spouse's job as equally important. This simply did not occur with the Southern women. While the first priority for working was money among respondents in both subsets, the Western respondents volunteered two other reasons for working more often than the Southern respondents: job satisfaction and fun (Item A-4).

Finally, the greatest disparity between the two respondent subsets of blue/pink-collar women workers concerns women's appropriate roles (Item A-5). In nearly all cases the Southern respondents specifically indicated that to be fulfilled a woman needed a home, husband, children, and sometimes a job if economically necessary. In marked contrast, the Western respondents allowed a consistent degree of choice or latitude and stressed this after specifically *rejecting* the idea that there is an appropriate role for women.

CONCLUSION

This paper has shown the strong cultural hegemony among contemporary Southern plain folk of a stereotypic gender role ideology—an ideology that has its roots in the cultural image of the antebellum Southern lady.[42] However, the great majority of the Southern populace were not plantation owners (with their ladies) but ordinary farmers and townspeople. Many of their descendants still live in the rural areas and small towns of the contemporary South. For such

women of the contemporary South—those primarily of the plain folk tradition
—daily life, especially in the domestic sphere, remains for the most part cir-
cumscribed by their multiple roles—wife, mother, daughter, housewife—that
are defined by their relationships to others.

Much of the imagery surrounding the antebellum Southern lady, however,
is alive and well among the plain folk of today despite the reality that dramati-
cally increasing numbers of Southern women (now more than half) have had to
seek work outside the home. They are beginning to come to grips with the
realities and contradictions of combining family responsibilities with the demands of a full-time double-duty work schedule. We have seen, through the
lives and responses of these women, how new (and sometimes startling) is the
concept that a woman can have needs as a person, or that she can seek to define
for herself her own identity.

Whereas the objective conditions of women in the two regions may not be
all that different, their *ideas* about their appropriate gender roles are quite different. The data presented here support my earlier suggestion that what is
striking about the South is the tenacity and consistency of the patterned *constellation* of sex-stereotypic images and ideas. Hill defines the " 'solid South' " as
"a *menial construct,* a state of mind characteristic . . . of white mainstream
society" (emphasis is Hill's). Speaking not specifically about gender role ideology, but much more broadly of the South, Hill continues, "The distinctiveness of the South may lie not in its empirical differences from other regions, but
in its unique belief system."[43] Without the gender role ideology encompassing
Southern womanhood, and indeed supported by many Southern women, the
South would not be the South.

The South's contemporary gender role ideology is clearly distinctive
enough for social scientists to speak meaningfully about a regional subculture
that features a social system of shared symbols surrounding Southern womanhood. As we have seen in this article, clear differences in gender role ideology
are indeed present, differences supportive of the contention that the South with
its rigidly stereotypic gender role ideology can realistically be referred to as a
distinct subculture. Comparison with other areas such as the West, where the
gender role ideology appears less consistently rigid and stereotypic, has highlighted these differences. These differences may well reflect changes less revolutionary and less pervasive by far than ardent feminists might hope and the
moral majority might fear.

NOTES

1. This article, condensed and in slightly different form, was presented at a conference,
   Southern Women: Portraits in Diversity, Newcomb College Women's Center, Tulane University, New Orleans, 1985.
2. See Carole E. Hill, "Anthropological Studies in the American South: Review and
   Directions," *Current Anthropology* 8(1977):309. Hill points out that studies *of* the

South are those concerned with delineating those characteristics that make the South a distinct culture area, that is concerned with defining "Southern culture." Studies *in* the South focus on the data collection to test concepts of a discipline, that is the conceptual framework applied to the data is paramount, the geographic region is of "little concern." However, as my own research demonstrates, these studies are not mutually exclusive.

3. Lillian Smith, *Killers of the Dream* (New York: Norton and Co., 1961, Revised Edition).

4. Anne Firor Scott, *The Southern Lady: From Pedestal to Politics, 1830–1930* (Chicago: The University of Chicago Press, 1970), pp. x–xi.

5. Frank Lawrence Owsley, *Plain Folk of the Old South* (Baton Rouge: Louisiana State University Press, 1949). This plain folk tradition was naturally linked in complex ways to the plantation tradition, just as in an analogous manner still today those of wealth and power serve as compelling icons of a culture.

6. Mary Frederickson, "The Southern Summer School for Women Workers," *Southern Exposure* 4(Winter, 1977):75–85.

7. Dickson D. Bruce, *And They All Sang Hallalujah* (Knoxville: University of Tennessee Press, 1974).

8. Hill, "Anthropological Studies in the American South: Review and Directions," p. 311.

9. Ibid.

10. Ibid.

11. Caroline M. Dillman, "Researching Southern Women in Transition: Definitional Complexities" (Paper presented in a symposium, Southern Women in Transition, at the meeting of the Mid-South Sociological Association, Jackson, Mississippi, 1982).

12. Pertti J. and Gretel H. Pelto, quoting Franz Boas in *Anthropological Research: The Structure of Inquiry* (London: Cambridge University Press, 1978, Second Edition), p. 55.

13. If we assume that those Southern women respondents willing to participate in my research were less closed to outsiders, hence, quite probably, less traditional, then the results reported here minimize, instead of exaggerate, the degree of cultural continuity and persistence of the Southern lady ideal as an icon among the plain folk; hence we have a conservative estimate of the contrasts noted between the two regions.

14. Data analysis has been completed for the entire Southern respondent set of 105 women. While these data have not been included in summary here, they have been reported elsewhere. [Susan Middleton-Keirn, "Contemporary Southern Women: Are They That different?" (Paper presented in a symposium, Southern Women in Transition, at the meeting of the Mid-South Sociological Association, Jackson, Mississippi, 1982); Susan Middleton-Keirn, "What's a Woman To Do?" (Paper presented in a symposium, Feminism and Femininity, at the meeting of the Southern Anthropological Society, Boone, North Carolina, 1982.)]

15. This area includes six counties: Tuolumne, Calaveras, Merced, Mariposa, Stanislaus, and San Joaquin. These Central Valley counties are located north and east of the "Silicon Valley" where a key industry is the production of microchips. Clearly using the term *microchips* to describe the Western respondents is as metaphorical as the use of the term *magnolias* to denote the Southern respondent set.

16. Louise Kapp Howe, *Pink Collar Workers: Inside the World of Women's Work* (New York: Avon Books, 1977).

17. Department of Finance, *California Statistical Abstract*, 22nd Edition (Sacramento: State of California, 1981), p. 27.

18. See Betsy Mahoney, "The Facts Behind the Myths," *Southern Exposure* 9(1981):5–8, who states that nearly 80% of Southern working women hold either blue-collar or pink-collar jobs. These jobs are not only low-paying, but they offer little or no opportunity for advancement.

19. See Lewis M. Killian, *White Southerners* (New York: Random House, 1970), who has defined Southerners in this way.

20. Dillman, "Researching Southern Women in Transition: Definitional Complexities."

21. Catherine Clinton, *The Plantation Mistress* (New York: Pantheon Books, 1983).

22. For an excellent, albeit eclectic, and very general bibliography of women in the South see *Southern Exposure*, 4(1977):98–103.

23. The author gratefully acknowledges the generous award of a California State University Chancellor's Office Affirmative Action grant which has supported and facilitated ongoing data collection and analysis.

24. These included a truck owner-operator (with her husband), a tractor-trailer rig driver, a bridge tender, an offset press operator, a fork lift driver, and a delivery truck driver (with her husband).

25. Mahoney, "The Facts Behind the Myths," p. 6.

26. Ibid., p. 7.

27. Ibid., p. 6.

28. In order to protect the anonymity of respondents, their names in this article have been coined, combined, or otherwise altered.

29. Howe, *Pink Collar Workers: Inside the World of Women's Work*, p. 261.

30. United States Department of Labor, *Equal Employment Opportunity for Women: U.S. Policies* (Washington, D.C.: U.S. Government Printing Office, 1982).

31. Responses total more than 100% since a woman often gave several reasons for working.

32. There were also three nonrespondents and one androgynous response ($N = 28$).

33. Susan Middleton-Keirn and Jackie Howsden-Eller, "Discrediting the Challenge: The Role of Deviance Assignments in Sex-role Ideology," *Quarterly Journal of Ideology* 10(1986):23–29.

34. Five respondents gave no definition, while two gave an androgynous response.

35. Although problems already described in the earlier section of the paper made it necessary to remove the word *feminism* during the Southern research, it was reintroduced to determine the responses of the Western women.

36. Middleton-Keirn, "Contemporary Southern Women: Are They That Different?" and Middleton-Keirn, "What's a Woman To Do?"

37. Middleton-Keirn and Howsden-Eller, "Discrediting the Challenge: The Role of Deviance Assignments in Sex-role Ideology," p. 25.

38. The remaining 12 women were divorced, never married, or single parents.

39. This number includes five respondents who said, "We discuss things but he's really in charge," or made a strikingly similar comment.

40. These figures do not total 100% because another 14% of the respondents were unclassifiable: single; living with parents or relatives; housekeepers, who said their boss was head of household; or no response.

41. Middleton-Keirn, "Contemporary Southern Women."
42. See Scott, *The Southern Lady,* pp. 4–21, who says these antebellum ladies were those relatively few of the plantation tradition. However, numerous authors (Clinton, *The Plantation Mistress;* Sara Evans, "Women's Consciousness and the Southern Black Movement," *Southern Exposure* 4[Winter 1977]:70–75; Sara Murphy, "Women's Lib in the South," *New South* 27:[Spring 1972]42–46; Smith, *Killers of the Dream*) have noted the behind-the-scenes hard-work activities of even these primarily plantation-tradition women in the system that stereotyped (according to Susan Hesselbart, "A Comparison of Attitudes Toward Women and Blacks in a Southern City," *Sociological Review* 17:[Fall 1976]45–68) both blacks and females.
43. Hill, "Anthropological Studies in the American South: Review and Directions," p. 310.

Chapter 14

AND THE GIRLS BECAME WOMEN: ASPIRATIONS AND EXPECTATIONS VERSUS ATTAINMENTS OF LOW–INCOME BLACK AND WHITE SOUTHERN FEMALES

WILLIAM F. KENKEL AND SARAH M. SHOFFNER

Robert Browning tells us that our reach should exceed our grasp "or what's a heaven for?" Yet, for some people, the gap between aspirations and achievements resembles a chasm. Often, the size of the aspiration-achievement gap varies systematically by social characteristics such as rural/urban orientation, ethnicity, race, class, and gender. Based on the results of a longitudinal study, this chapter examines the differences between the aspirations and achievements of Southern females and focuses on the role of race in such differences.

Researchers have examined the aspiration-achievement gap between rural and urban populations, between males and females, between the lower class and the middle class, and among various ethnicities and races.[1] However, little or no research has been conducted using region as a variable. Although this presentation makes no comparison concerning regions, it does establish a baseline for aspiration and achievement levels among one segment of the population of the American South—rural, working-class females of two races—and presents findings of the differences in levels between the black and white females in the region.

The first wave of the study was conducted in 1969, five years after the Civil Rights Act forbade discrimination on the basis of sex and race and six years after Betty Friedan wrote about the malaise of women who were trapped in their mother-wife-homemaker roles.[2] The consciousness of American women had been raised, and the movement toward equality in education, in employment, in the home, and in politics had, at least, begun. The emerging concept was that the new role of women should include formal education and full participation in the work force. This was, in part, the social context in which our study began. The first wave of what was to become a longitudinal study concentrated on what were the occupational and educational aspirations and expectations of young children in low-income subcultures and what home, school, personal, and other factors influenced these aspirations and expectations.

THEORETICAL BACKGROUND

The factors of class, region, and race are significant components of the social world in which the respondents lived and, accordingly, would be assumed to have an influence on their aspirations, expectations, and achievements. How does "growing up rural" affect the occupational aspirations and achievements of children and youth? One approach to answering this question deals with the nature of the labor market in rural areas. Nilsen, in contrasting metropolitan and nonmetropolitan areas, found that nonmetro workers were concentrated in "low-earnings occupations."[3] Put differently, rural workers are most likely to be working class, rather than middle or upper class. Another approach to explaining the influence of rural residence uses a social-psychological model rather than a labor market one. As Falk puts it, the general notion of "others" has been used to explain how people are influenced by other people.[4] A child growing up in a rural, working-class area is most likely to observe "others" who have low prestige jobs rather than high prestige ones. Furthermore, the range of occupations encountered by rural youth will be relatively restricted. Both the nature and range of the occupations held by "others" constitute a disadvantage for rural children and youth in any attempt to make life plans, and they affect the size of the gaps between aspirations and/or expectations and achievements.

Cosby has elaborated a dualistic framework for explaining the developmental process of status attainment.[5] For those with reasonably high opportunities for achievement, such as white, middle- and upper-class males, the occupational aspirations tend to become increasingly more realistic. That is, with age and maturity, the aspirations are "adjusted" with the result that there is a relatively small gap, if any, between what one wants to achieve and what he or she actually achieves. The process is quite different for the disadvantaged, those whose chances for success are not high. Growing up in America, they are aware of the occupational and educational symbols of success and are likely, as children, to have high occupational and educational aspirations. As they mature, they do not necessarily "adjust" their aspirations to conform with what they are likely to achieve. Rather, as Cosby explains, one psychological adjustment to low attainment, or expected low attainment, is to retain the higher aspirations.[6] Planning, expecting, and predicting success in the future serves to compensate for not being really successful in a success-oriented society. The dream is not really forsaken; it is just postponed. The result is that for rural, low-income youth there is likely be a sizable gap between aspirations and attainments.

Being black is a disadvantage in the status-attainment process. The psychological adjustment of retaining high aspirations, despite probable lower attainments, is again operative. In the present study, we should therefore expect a large gap between the occupational and educational aspirations of the black respondents and their actual attainments.

One other factor enters the picture here: regionalism. In addition to taking into account the rurality of the population studied and its lower-class status, the special culture of the region and its effect on aspirations and achievements for females, both black and white, needs to be considered. To assess the effect of the regional culture, it is necessary to examine first the historical foundations of the two racial sets of females and the possible impact that could affect differences in the gap between aspirations and achievements.

Southern White Women

To be Southern and white is to be enmeshed in a culture with roots that stretch back before the Civil War. Particularly relevant here are the cultural traditions and prescriptions regarding the role of women. Social historians and others agree that there was something distinct about the role of the Southern woman.[7] The woman enacted a clearly subordinate role in the strong patriarchal family and society of the South. Home and family were supposed to be central in her life. Personality traits compatible with her role included meekness, self-control, self-abnegation, and long-suffering patience. To be sure, the world has turned many times since the heyday of the antebellum South. In recent times, the new ideas on the roles of the sexes and of opportunities for women that form the women's movement have reached the South. Dillman reminds us, however, that even among younger women there are those who have not accepted the role of "new Southern woman" and that there are others "who are struggling with the painful transition from traditional to modern Southern woman."[8] All of this suggests that the mothers and teachers of the girls in the present study probably had more traditional attitudes on the roles of the sexes than could be found elsewhere in the United States in the late 1960s.[9]

The role of the Southern lady in its pure and historic sense could be enacted only by the privileged few, although it could be emulated and partially enacted by those with at least adequate means. But the mothers of the Southern girls who are the respondents in the present study are from the low-income, working class and thus share different cultural traditions. It was a world, as Janiewski points out, in which women worked hard in the home and in the farm or factory economies marked by a strong division of labor according to gender.[10] There was men's work and women's work, and that was that, except, of course, that men's work was better paid. Abbott contends that even recently "Southern working women fare worse than any in the nation."[11] There is little room to dispute her conclusion, especially since she notes that in 1975 (six years after the first wave of the present study) women made up only one percent of all skilled workers in 16 Southern cities.[12]

White, Southern lower-status women experience a number of disadvantages in the quest for status attainment, and the disadvantages are hypothesized to affect the size of gap between their aspirations and achievements. The sociohistoric features of the South hinder white Southern women's progress away from tradition and into women's equal place in the world of work. Gender is a disadvantage to high achievement and, as noted previously, so are low-income and rural backgrounds. Education is devalued in rural areas, in part, as Hobbs and Hobbs point out, because the local job opportunities do not require much education.[13] Kohn's social class studies found that, in general, the working class does not place a high value on education.[14] What then, can be predicted about the gap between aspirations and achievements of white females?

The impediments and barriers to high occupational achievements faced by white, low-income, Southern women are so far-reaching that it is predicted that they serve also to lower the aspirations of the children and youth. With lowered aspirations, the gap between aspirations and achievements should not be too large. We are predicting, however, that on the average aspirations would be higher than achievements. This is because of the psychological mechanism referred to earlier according to which one tends to hold on to the dream, the higher aspirations, rather than admit to failure.

Southern Black Women

Historically in the South, as Janiewski has noted, there has been a division of labor by race imposed on and in addition to that by gender, as mentioned earlier.[15] In the tobacco and textile industries, for example, there were some jobs for black women, others for white women. Domestic service jobs were almost always held by black women who worked in the homes of white women. In short, a girl growing up in a working-class, black household has different subcultural experiences and different role models than does a girl growing up in a working-class, white household. How does this difference affect the aspirations of black girls and young women and how does it affect the gap between their aspirations and achievements?

The paucity of higher-status and diversified black occupational role models would suggest that young black girls would have low occupational and educational aspirations. Yet Howell and others have found that blacks place a higher value on education than do whites.[16] Thus, holding rurality and social class constant as in the present study, we would expect to find that the black females have higher aspirations than do the white females. Yet the experience of blacks in achieving higher educational levels and in translating their education into well-paying, higher-status jobs has not been remarkable. The combination of factors leads to the hypothesis that among the black females there will be found higher aspirations and lower achievements relative to white females.

METHODOLOGY

The data for this study came from two regional research projects sponsored by the Agricultural Experiment Stations in six Southern states. A full description of the methodology of the study can be found in the regional publication, *On the Road to Adulthood*.[17] In each state, the principal investigator selected schools that served essentially depressed areas as defined by unemployment rates and poverty levels. Both black and white students were included in the study.

A look at a few background factors should help describe the respondents and their families. The parents of the students had a fairly low level of education. Among whites, about 85% of the fathers and 80% of the mothers had not finished high school. Among blacks, 95% of the fathers and almost 90% of the mothers had less than a high school education. Of the white fathers, about one-fourth were employed as craftsmen, another quarter as operatives, and 14% as nonfarm laborers. The most frequently named occupational category for black fathers was nonfarm laborer, with about 30% in this category. About 7% of the black fathers were in each of the occupational categories of craftsmen, operatives, and service workers.

Approximately half of the white mothers were working outside the home when the child was in the fifth or sixth grade of school and this was true of 60% of the black mothers. The most common occupations of white mothers were operatives (12%), clerks (6%), laborers (5%), and service-household workers (5%). By contrast, 40% of the black mothers were engaged in service-household work; smaller numbers worked as laborers (8%) and operatives (5%).

The first phase of the study gathered data from 1,412 fifth- and sixth-graders in their schools and from the mothers of these students in their homes. Half of the students were girls and, of these, 416 were black and 290 were white. The second phase was conducted in 1975 when the youth were, or could be expected to be, juniors or seniors in high school. The total number of respondents was 938 (66% of the original sample). The loss is partially explained by the fact that one state, with 210 blacks in its sample, was unable to collect data for the second phase. The third phase was conducted in 1979, three to four years after the young women could be expected to have graduated from high school. By this time, the young women should have been almost through college, if they had attended at all, and others had had time to start their occupational careers. A mailed questionnaire was used for the third wave. Completed questionnaires were received from 196 white and 91 black females or 61% of those contacted at high school age.

Most of the analyses use those cases for which both first- and second-wave data are available. Thus, the analyses for the grade school and high school students utilize 473 cases. For the young adults, the analysis utilizes 287 cases.

The key variables in this study are those that deal with occupational and educational aspirations, expectations, and achievements. Occupational aspirations were measured by the question, "If you could choose any job you *wanted,* what kind of job would you *really like* to have when you grow up?'' Occupational expectations were measured by the question, "What kind of job do you think you *really will* have when you grow up?'' Both occupational aspirations and expectations were given an appropriate occupational prestige score, ranging from 42 to 89, according to Duncan's Socioeconomic Index.[18] The occupational choices were also categorized according to the nine-point Census classification system, which ranges from professional-technical worker (1) to laborer (9).

The educational aspirations and expectations of the students were also measured by two questions. Educational aspirations were measured by the question "How far would you like to go in school?'' with the choices ranging from completing eighth grade to four or more years of college. Educational expectations were measured by the question "How far do you think you will go in school?''

FINDINGS

The findings of the study are reported here in a chronological manner, beginning with the educational and occupational aspirations and expectations of fifth- and sixth-grade girls and looking at some of the more important factors found to be related to the girls' goals. A similar analysis is repeated for the youth at high school age and then we look at the educational and occupational levels actually achieved by the young women four years after high school age. The discussion concludes with the examination of the occupational plans of the girls in more detail, looking particularly at the proportion who aspired to "gender appropriate" jobs and otherwise restricted their choices. Throughout the various analyses, black-white comparisons are made and show that race had a profound effect on life plans and, particularly, on the girls' chances of achieving their ambitions.

Educational Plans of Grade School Girls

The fifth- and sixth-grade girls had high educational aspirations and expectations. As shown in Table 1, 71% of the black and 59% of the white girls said they wanted to graduate from college. Expectations were lower, but 45% of the black and 37% of the white girls expected to graduate from college. At the other extreme, fewer than 1% of the black and 3% of the white girls said that they hoped to finish their education with about two years of high school or less.

The higher the girl's occupational aspirations and expectations, the higher were her educational aspirations and expectations. This suggests that even at fifth- and sixth-grade levels the girls recognize that jobs in American society have certain educational prerequisites or expectations. A strong factor affecting educational goals is race, with the black girls having higher aspirations and expectations than white girls. Other characteristics of the girls associated with educational plans included academic motivation, achievement motivation, and

TABLE 1   Educational Aspirations and Expectations of Grade School Girls, by Race

	Blacks		Whites	
	Aspirations	Expectations	Aspirations	Expectations
Educational	(N = 186),	(N = 186),	(N = 281),	(N = 281),
Level	%	%	%	%
Finish college	71.0	59.1	45.2	36.7
Two years of				
college	9.7	6.8	19.9	10.7
High school and				
trade school	4.3	5.7	4.3	6.4
Finish high school	14.0	24.2	26.9	40.2
Trade school	.5	.4	.5	.4
Two years high				
school or less	.5	3.9	3.2	5.7

self-concept, with the higher the scores on these scales, the higher the educational goals.

Parenting factors related to the girl's educational goals included mother's job and educational choices for her child and how strongly the parents feel about the child finishing high school. The higher the mother's scores in response to these questions, the higher the daughter's educational goals.

Educational Plans at High School Age

By high school age, the girls, now young women, had extensively lowered their educational goals. Instead of 71%, now 27% of black girls wanted to finish college; instead of 59%, now only 23% of the white girls aspired to college education. Only 13% of the black and 8% of the white girls, as shown in Table 2, actually expected to graduate from college. Fewer than 2% of the black

TABLE 2   Educational Aspirations and Expectations of High School Girls, by Race

	Blacks		Whites	
	Aspirations	Expectations	Aspirations	Expectations
Educational	(N = 186),	(N = 186),	(N = 281),	(N = 281),
Level	%	%	%	%
Finish college	26.9	13.5	23.1	7.8
Two years of				
college	13.4	10.0	12.9	8.9
High school and				
trade school	24.2	28.8	25.8	19.6
Finish high school	12.9	24.9	23.7	32.7
Trade school	1.1	3.6	2.2	1.8
Two years high				
school or less	1.6	5.7	4.9	24.5
No response	19.9	13.5	7.4	4.7

girls wanted to complete their education with less than high school graduation but 6% expected to stop at that level. Almost 5% of the white girls aspired to less than high school graduation while 24% expected that in reality they would stop at that level.

A number of factors showed a modest, but statistically significant, relationship with the girls' educational goals. Their occupational plans, academic motivation, achievement motivation, and high school grade point average all were in the predicted direction—the higher the scores, the higher the educational goals. The older the age at which the high-school-age young woman expected to marry, the higher were her educational aspirations and expectations. The more she had thought about her future job and the more she had talked about it with parents and others, the higher were her educational goals. The girl's parents had an influence on the daughter's goals. How far the parents wanted her to go in school, how strongly they felt about her not dropping out of high school, the higher were the daughter's educational goals.

Educational Attainment at Young Adulthood

The number of years of schooling attained by the respondents by age 21 or 22 are shown in Table 3.

Let's look at the educational attainments of the young women as compared first to their *aspirations* at high school age and then to their *expectations* at the same age. Four years after they were juniors or seniors in high school, or could have been expected to reach this level, 5% of the black and 2% of the white young adult women had finished college. Another 7 and 5%, respectively, had finished two years of college. These attainments are a far cry from their aspirations. Just a few years before, 27% of the black young women said that they wanted to finish college and another 13% said that they wanted to finish at least two years of college. Forty percent thus *aspired* to some college; 12% reached this level of education. Thirty-six percent of the white young women aspired to complete some college or to graduate from college; 7% did so. It would be easy to conclude that the girls aimed too high or dreamed the wrong dreams. Yet our analyses revealed that those who aspired to a college education were considerably more likely to achieve it than those who did not. For example, almost half

TABLE 3   Educational Attainment of Young Adult Women, by Race

Educational level	Blacks ($N = 97$), %	Whites ($N = 199$), %
College graduate	5.1	2.0
Two years of college	7.2	5.0
High school and trade school	48.4	24.1
Finish high school	28.9	40.2
Trade school	—	1.0
Two years high school or less	10.4	27.6

of the black grade school girls who wanted to attend college did so, as opposed to about a quarter of those who aspired to high school graduation only and none of the black girls who said that they wanted to complete their education with only about two years of high school. White girls showed the same trend but mostly when we compared their aspirations at high school age and later achievements. An uncomfortably large proportion of the high aspirers missed the mark but, at the same time, more of the high aspirers had high achievements than did those with lower aspirations.

In some respects, it is more meaningful to compare the educational *expectations,* rather than *aspirations,* with the adult attainments. The question on expectations asked how far in school the high school girls thought they really would go. Just four years later we determined how much education they had actually achieved. Restricting the comparison to the higher levels of education, almost one-fourth of the black girls actually expected to attend or to graduate from college, but only 12% did so. Almost 17% of the white girls expected that they would attend or graduate from college, but only 7% achieved this level of education. The difference between expectations and achievements suggests that there was considerable disappointment among these young women.

Occupational Plans of Grade School Girls

Remarkably, as shown in Table 4, a quite high proportion of girls, 75% of the black and 70% of the white, aspired to jobs at the professional-technical level, the highest level possible using the Census categories. The girls' expectations were a little lower; 71% of the black and 60% of the white girls actually expected to hold the higher level jobs they said they wanted.

TABLE 4 Occupational Aspirations and Expectations of Grade School Girls, by Race

Occupational Category	Blacks		Whites	
	Aspirations (N = 182), %	Expectations (N = 171), %	Aspirations (N = 271), %	Expectations (N = 236), %
Professional, technical	75.3	70.8	70.1	60.2
Farm, farm manager	—	—	—	—
Manager, official, proprietor	—	—	—	—
Clerical, sales	9.3	11.1	14.8	13.6
Craftsman, foreman	1.1	1.8	0.7	0.4
Operative	1.1	1.8	3.7	11.4
Service, private household	12.1	11.7	10.0	12.3
Farm laborer, foreman	—	—	—	—
Laborer	1.1	2.9	0.7	0.9

TABLE 5   Occupational Aspirations and Expectations of High School Girls, by Race

Occupational Category	Blacks		Whites	
	Aspirations (N = 178), %	Expectations (N = 248), %	Aspirations (N = 146), %	Expectations (N = 182), %
Professional, technical	59.6	48.0	43.2	23.6
Farm, farm manager	—	0.4	—	0.6
Manager, official, proprietor	3.9	1.2	1.4	1.7
Clerical, sales	23.6	33.1	30.8	28.6
Craftsman, foreman	1.7	2.0	4.1	1.1
Operative	1.7	2.4	4.8	18.7
Service, private household	8.4	11.3	12.3	11.5
Farm laborer, foreman	—	—	—	—
Laborer	1.1	1.6	3.4	14.3

Among the girls who did not aspire to high-level occupations, about 10% of the black and 15% of the white girls aspired to middle-level occupations such as sales and clerical work. Thirteen percent of the black and 11% of the white girls said that they wanted to be service workers or laborers.

The factor most strongly related to girls' occupational plans was the mothers' occupational expectations for the daughters. The higher the mothers' expectations, the higher the girls' aspirations. Other parental factors positively associated with a girl's occupational goals were the prestige of the mother's occupation and the mother perceived as a loving person, as opposed to a punishing or demanding one, using the Bronfenbrenner Parent Behavior Questionnaire.[19]

It was also found that the higher the girl's self-concept, the higher her occupational goal. And the higher the girls' educational aspirations and expectations, the higher their occupational goals.

Occupational Plans at High School Age

Data from the second set of interviews, reported in Table 5, show two important changes in occupational goals. First, for both races, the occupational aspirations and expectations dropped. Where at grade school age 75% of the black girls aspired to the highest level occupations and 71% expected to hold such jobs, by high school age the corresponding proportions were 60 and 48%. Among white girls in the fifth and sixth grades, 70% aspired to and 60% expected to fill an occupation at the highest level. By high school age, these proportions had dropped to 43 and 24% respectively.

The lowering of occupational goals is perhaps to be expected. As they approached high school graduation, some of the girls realized that they were not going to fill high-level positions. Perhaps more surprising is that 60% of the black girls and over 40% of the white girls held on to their high occupational aspirations. The difference between the races is striking. Not only did more black girls than white girls have high aspirations, but almost half of the black girls and only 23% of the white girls actually expected, at late high school age, to hold an occupation at the highest level. At the other extreme, fewer than 2% of the black girls expected to be laborers but 14% of the white girls said that was the job they really expected to hold.

Occupational Attainment at Young Adulthood

The occupational attainments of the young women at about age 21 or 22 are shown in Table 6. While almost 60% of the black high school girls aspired to be employed at the professional-technical level, about 7% were employed at this level. Forty-three percent of the white girls aspired to the highest levels of occupations; 6% attained this level.

The attainments at young adulthood were also compared with the *expectations* reported by the girls four years earlier. Three occupational levels were created by considering the highest three Census categories as high-level jobs, the next three as medium-level jobs, and the lowest three as low-level jobs. A cross-tabulation was then made showing the occupational expectations of the young women at high school age and their own attainments as young adults. We can thus see how many of the young women who expected to fill a high-level occupation, for example, actually achieved a job at that level, how many of them achieved a medium-level job, and how many were found in a low-level occupation.

It might be assumed that the girls' occupational expectations at high school age would be closely related to the jobs they attained as young adults. After all, the measures were taken only four years apart and the questions con-

TABLE 6 Occupational Attainment of Presently Employed Young Adult Women, by Race

Occupational Category	Blacks (N = 44), %	Whites (N = 112), %
Professional, technical	6.8	6.3
Farmer, farm manager	—	—
Manager, official, proprietor	—	1.8
Clerical, sales	36.6	39.3
Craftsman, foreman	6.8	4.5
Operative	13.6	19.6
Service, private household	27.3	9.8
Farm laborer, foreman	—	0.9
Laborer	9.1	17.9

cerning expectations asked what occupation they really expected to hold. In Table 7, the percentages in parentheses indicate the proportion of those who expected a specific occupational level and achieved that level. Thus, only 9.5% of the black and 25% of the white young women who at high school age expected to attain a high level occupation were actually working at such a job. This gap between expectations and achievements suggests considerable disappointment and potential frustration.

The discrepancy between occupational plans and occupational reality was more severe for black than for white young women. Many more black young women (55%) expected to hold a high level job than did white young women (30%). Yet a higher proportion of white than black women achieved their goals. At the other extreme, half of the black women who expected to hold a low-level job ended up with such a job, but only 26% of the white women with such an expectation achieved such a job. Most of the remaining white women achieved medium-level jobs, but 5% of those with the lowest expectations actually achieved the highest level jobs.

DISCUSSION

What happened to the hopes and plans of the Southern girls and youth? Did they aim too high and expect too much or were they unaware of the barriers to their dreams created by their lack of knowledge of how to get to where they wanted to go? With regard to the black young women, it is likely that some, at least, were not fully aware of how difficult it would be for a black woman in the South to reach the dreams they dreamt. The young women were compared to the young men in the study with regard to the rewards they sought in occupations. Men were more likely to stress the chance to make money and steady employment while women stressed the opportunity for helping others and a chance to

TABLE 7 Occupational Expectations of High School Females by Adult Attainment

High school occupational expectations	Level of occupational attainment			Total at high school	
	Low	Medium	High	n	%
Black females (N = 38)					
Low	(50.0)	50.0	—	4	.5
Medium	30.8	(69.2)	—	13	34.2
High	38.1	52.3	(9.5)	21	55.3
White females (N = 94)					
Low	(26.3)	68.4	5.3	19	20.2
Medium	27.7	(68.1)	4.3	47	50.0
High	28.6	46.4	(25.0)	28	29.8

Note: Percentages within parentheses indicate proportion of those who expected a specific level and achieved that level.

do interesting work. This suggested that we investigate further the nature of jobs the girls and youth said they wanted. Perhaps there was something about the *kinds* of jobs to which they aspired that foredoomed so many to disappointment.

Analyses revealed two basic features of the nature of the occupational choices of the girls and youth: (a) they aspired to occupations that are usually considered feminine occupations, and (b) they aspired to occupations within a narrow range of all occupations.[20] At grade school level, 92% of the girls' occupational choices were for jobs that traditionally have been considered feminine jobs; at high school age, 78% of the choices were for feminine jobs and another 13% were for jobs that are gender neutral.

Not only did the girls and youth tend to choose feminine jobs, they tended also to restrict their choices to a relatively few jobs. At grade school age, the jobs of teacher, nurse, secretary, and beautician accounted for 77% of the girls' choices. At high school age, these same four occupations, plus that of social worker, accounted for 57% of the youths' occupational choices. Between grade school and high school ages, the girls did change their occupational choices, but our analyses found that only slightly more moved away from feminine jobs as moved toward them.

Why did the low-income girls choose "gender appropriate" jobs when in grade school and basically choose the same types of jobs when nearing high school graduation? Earlier we noted that there is a restricted range of role models in most rural areas. In the sample, about half of the mothers of the respondents worked outside the home and most of these were in low-prestige occupations. If the daughters have high aspirations, as they do, they are faced with choosing jobs that are not being modeled by their mothers, the mothers of their friends, or even women within their subculture.

The unique nature of women's roles should also be considered. The division of labor by sex still generally results in women having primary responsibility for home management and child care. Perhaps Southern women perceive that teaching, nursing, and secretarial work have high turnover rates and would allow them to move in and out of the job market in keeping with their family responsibilities.

Traditional family ideology is alive and fairly strong among young Southern women. When asked what jobs they would consider other than the one they preferred, 24% of the young women checked "housewife only." These cases were in addition to the 12% who wrote in "housewife" in response to the question that asked what kind of job they would really like to have in the future. Four years after high school age the young women were asked how they felt about married women working outside the home,[21] and four choices were allowed, ranging from the most traditional that stated that a woman should not work unless her husband is unable to do so, she should work only if she has no children or the children are in high school, it is all right to work if all the children are in school or if she has a good sitter, to the most liberal choice that stated that she should be able to work if she wants to since the children are her husband's as much as hers. Only 18% of the white and 32% of the black young women agreed that married women should be able to work outside the home if they want to do so. The proportion of young adult women saying that women should have full control over their occupational role is actually lower than the proportion of high-school-age young women granting such control to married women.

The traditional family ideology of young, low-income, Southern women is also evidenced in their marriage plans. Almost 42% of the white and 13% of the black high-school-age youth said that they expected to marry at age 19 or younger. Almost 31% of the white and 26% of the black youth expected to marry at age 20 or 21. Investigation is under way now to see how many achieved their marital goals, but the expectations for youthful marriage, whether or not achieved, are really not compatible with the emerging role of modern woman.

The cynic contends that the best advice for success we can give to a child is to "choose your parents carefully." Many of the Southern girls and young women in our study bought into the American dream and set high goals for themselves. But not many reached their goals, particularly if they were black. The line from Shakespeare, "The fault, dear Brutus, is not in our stars but in ourselves, that we are underlings" needs to be amended for Southern women. The fault is neither in their fates nor selves, except in the sense that they chose underclass parents and found it exceedingly difficult to rise above their backgrounds.

NOTES

1. See, for example, Bernice Moore, *Factors That Influence the Career Choices of Rural Minority Students,* Research Bulletin No. 31 (Orangeburg, SC: South Carolina State College, 1983); Arthur G. Cosby and Ivan Charner, eds., *Education and Work in Rural America: The Social Context of Early Career Decision and Achievement* (College Station, TX: Texas A. & M. University, 1978); and Frank M. Howell and Wolfgang Friese, *Making Life Plans: Race, Gender, and Career Decisions* (Washington, DC: University Press of America, 1982).

2. Betty Friedan, *The Feminine Mystique* (New York: Dell Publishing Company, 1963).

3. Sigurd R. Nilsen, *Assessment of Employment and Unemployment Statistics for Nonmetropolitan Areas* (Washington, D.C.: Economics, Statistics, and Cooperative Service, U.S. Department of Agriculture, Rural Development Research Report 18, 1979).

4. William W. Falk, "Career Development in Theoretical Perspective," in *Education and Work in Rural America,* Arthur G. Cosby and Ivan Charner, eds.

5. Arthur G. Cosby, "Occupational Expectations and the Hypothesis of Increasing Realism of Choice," *Journal of Vocational Behavior* 5(1974):53–65.

6. Ibid.

7. For example, see Anne Firor Scott, *The Southern Lady* (Chicago: University of Chicago Press, 1972). See also Julia Cherry Spruill, *Women's Life and Work in the*

Southern Colonies (Chapel Hill, NC: The University of North Carolina Press, 1938), and Catherine Clinton, *The Plantation Mistress* (New York: Pantheon, 1982).

8. Caroline M. Dillman, ''The Making of the Southern Woman: Socialization Then and Now'' (Paper presented at the meeting of the Southern Anthropological Society, Boone, North Carolina, 1982), p. 8, and Caroline Matheny Dillman, ''Southern Women: In Continuity or Change?'' (Paper presented at the meeting of the Southern Anthropological Society, Atlanta, 1987), to be published in *Southern Women: New Issues—New Perspectives,* Holly Mathews, ed. (Athens, GA: The University of Georgia Press, forthcoming).

9. An item on the mother's schedule revealed that most of the women had never lived outside the South.

10. Dolores Janiewski, ''Sisters Under Their Skins: Southern Working Women, 1880–1950,'' in *Sex, Race, and the Role of Women in the South,* Joanne V. Hawks and Sheila L. Skemp, eds. (Jackson, MS: University Press of Mississippi, 1983), p. 28.

11. Shirley Abbott, *Womenfolks: Growing Up Down South* (New York: Ticknor and Fields, 1983), p. 166.

12. Ibid.

13. Daryl J. Hobbs and Vickie Hobbs, ''A Research and Development Approach to Rural Education'' (Paper presented at the meeting of the American Education Research Association, San Francisco, 1979).

14. Melvin Kohn, ''Social Class and Parent-Child Relationships: An Interpretation,'' *American Journal of Sociology* 38(1963):471–480; Melvin L. Kohn, ''Social Class and Parental Values,'' in *The Family: Its Structures and Functions,* Rose Laub Coser, ed. (New York: St. Martin's Press, 1974), pp. 334–353; and Melvin L. Kohn, *Class and Conformity, A Study in Values,* 2nd ed. (Chicago: The University of Chicago Press, 1977).

15. Janiewski, ''Sisters Under Their Skins,'' p. 28.

16. Frank M. Howell, George W. Ohlendorf, and Lynn W. McBroom, ''The 'Ambition-Achievement' Complex: Values as Organizing Determinants,'' *Rural Sociology* 46(1981):465–482.

17. Sarah M. Shoffner and William F. Kenkel, eds., *On the Way to Adulthood: Changes and Continuities in the Life Plans of Low-Income Southern Youth* (Raleigh: North Carolina State University Press, 1986).

18. Albert J. Reiss, *Occupations and Social Status* (New York: The Free Press, 1961), pp. 109–138.

19. E. C. Devereaux, U. Bronfenbrenner, and R. R. Rodgers, ''Childrearing in England and the United States,'' *Journal of Marriage and the Family* 31(1969):257–270.

20. William F. Kenkel and Bruce A. Gage, ''The Restricted and Gender-Typed Occupational Aspirations of Young Women: Can They Be Modified?,'' *Family Relations* 32(1983):129–138.

21. William F. Kenkel and Bruce A. Gage, ''Attitudes Toward Working Wives Among Low-Income Youth,'' *Free Inquiry in Creative Sociology* 10(1982):150–152. See also Susan Middleton-Keirn, ''Magnolias and Microchips: Regional Subcultural Constructions of Femininity,'' in this volume.

Chapter 15
SOUTHERN WOMEN AND TEXTILE WORK: JOB SATISFACTION[1]

JAN K. BRYANT

Although the textile industry, one of the major employers in the South, has been characterized by low wages and poor working conditions, textile work can be a relatively attractive occupation for many Southern women. That satisfaction can be derived from textile work under specific circumstances is supported by a study of 10 white female workers at Firestone Textiles in Gastonia, North Carolina, and from the author's own experiences in working at this particular mill full time during high school and two years of college.[2] This chapter focuses on the findings concerning the women's job satisfaction, only one aspect of the original research, which also studied the group consciousness and self-image of these female textile workers.

There exists a complex and conditional set of factors that affected the job satisfaction of the small group of workers interviewed: first, the labor market of the community determined the type of jobs available; second, certain characteristics of the work at Firestone Textiles satisfied the workers; third, the human capital of these women affected their eligibility for alternative occupations; and finally, attention must be given to Southern culture—the strong sense of individualism, the importance of place and family ties, and stoicism—that affected the way these women perceived their work.

Beginning in the late 1800's, Gastonia, North Carolina, and the surrounding country grew to be one of the major textile centers of the South. Despite the decline of the textile industry in the early 1970s in Gastonia as well as the rest of the South, a significant proportion of the city's labor force has been and continues to be either employed by the textile industry or in firms providing support services or products to the industry. Although the Gastonia area offers a greater number of more diverse job opportunities compared to small mill villages, alternative low-skill employment for most women is limited to low-level service jobs and retail sales. This fact especially affects women since textiles, as an industry, is unusual in its employment of women. Unskilled Southern men have a greater chance of employment with other industries and in construction work.[3]

Firestone Textiles[4] of Gastonia, located west of downtown Gastonia, is one of the largest textile operations under one roof in the world and is a major producer of synthetic tire cord. Unlike many textile mills in the South, Firestone has never truly been a focal part of a "mill village." In addition to the fact that Firestone has always been a very large mill owned by outside management, and that Gastonia is quite large compared to many mill communities, it was also only one mill among many textile employers in the area. Firestone Textiles, however, was distinguished from the other mills for its reputation of providing physically demanding work for its workers, relatively high wages, and generally "fair" employment policies. People working at Firestone expected to do "hard work," but they also expected to be treated "fairly."

This study focused on only one occupation of the many necessary to the production of tire cord at Firestone: respooler operator. Respooling is a female occupation in that only women are hired to do this task. In explanation, respoolers are assigned to machines with 80 top spindles and 80 lower spindles. Respooler operators walk up and down their respective alleys tying small bobbins (yarn) to larger bobbins (tops) with a double weaving knot. The women continuously replace empty small bobbins and remove the full large bobbins, which weigh several pounds. The object is to empty as many small bobbins as humanly possible since their number determines respoolers' pay. Production is set at about 1,300 small bobbins per eight-hour shift, with each worker emptying between 1,200 and 1,800 each night. Respooling is both incredibly menial—the only thought involved is to make sure that large bobbins do not overfill—and physically exhausting—the women are constantly walking, bending over, and lifting.

Work at Firestone as described above does not appear to be very "satisfying." Nonetheless, 9 of the 10 women said that they were indeed satisfied. This supports other research in which it has been found that working-class women do derive satisfaction from jobs that objectively lack aspects providing any self-fulfillment.[5] The women at Firestone were not unlike those described by Ferree in that "while financial need may bind them to their present jobs or work conditions, there are relatively few who would wish to give up the sense of participation and purpose in society that having a job can provide."[6] The women in this study suggested that work, in and of itself, was very important to them. They liked working because it got them out of the house and gave them something to do. However, if given the hypothetical situation in which they didn't need the money, they would not work at Firestone. They saw work at Firestone as "satisfying," given their limited alternatives.

The women identified the high pay and the autonomy of respooling as the aspects they most liked about their jobs. The women themselves noted that "Firestone was the best paying mill in town." Eight of the ten workers agreed that it would not be easy for them to find another job with comparable pay and benefits. Several of the women emphasized their job autonomy and the individualized nature of their work as what they most liked about their work. The women worked at their machines alone; they appreciated not having to cooperate with others or having to serve others. Being "bothered with others" on their jobs was something they wanted to avoid and had experienced in other service jobs such as being a waitress. Related to this, the women emphasized that they liked their jobs because there was a lack of close supervision. The women were provided with a strong sense of autonomy. They were able to set their own pace at work, and, as long as they performed at the minimum level, the supervisor left the workers alone.

Despite their overall job satisfaction, there was also evidence of job dissatisfaction in particular areas of specific tasks. They did not like lifting heavy tops, getting so filthy, and having to "make production" every day. Two of the women complained that the pay was good, but it was not enough for the hard work they did. Even though their pay was better than that paid for most mill work, they were still not doing that well monetarily. One women exclaimed: "It takes a lifetime to get what you got and you still don't have anything working in a mill. You're just surviving."

One characteristic of the workers that strongly influenced their satisfaction and alternative opportunities was their low level of education (the median was 10 years). None of the women had graduated from high school. The women were very aware of their limited alternative job opportunities. Among these women, aged 21 to 57, there was not a trend of greater years of education for the younger workers. Leiter similarly points out that textile workers' limited education encourages increased dependence on the mills: "We have seen that poorly educated mill workers have little alternative for steady employment."[7] In addition, for most of these women their job experiences were limited to working in textile mills and fast food restaurants. These women realistically did not foresee any better job opportunities, given their educational level and job training.

In addition to the limits posed by the labor market and the women's lack of human capital, it is very possible that the cultural characteristics of these women further encouraged their overall satisfaction with work at Firestone. First of all, the women appear to be exceedingly individualistic. The importance of individualism for Southerners has been emphasized in other research on the South and in research on textile workers, specifically.[8] Wilbur J. Cash has argued that the root of Southerners' strong sense of individualism comes from the interaction of their Scotch-Irish ancestry and frontier past.[9] For the women at Firestone, their strong sense of individualism was evidenced by their desire not to work in groups with others and by their view of themselves as individuals and as being different from other textile workers. Several women stressed that they were "whole individuals." One woman in particular described her self-view: "I'm a whole individual person. I don't view myself according to others' images. I have very little communication with the other workers. I don't see a low picture—not the same scale as others at work see themselves." The women's individualism added to their job satisfaction in that they didn't see job-specific problems as being tied to the job. Work-related difficulties were viewed by them as isolated to themselves or as one-time-only events.

Another Southern trait, localism, may have affected these women's view of work at Firestone. Reed notes that the tendency of Southerners to focus on the uniqueness of individuals generalizes to their sense of place: "Comparable to the way Southerners see the uniqueness of individuals, they also see their home-towns as unique, special and better."[10] Southerners have a greater tendency to be attached to their towns. According to Reed, "Southerners seem more likely than other Americans to think of their region, their states, and their local communities possessively, as theirs, and distinct from and preferable to other regions, states, and localities."[11] In addition, Reed found the least educated, least urbanized people working in low-skilled, low-paying occupations to have the highest degree of localism.[12] Likewise, Leiter expressed in his study of textile workers at Roanoke Rapids, North Carolina, that, "Mill workers love their towns."[13] These women may have been especially stuck in their jobs since none of them expressed the desire to leave Gaston County to search for better work opportunities, and only two expected to leave Firestone, one to retire and one to enter the ministry.

Another characteristic, found in other research to be more highly valued by Southerners and especially by textile workers, was these women's strong sense of family.[14] Reed points out, "[T]he Southern concern with kin in general is indeed well-known—to the point of stereotypes."[15] On top of this, historically in textiles, the family, rather than the individual, has been the work unit.[16] Although the phenomenon of generations of mill workers working side by side has declined, it is very possible that familial values haven't changed radically. For example, Quinney notes that, in growing up in a Southern mill village, childhood tales expressed the sentiment "that a strong family can get through the hardest times," while also emphasizing "the importance of hard work and thrift."[17] The women at Firestone stressed that their work fulfilled only their need to provide monetarily for themselves and their families. The women interviewed said that their families were the most important thing in their lives; working was only a means to an end. Their "real life" was at home with their family, especially their children. The expression, "When I go home, I leave the job at the gate," was common to these women. Other indications of the importance of family life for these women were that all of the women except one lived with other family members and that all but two had children.

Finally, one other characteristic of Southerners that may have influenced the attitudes of these women was their stoicism. They have very low expectations and were unlikely to question existing authority relations. One source of their stoicism was most likely their substantial experience with hardship in their lives. Related to this, most of these women had parents who had been mill workers. Consequently, it is most probable that the cultural roots of these women were based in a more rural society where stoicism was often highly valued.[18] Additionally, they had little reason to expect life to get better. It also has been argued that the religious fundamentalism of Southerners, with its elements of fatalism and predestination, has contributed to their stoicism in that its inherent strong self-denial has led them to expect little enjoyment from life. As Reed points out, "Another characteristic of the Southern religion is its hard line on private morality, an 'anti-fun highly individualistic moral orientation,' an emphasis on the 'Thou shalt nots' of moral restriction."[19] Several of these women were very religious and fundamentalist.

In summary, the findings of this study provide an example of textile work in which female workers view their jobs as satisfying and add to our understanding of their lives. First and foremost, the community itself had limited alternative employment opportunities, and textile work was an important part of the industrial makeup of the local economy, making textile jobs available and acceptable work for women in the study. The work itself has aspects that they liked, in particular, the higher pay and autonomy. The women deemed work at Firestone superior to other mills for these reasons. Secondly, the workers lacked human capital, investments in education, and alternative training that would have prepared them for better jobs. In addition to these factors, their Southernness both encouraged them to value textile work and discouraged them from demanding better working conditions.[20]

NOTES

1. Portions of this article were included in a paper, "A Study of Women Workers at Firestone Textiles, Gastonia, North Carolina," presented at the meeting of the Midwest Sociological Society, Chicago, April 19, 1984.
2. I grew up in a working-class family only a few blocks from Firestone Textiles. My family background is not very different from the backgrounds of women in this study. I, however, was atypical in one area: I had a great desire to go to college and was incredibly motivated and lucky enough to receive a combination of scholarships and federal grants to make it possible.
3. See Jeffrey Leiter, "Continuity and Change in the Legitimation of Authority in Southern Mill Towns," *Social Problems* 29(June 1982):542; Linda Frankel, "Southern Textile Women: Generations of Survival and Struggle," in *My Troubles Are Going to Have Trouble with Me: Everyday Trials and Triumphs of Women Workers,* eds. Karen Rodkin Sacks and Dorothy Remy (New Brunswick, NJ: Rutgers University Press), p. 51.
4. Firestone Textiles is also unusual in that it is the site of the previous Loray Mill strike of 1929 which is described in Liston Pope's *Millhands and Preachers: A Study of Gastonia* (New Haven, CT: Yale University Press, 1942).
5. See Lillian B. Rubin, *Worlds of Pain: Life in the Working Class Family* (New York:

Basic Books, 1976), pp. 167–184; Myra Marx Ferree, "Sacrifice, Satisfaction, and Social Change: Employment and the Family," in *My Troubles Are Going to Have Trouble With Me: Everyday Trials and Triumphs of Women Workers*, eds. Sacks and Remy, pp. 61–79.

6. Ferree, "Sacrifice, Satisfaction, and Social Change," p. 77.
7. Leiter, "Continuity and Change in the Legitimation of Authority in Southern Mill Towns," p. 547.
8. See John Shelton Reed, *The Enduring South: Subcultural Persistence in Mass Society* (Lexington, Mass.: Lexington Books, 1972), p. 33; Richard L. Simpson, "Labor Force Integration and U.S. Textile Unionism," *Research in the Sociology of Work*, vol. 1, eds., Richard L. Simpson and Ida Harper Simpson (Greenwich, CT: JAI Press, 1981), pp. 385–386.
9. Wilbur J. Cash, *The Mind of the South* (New York: Alfred A. Knopf, 1941), p. 31.
10. Reed, *The Enduring South*, pp. 33–43;
11. Ibid.
12. Ibid., p. 40.
13. Leiter, "Continuity and Change in the Legitimation of Authority in Southern Mill Towns," p. 547.
14. See Maxine Alexander, ed., *Speaking for Ourselves: Women of the South* (New York: Pantheon Books, 1984); George L. Hicks, *Appalachian Valley* (New York: Holt, Rinehart and Winston, 1976).
15. Reed, *The Enduring South*, p. 85.
16. Simpson, "Labor Force, Integration and U.S. Textile Unionism," pp. 393–394.
17. Valerie Quinney, "Mill Village Memories" in *In Growing Up Southern: Southern Exposure Looks at Childhood, Then and Now*, ed. Chris Mayfield (New York: Pantheon Books, 1981), p. 229.
18. Hicks, *Appalachian Valley*, p. 90.
19. Reed, *The Enduring South*, p. 69. See also Joseph H. Fichter and George L. Maddox, "Religion in the South, Old and New," in *The South in Continuity and Change*, eds., John C. McKinney and Edgar T. Thompson (Durham: Duke University Press, 1965), p. 365; Robert Raymond Brown, "Southern Religion, Mid-Century," in *The Lasting South*, eds., Louis D. Rubin, Jr., and James Kilpatrick. (Chicago: Henry Regnery Company, 1957), p. 138.
20. This research was conducted in 1981 and around that time serious changes began to take place at Firestone. The unfortunate consequences for workers have been pay reductions, workload increases, and layoffs. In response to workers' disaffection, the United Rubber Workers led a union drive at Firestone in early 1987. Consistent with the fact that unions have historically done poorly in the South's textile industry (see Note 3), the union vote was not successful. Perhaps of greater importance, however, is that such changes in the workplace could have very serious consequences for Southern women in textile mills. It is likely that these women, whether or not they retain their mill jobs, will be subject to decreases in their standard of living, quality of work life, and sense of self-worth.

Chapter 16

STRONGER THAN LOVE: LOUISIANA'S SUGAR CANE WOMEN

JULIA BURKART

Sugar cane is a vital part of Louisiana's economy and has been raised for commercial purposes there for more than two centuries.[1] The State Department of Agriculture celebrates this plant with a brightly colored poster with this slogan: "Sweeter Than Love: Louisiana Sugar Cane." Sugar cane has brought the sweetness of wealth to a few white people and poverty to many black people.

Black women are twice removed from public attention vis-à-vis the sugar cane industry: the media generally ignore blacks who are the direct producers or workers and focus on white men who own or operate the plantation or on young white women who adorn the floats during the annual Sugar Cane Festival. Traditionally, black women have been an auxiliary work force who are denied recognition and who have had to manage several roles—field hand, wife, and mother.

This chapter is based on a study in the cane region of South Louisiana[2] and focuses on those black women who were "born and raised" on sugar cane plantations in Louisiana, women whose lives are almost unknown by the world outside the plantation. Thirty-one families that had lived on plantations and had left this situation to build their own homes were interviewed. They had received loans from the Farmers Home Administration and direction from the Southern Mutual Help Association, an advocacy group. To appreciate the achievement of the home builders, it was necessary to compare current life on the plantation; for this reason, 13 families still living in the quarters were also included in the study. Of particular interest here are the women and how they viewed life in the quarters and how that life compared with the new one as home builder and owner away from the quarters.

The sugar cane plantation as known to the subjects in the study is not that of the Big House with white pillars and free-handed hospitality. Neither is it the plantation of sharecroppers' cabins scattered over the land. Sugar cane culture is capital intensive; on plantations profit comes from large-scale operations that employ "a relatively large number of unskilled laborers whose activities are closely supervised."[3] Field hands are paid by the hours worked and not by a share of the crop produced. Historically, one of the benefits of plantation work was that of free housing; this arrangement persists today. Each plantation visited during the research had a group of "quarter" houses. Some quarters were like small villages; others were only a row of about five houses. All of them were removed from the manor house of the owner. Free housing enables the worker and family to survive even when the former is out of work and in debt; it also insures an available labor force for the plantation.

Living in a house owned by one's employer, removed from the larger society, and subject to some degree of observation by the employer is part of a paternalistic system that has influenced labor relations on plantations. In general, the "free" house is given to the male head of a family because he is more or less a full-time worker. A woman who heads a family would have to pay rent because she can do only seasonal work.[4] Because the worker lacks transferable skills and is dependent on his or her boss for housing, the worker often feels unable to leave the plantation for a more competitive situation. The results of this system can be seen from the economic levels of plantation families. Of the 13 resident families interviewed, all were found to be at or below the official poverty level for that year.[5] Previous studies had similar findings: in 1979 full-time, permanent workers averaged less than $6,000 a year.[6] The setting, then, includes different degrees of poverty.

One can recognize plantation quarters by their appearance—several old frame houses off the main highway, set next to each other, perhaps painted the same color would indicate plantation quarters. Often the houses are identical in appearance and reflect common ownership; sometimes they are unpainted and in disrepair. Whether the quarters are seen as normal or depressing depends on one's viewpoint; to the residents the quarters represent what is known and familiar. Let's turn, then, to three case study examples of women who tell us about life in the quarters. One of the women has moved into her own house away from the plantation and compares the two lifestyles.

Ella Mae is 35 and has no teeth.[7] Malnutrition, gum disease, and lack of dental care have turned her face into that of an old woman. She confided that when she was first married, before the children came along, she had started to save for dentures. One thing after another happened, and now she has given up the hope of eating with teeth and not "gumming" her food.

Her home in the quarters has a living room, a kitchen, two large bedrooms, and a small room where her only daughter sleeps. Ella Mae has five children and prays that she doesn't conceive again. She doesn't like birth control, and sterilization is abhorrent to her. Her husband, Paul, is a tall, good-looking man who came from north Louisiana, from the cotton region. He began his life in the fields when he was 10 years old. "There wasn't any choice," he commented.

During planting and grinding (i.e., harvesting) season Ella Mae works in the cane fields for $3.40 an hour.[8] At planting time she and two other women follow a tractor-pulled cart filled with cane; they pull out two stalks and drop them in the deep furrows of the rich soil. The work is hard. It requires mainly the use of arm muscles, and most of the women, however frail, have well-developed biceps. The women must walk behind a moving tractor—human beings keeping up with a machine. They get a break only when the cart has been emptied. For the few minutes it takes to refill the cart with a full load, the women sit on the furrows and drink from thermos bottles of cold water.

Around October the harvest time begins and the women scrap cane—they cut down with a long cane knife any errant stalks left by the mechanical harvester. One winter evening as I was leaving the plantation, I saw Ella Mae trudging home. She was bundled up in three sweaters and had mud on her rubber boots—the fields are often wet and muddy. Ella Mae's face was smudged from the smoke of burning cane stalks and she looked like the embodiment of weariness. Like the other women of the cane, she got up early and would have more work waiting for her when she reached home. She greeted me and I thought of the question I had asked her as part of the interview I conducted with plantation families. "What kind of work do you think your children will do?" Ella Mae answered without hesitation, "I know what kind of work they *won't* do: they won't work in the fields!"

Ella Mae hopes for her children's betterment; perhaps the fact that schools are now integrated will help them realize her hope. She also wants to advance herself and has dreams of getting a GED (General Education Diploma). Her ambition just now has one outlet, her housekeeping. The old house is immaculate inside; often when I went to visit her the kitchen chairs were stacked on top of the table while the floor dried. I noticed three layers of old linoleum on the floor. The beds were visible since the bedroom doors were open; none of the beds had a spread, but the sheets that served this purpose were smooth and without wrinkle. The very cleanliness of her home had something pathetic about it, and I imagined what she could do with more income.

Ella Mae is courageous and optimistic, but from my observations of how plantations work, I believe that she will be in this house until she dies, probably prematurely. Not only childbearing and hard work have drained her, but exposure to pesticides on the cane and in the air she (and her children) breathe. I am somewhat awed by Ella Mae's optimism and hopes, but her indifferent health may get worse and her husband will probably never advance beyond his routine job of repairing tires on the big tractors. She and her family will undoubtedly sink deeper into poverty, and, finally, she will lose the war against roaches in her immaculate kitchen.

Maywel, a widow, receives a small social security pension and some money for keeping three foster children.[9] She is 64 and has never left the plantation; she lives in a quarter house valued at $1,000.[10] From her front porch she can survey her neighbors, and she knows the history and present situation of most of them. "I was born and raised at Mamou Plantation and I came here when I got married." she said. "We used to live where the McCraes are now, but when all my children left and my husband died, I got this little place. I never want to leave Falwyn Plantation."

Inside her house there are two rooms and a kitchen; there are beds in each room for her and the three children she is raising. On cold days when I visited her, we sat in the front room where a small gas heater fights the dampness in the high-ceiling room. On the back of the door, swathed in plastic is Maywel's church dress, a white, long-sleeved garment. She goes to church every Sunday and does "floor duty" once a month. Church is the major social meeting place for Maywel and many of the other women. Perhaps the clothing and the occasion remind the plantation dwellers that they, too, are important.

Maywel recalled how she met her husband, Ben.

I was visiting some friends here at Falwyn and we walked over to the sugar house [mill]. Ben was new here and didn't know many people. He was just getting off work, it was about four o'clock when he saw me by the bridge. He asked somebody, "Who is that girl? I want to meet her." So that started the whole thing. He told me after we were married that he knew then he wanted me for his wife.

He was a good man and we raised eight head of children together. When he got paid he would give me the money and I would buy what we needed; he trusted me all the way. I tried to save some each month, and Ben knew this. He would ask me, "Do we have any money left?" I would say, "Yes." He never asked how much or what I did with it. With all the children I never saved the money too long.

Maywel was poor and lived poor, but she had a natural intelligence that could size up a situation. Before leaving at the end of my research, I went to say good-bye. "Miss Julie, I hope you don't forget us poor people," she said.

Not wanting to emphasize the difference between us, I protested, "Maywel, I'm not so rich myself, you know."

Maywel then gave this illustration: "I know you're not rich, Miss Julie, but if you go to the courthouse they will wait on you. If I go down, they will let me stand there. Your *life chances* [emphasis mine] are better than mine." Maywel did not need to study sociology to know what her prospects were, but she was happy in her $1,000 house because the quarters provided her with memories and opportunities to serve.

Hazel was 55 when I met her, had left the plantation, and was learning to read again. She was in the fifth level of the Laubach Literacy Program; I was her instructor. It was hard to focus on the stories in her book like "The Battle of Stone Mountain" when the warmth of her personality and her eagerness to communicate reached out to my wish to know more about her life and how she got to be mistress of her own home.

Hazel looked at the cheerful living room with the carpeted floor and upholstered furniture. This was quite different from the house she left behind.

> *My house on Beaumont [Plantation] had a roof that leaked and we had to shift the furniture every time it rained. And we had lots of roaches, and the rats would come in from the fields after grinding [harvest season]. But that's what I was used to, and, when that lady from the Southern Mutual [the organization that facilitated the housing program] came around, some people just didn't believe her—how could we own a house, much less build it? Now Jake, my husband, said, "This is our chance, let's go!" I just wasn't for it—I didn't want to leave the plantation. Jake told me, "I'm going ahead, if you want it or not." Now I was too old to get me another husband, I thought, and I shouldn't be so against him in this. So one day on my lunch hour—I was working at the Chicken Shack in town[11] —I walked on over here and saw the cement floor they just poured. This is where our house is now. I prayed that I would be for it, that God would change my mind. I walked back to work and after a while I felt better about the house and was glad that Jake decided to go through with it.*

Going back further in time, Hazel reminisced about her marriage and life in the plantation quarters.

> *I married Jake on Beaumont Plantation and ole Mister Bud, the boss, gave us a house of our own, but it just had one room. Soon after we were married, Jake's brother and his wife and little boy moved in with us—they had no place to go. It was crowded, and my first child came along, and that made six of us in one room. Well, they moved out but then our children kept coming. My husband always worked hard, but sometimes it would rain on the paycheck,[12] and we didn't have nothin'. Jake used to get so worried about our debts, I wanted to save him, so I would make [sic] groceries in my own name—I went to Mr. Pete at the grocery store and told him to write down the bill in my name. I would tote the groceries home, and that way, Jake didn't know and he didn't worry. That was a long time ago, and now I thank God we are here.*

Hazel talked with pride about the house she and her husband now own.

This is the first thing I ever owned in my life. I work for a dentist and lawyer—I clean their place at night, and Jake has a job at the cemetery, so we can keep up the notes. I love to look at my house and enjoy it. See that panelling on the walls? Well, I did all of that. Jake and Mr. Dane, our neighbor, they nailed all the roofs for these houses. They weren't afraid of getting on a ladder, so they did it for everybody.

Hazel was an eager student and told me about her early education.

I want to learn how to read better; I used to read a long time ago, but then I forgot. When I was little we had to walk three miles to the school for coloreds; that was all in one room. In the winter it would be so cold I couldn't feel nothin' below my knees. One time a school bus passed us children from the plantation when we going to school. They were white children and they stuck out they heads and laughed at us. I didn't stay in school too long.

So Hazel and I continued with tutorial sessions. Sometimes I would feel guilty because she and I were about the same age and I had about six times as much schooling as she did. An accident of birth put us on either side of the table as student or teacher. She was always involved in her family's affairs, cooking food for this one, minding the baby of that one. I remember Hazel more as a friend than as a student. The last time I saw her was at a funeral in the plantation church. She and many others had come to pay their respects to the deacon, who had a heart attack suddenly while riding a tractor in the fields. She and Jake filed past where I was standing—the church was packed—and she reached out to kiss me. Tears were on her face because the deacon was well loved. Hazel seemed like a middle-aged, middle-class matron at that time. She had come a long way over a hard road.

While the stories of Ella Mae, Maywel, and Hazel do not exhaust the types of plantation women, they do represent that narrow world of the sugar cane plantation in 20th-century America. These women may not realize that the plantation is an anachronism in an industrialized country, but they do know how their lives have been shaped by this enterprise.

NOTES

1. Center for Louisiana Studies, *Green Fields: Two Hundred Years of Louisiana Sugar Cane* (Lafayette, LA: Southwestern Louisiana State University, 1980).
2. Julia Burkart, "From Quarters to Castle: Home Ownership Among Black, Sugar Cane Plantation Families" (Ph.D. diss., Texas Woman's University, 1983).
3. William Jones, "Plantations," *International Encyclopedia of the Social Sciences,* vol. VI (New York: Macmillan, 1968), pp. 155–199.
4. Women work in planting cane (September and October) and in "scrapping" cane during grinding, or harvest, season. Men work driving tractors, pumping water,

cleaning drains, repairing tires, fixing vehicles, and so forth. I met one woman who also drove the tractor, but she was (and is) exceptional. Also some of the black men are overseers. A strict division of labor according to sex probably explains why more work is given to men. During the slack season, women look elsewhere for work, usually as domestics. Depending on the plantation, disabled male workers usually pay rent.

5. Burkart, "From Quarters to Castle," p. 78.

6. Gulf South Research Institute, "A Wage and Employment Conditions Survey of Sugar Cane Farms in Inberia and West St. Mary Parish," mimeographed (Baton Rouge, LA: Gulf South Research Institute, 1979).

7. Names of plantations and of persons are fictitious, and case studies are composites. Tape recorders were not used in the interviews because it was very important that trust be established and that nothing hinder the establishment of the relationship. Therefore, the quotations from the conversations are not exact but are representative and are nearly the same as would have been recorded. Out of respect for the respondents little poor grammar and pronunciation have been included.

8. The prevailing minimum wage remains about the same currently in 1987.

9. Though rules vary from plantation to plantation, widows are allowed to remain in the quarters of some plantations but of course must pay rent.

10. From records in the Tax Assessor's Office of the local parish courthouse.

11. Hazel was working in town during the slack season. Often the women work as domestics; it is quite convenient for white families that black women from the sugar plantations are not working during the summer and thus can take care of the white children. There is usually a scramble among the younger black women for domestic work or service jobs in the spring and summer.

12. "Rain on the paycheck" means pay is less because the people do not work in the fields when it rains.

Chapter 17

WOMEN AND VIOLENCE: THE INTERSECTION OF TWO COMPONENTS OF SOUTHERN IDEOLOGY

BECKY L. GLASS

This study explores the interaction of two elements of Southern culture that have been the subjects of much discussion but little empirical attention: (1) the attitudes and experiences of the Southern woman and (2) Southern attitudes and behavior with regard to violence.

The South has been characterized by many authors as more violent than other geographical regions.[1] This violence has been attributed to Southern feelings of "social insecurity" and belief in a "passionate [Southern] temperament,"[2] to weapons as an important part of Southern culture,[3] and to the Southern glorification of war and the military.[4] However, the data that have been used to support this characterization have generally been either impressionistic,[5] based on homicide rates,[6] or indirect, based on opinion polls about gun ownership and corporal punishment in school.[7]

One study that explicitly compared the East, West, Midwest, and South on acceptance of and experience with various levels of physical violence found that the South was not significantly different from the other regions on the following items: percent who had ever been slapped or kicked, percent punched or beaten, percent threatened with a knife or gun; percent who had slapped or kicked another person, punched or beaten another person; percent who approved of a husband or wife slapping his or her spouse's face.[8] Respondents from the South were slightly more likely to have been spanked as a child, to agree that "young people need strong discipline by their parents," and to own firearms, but these differences were not significant.

It has been suggested that the Southern attitude toward violence may be "schizophrenic," in that one should never raise one's voice in anger; but, if necessary to defend one's honor or one's family, a Southerner must be prepared to respond with violence.[9] This interpretation may explain the discrepancy between the high homicide rates in the South and the findings of no regional differences in attitudes toward violence in the study cited above.

In all of this literature on Southern violence, however, distinctions are generally not made between Southern women and Southern men in attitudes or behavior.[10] This is not surprising in view of the well-documented fact that women are not included in most writings about the South.[11] However, it seems that the subject of violence is one area in which it is particularly important to include the perspective of the Southern woman, due to the unique and paradoxical relationship between men and women in the South.

On one hand, there is a glorification of the Southern lady that has its roots in the uneven sex ratio in the South during its early settlement[12] and as a symbol of Southern ideology which provided a foundation for oppression of blacks.[13] This is accompanied by notions of male chivalry and the Southern gentleman, who is quick to resort to violence to defend his lady but would never raise a hand to hurt her.[14] On the other hand, there is the "Southern mythology," as Gastil calls it,[15] that "the woman is worshipped, but it is the man who rules,"[16] and that, as most authors emphasize, whether writing of historical periods or of modern times, patriarchal power is an integral part of the Southern family.[17] Finally, there is the characterization, found in the writings of female Southern authors, that Southern women put on an appearance of being superficial and vacant-headed but in reality are stronger than men and have a core of steel.[18]

Given the confusing literature of Southern violence in general and the contradictory descriptions of women's place in Southern culture, the area of Southern women and violence is one that is worth investigating. The general research questions that are addressed in this study are the following: Are Southern women different from non-Southern women in their attitudes toward violence and the circumstances under which they find violence acceptable? Are Southern women's experiences as victims of violence different from non-Southern women? To what extent are Southern women different from Southern men in their attitudes toward violence, and are their relative positions different from the relative positions of men and women in other regions?

HYPOTHESES

Despite some countervailing evidence, most authors characterize the South as more violent than other regions. In the absence of information about sex differences regarding this regional violence, the first hypothesis is the following: Southern women are more accepting of violence than non-Southern women.

With regard to the circumstances under which violence may be acceptable, Southerners (meaning Southern men) have been characterized as being quick to come to the defense of (1) their family and (2) their women.[19] While it is generally assumed that the men are doing the defending, it may be expected that Southern women have also received this socialization. Thus, we have the second hypothesis: Southern women are more accepting of violence in defense of a family member or a woman than for other circumstances for violence, and this attitude is significantly different from non-Southern women.

Despite the presumption that Southern men will go to great lengths to defend their wives, the patriarchal heritage of the Southern family[20] and the traditionalist values of the South[21] suggest that these men, themselves, may be likely to commit violence against their wives. This leads to the third hypothesis: Southern women are more likely to have been the victims of violence than are non-Southern women.

Finally, because of the unique roles of the "Southern Lady" and the "Southern Gentleman," which have no counterpart in other geographic regions, it is expected that the relative positions of Southern men and women in their attitudes toward violence will be different from the relative positions of non-Southern men and women. However, the direction of the difference is difficult to predict. If the extreme femininity attached to the Southern lady and the extreme masculinity associated with the Southern male are salient, then we would expect their attitudes to be farther apart than those of non-Southern men and women. On the other hand, if their socialization as Southerners is the salient factor and the idea that the South is more cohesive than other regions is valid,[22] then we would expect their attitudes to be more alike than those of non-Southern men and women. Since we cannot predict which factor is more powerful, the fourth hypothesis is the following: The relative positions of Southern men's and women's attitudes toward violence are different from the relative positions of non-Southern men and women, but the direction of the difference is unspecified.

METHODOLOGY

The data used in this study are from the "General Social Surveys" conducted by the National Opinion Research Center on random, nationally representative samples from 1972 to 1986.[23] A particular advantage of this data set for our purposes is that it is possible to separate the samples not only by the geographic region in which the respondents are currently living, but also by whether a given respondent was living in the same state as a child. Thus, we can differentiate long-term Southerners from newcomers to the South.[24] By pooling samples for the eight years[25] in which questions about violence were asked and using only long-term residents of the geographic regions,[26] who are white,[27] a sample of 7,205 cases is available for analysis.

The acceptance of violence item reads, "Are there any situations that you can imagine in which you would approve of a man punching a male stranger?" Possible responses are "yes," "no," and "not sure." Only the "yes" and "no" responses were considered for these analyses.

The item is followed by five questions which ask "Would you approve if the stranger . . ." a) "was in a protest march showing opposition to the man's views?" b) "was drunk and bumped into the man and his wife on the street?" c) "had hit the man's child after the child accidentally damaged the stranger's car?" d) "was beating up a woman?" and e) "had broken into the man's house?" These situational questions are taken to imply more abstract variables related to approval of violence. That is, they can be interpreted to be asking whether violence is acceptable a) in defense of one's values, b) in defense of one's wife, c) in defense of one's children or family, d) in defense of women in general, and e) in defense of one's property.

The item about experience with violence reads "Have you ever been punched or beaten by another person?" This is followed by the item "Did this happen to you as a child or as an adult or both?" While these questions do not explicitly ask whether the person who did the punching was a relative, the literature on domestic violence indicates that virtually all such incidents are intrafamilial.[28]

Cross-classification analysis is used to analyze the data, in that the major variables of interest are categorical (i.e., sex, geographic regions, yes-and-no responses to the violence questions).

FINDINGS

The first hypothesis, which proposes that Southern women are more accepting of violence in general than non-Southern women, is not supported. As shown in Table 1, Southern women and Northeastern women have the lowest levels of approval of violence in general, while Western women have the highest levels.

TABLE 1 Approval of Violence in General, by Southern and Non-Southern Women

	Northeast	Midwest	West	South	All Regions
Would approve of violence in some situations*	63.9% (612)	67.2% (917)	73.3% (426)	63.7% (900)	66.2% (2855)
Would not approve	36.1% (345)	32.8% (448)	26.7% (155)	36.3% (512)	33.8% (1460)
Total Ns	(957)	(1365)	(581)	(1412)	(4211)
χ^2, 3 d.f. = 19.73, $p < .000$					

* Answered "yes" to the question "Are there any situations that you can imagine in which you would approve of a man punching a male stranger?"

When, however, specific circumstances are taken into account, as suggested by the second hypothesis, Southern women do hold different views from women in other regions. Table 2 shows that Southern women are significantly more accepting of violence when their values are opposed and when someone's wife or child is threatened. On the other hand, they are less accepting of violence in defense of women in general or private property.

The third hypothesis, which posits that Southern women are more likely to be victims of violence, is not unequivocally supported. Southern women report the least experience with being punched or beaten (see Table 3). However, for women who have been punched or beaten, Southern women are more likely than non-Southerners to have experienced this abuse as adults rather than in childhood, and Southerners are more likely than Northeastern or Midwestern women to report being hit "four or more times" rather than one to three times. (They are tied with Western women; analyses not shown.)

In comparing men's and women's attitudes toward violence, Southern men and women tend to be more alike than men and women in other regions (see Table 4). While the other regions have two to three significant differences in men's and women's responses about violence in general and violence in specific situations, there is only one significant difference for the South. This difference is for the situation of defending one's wife, and, although the sex differ-

TABLE 2 Approval of Violence, by Situation, for Southern and Non-Southern Women*

	Northeast	Midwest	West	South	All Regions
Violence against protest marcher (defense of values) N = 4146					
Approve	3.2%	2.4%	2.7%	5.2%	3.5%
	(29)	(32)	(15)	(70)	(146)
χ^2, 3 d.f. = 17.75, $p < .000$					
Violence against drunk bumping into couple (defense of wife) N = 4134					
Approve	4.8%	6.4%	5.8%	12.4%	7.9%
	(43)	(86)	(32)	(166)	(327)
χ^2, 3 d.f. = 57.16, $p < .000$					
Violence against someone hitting one's child (defense of family) N = 4091					
Approve	50.5%	47.9%	54.1%	56.5%	52.1%
	(454)	(630)	(294)	(754)	(2132)
χ^2, 3 d.f. = 21.18, $p < .000$					
Violence against someone beating a woman (defense of women in general) N = 4107					
Approve	85.7%	85.6%	89.5%	83.3%	85.4%
	(760)	(1134)	(487)	(1125)	(3506)
χ^2, 3 d.f. = 12.39, $p < .007$					
Violence against someone breaking into one's house (defense of property) N = 4148					
Approve	85.9%	82.2%	82.3%	85.2%	84.0%
	(778)	(1098)	(452)	(1157)	(3485)
χ^2, 3 d.f. = 8.01, $p < .05$					

* In the interest of space and clarity, only the percent approving of violence is reported here; percent disapproving can be calculated by subtracting from 100%.

TABLE 3   Women as Victims of Violence, by Region

	Northeast	Midwest	West	South	All Regions
Have been punched	19.0%	20.1%	31.1%	17.5%	20.4%
or beaten at least	(190)	(289)	(184)	(264)	(927)
once in lifetime					
Never punched	81.0%	79.9%	68.9%	82.5%	79.6%
or beaten	(809)	(1149)	(408)	(1246)	(3612)
Total *N*s	(999)	(1438)	(592)	(1510)	(4539)

χ^2, 3 d.f. = 50.71, $p < .000$

ence is statistically significant, it is clear that Southern men and women are very different from the rest of the country on this item and certainly closer to each other than to the other regions.

DISCUSSION

One of the most notable findings of this study, which directly addresses the question of whether the South ascribes to violence more than other regions, and whether Southern women ''buy into'' such approval of violence (if it exists), is that Southern women's approval of violence in general is the lowest of

TABLE 4   Sex Differences in Approval of Violence, by Region

	Northeast		Midwest		West		South	
	Men	Women	Men	Women	Men	Women	Men	Women
$N =$	(711)	(884)	(1029)	(1274)	(434)	(540)	(922)	(1118)
Approve, in general	70.2%	64.7%	68.7%	68.3%	72.1%	75.0%	71.4%	68.7%
	($p < .03$)		(NS)		(NS)		(NS)	
Approve for protest	2.6%	3.0%	3.3%	2.5%	3.6%	2.7%	6.2%	4.7%
marcher (defense	(NS)		(NS)		(NS)		(NS)	
of values)								
Approve for drunk	5.8%	4.8%	8.7%	6.6%	9.1%	5.8%	18.4%	13.0%
bumping husband	(NS)		($p < .09$)		($p < .08$)		($p < .002$)	
and wife (defense								
of wife)								
Approve for someone	59.0%	51.1%	57.8%	48.2%	62.1%	56.1%	62.9%	59.4%
hitting one's child	($p < .003$)		($p < .000$)		($p < .08$)		(NS)	
(defense of family)								
Approve for someone	85.8%	86.9%	87.7%	86.7%	85.3%	91.5%	87.5%	86.1%
beating woman	(NS)		(NS)		($p < .005$)		(NS)	
(defense of women)								
Approve for someone	90.6%	85.6%	89.2%	81.9%	83.9%	83.6%	88.9%	86.6%
breaking into house	($p < .005$)		($p < .000$)		(NS)		(NS)	
(defense of								
property)								

all the regions, but their approval of violence in specified situations is the highest of all regions for three of the five situations. This supports some of the impressionistic notions about the socialization of Southern women—that harmony, courtesy, gentleness, and self-discipline are highly valued,[29] but at the same time, threats to the Southern way of life or to family or to other important values are to be taken seriously and dealt with decisively.[30]

The conditions under which violence is approved by Southern women also provide insight into the ideology of the region and, again, empirically support certain aspects of the anecdotal characterizations of Southern women. For example, compared to women of other regions, Southern women are very approving of a man defending his wife, even from an accidental insult, but are less approving of violence in defense of a non-kin woman.[31] The high support for defense of a family member, especially the wife, is congruent with the notion that the South is characterized by strong family ties and strong family loyalty,[32] and with characterizations of Southern chivalry, in which an insult or threat to a man's wife is the most serious kind of affront to him personally.[33] Relatedly, the lower support, compared to other regions, for the defense of an unknown woman coincides with the paradoxical role of women in the South—that the idealization of women in the abstract is/was useful for maintaining class and race boundaries, but that the evaluation of women qua women is quite low; that is, women's position in the family and elsewhere is subordinate to men, and any attempts to change this traditional ordering can justifiably be met with strong measures.[34] Scott points out that the invention of the Southern lady was an integral part of the slaveholding society and it was put on women's shoulders to enforce the system.[35] These data about contemporary Southern women's attitudes toward woman beating suggest that Southern women continue to "buy into" the system and subordination of women to some extent.

In light of the above discussion about women's place in the South, it is noteworthy that Southern women are least likely of all regions to have been punched or beaten. There is more than one possible explanation for this finding. It may be a true difference and reflect the Southern value on harmony, self-discipline, and the veneration of family members. Alternatively, it may reflect a greater reluctance on the part of Southern women, compared to non-Southern women, to report having been hit. Since virtually all attacks on women occur within the family, admitting to being hit may be considered by Southern women a violation of the sacred privacy of the family.[36] Further, due to Southerners' awareness that other parts of the country consider them "backward" (what Bruce calls "social insecurity"[37]), Southern women may be hesitant to report violence against "ladies" for fear it will reflect badly on their nativity and heritage.

The suggestion that Southern women accept and support Southern socialization and Southern values, despite their relatively disadvantaged position, is further corroborated by the comparison of men's and women's attitudes toward violence across regions. While men and women tend to be similar to each other within each region, the similarity is the greatest in the South. This overlaying of sex differences may be an indication of the pervasiveness of Southern culture relative to Western culture or Northeastern culture or Midwestern culture. Despite the phenomenon of the Southern lady, for which there is no parallel in other parts of the country, and the Southern historical tradition of men's and women's proper places, the ideology of the Southern region is shared by its residents, regardless of sex. This implies that the "men's reality" and "women's reality" that have been posited in other contexts[38] are superseded by a "Southern reality."

The distinctiveness of Southern women's attitudes toward violence compared to other women and their relative agreement with Southern men's attitudes toward violence has implications for those who would advocate the "liberalization" of men's and women's roles in the South. Proposals to Southern women to change their attitudes and their endorsement of "the system" may be expected to be met with resistance to the extent that altering their role as Southern women is perceived as threatening to their regional identity and to the extent that they tacitly believe the Southern woman ideology that they are indeed the stronger sex, regardless of outward appearances. At a stereotypical level, such resistance might be interpreted as unnecessarily conservative and damaging to women personally and generally, but the reasons behind the support of Southern values must be considered. Men and women in the South have a claim to a unique set of self-perceptions, values, and traditions derived from their geographic region, which provide them with a sense of belongingness that other groups attain through ethnic or racial or genealogical connections.[39] Thus, to suggest that they change their concept of gender relations without recognizing how their sex roles are interdependent with other aspects of Southern identity, ignores the complexity of the situation. This would be analogous to suggesting to members of some ethnic group that they stop observing a particular ethnic festival because the food that is traditionally consumed is carcinogenic. While the goodness of the outcome (better health for the ethnic group; greater observable equality for Southern women) cannot be denied, the ramifications of the change are greater than its specified objective.

In conclusion, the positions of women and of violence in Southern culture should not be dismissed as either simplistic or dogmatic, but rather as elements of a complex world view, with definable precedents, which serves as an important source of self-identity for a significant proportion of the U.S. population. Even if one disagrees with the Southern position, understanding how its elements are interrelated is necessary for an understanding of Southern women.

NOTES

1. For example, Sheldon Hackney, "Southern Violence," *American Historical Review* 74(1969):906–925; Frank Vandiver, "The Southerner as Extremist." in *The South: A Central Theme?,* ed. Monroe Billington (New York: Holt, Rinehart, and

Winston, 1969); John Shelton Reed, "To Live and Die in Dixie: A Contribution to the Study of Southern Violence," *Political Science Quarterly* 76(1971):429–445; Dickson Bruce, *Violence and Culture in the Antebellum South* (Austin, TX: University of Texas Press, 1979).

2. Bruce, *Violence and Culture in the Antebellum South*, p. 11.
3. Raymond Gastil, *Cultural Regions of the United States* (Seattle, WA: University of Washington Press, 1975).
4. John H. Franklin, *The Militant South 1800–1861* (Cambridge, MA: Harvard University Press, 1956).
5. For example, Howard Odum, *The Way of the South* (Chapel Hill, NC: University of North Carolina Press, 1947).
6. Reed, "To Live and Die in Dixie."
7. John Shelton Reed, *The Enduring South* (Lexington, MA: Lexington Books, 1972).
8. Rodney Stark and James McEvoy, "Middle-Class Violence," *Psychology Today,* November 1977, pp. 52–54, 110–112.
9. Bruce, *Violence and Culture in the Antebellum South*, p. 18.
10. See Reed, *The Enduring South,* for an exception.
11. Caroline Matheny Dillman, "The Sparsity of Research and Publications on Southern Women: Definitional Complexities, Methodological Problems, and Other Impediments," in this volume.
12. Bernard Murstein, *Love, Sex, and Marriage Through the Ages* (New York: Springer Publishing, 1974); Stuart Queen, John B. Adams, and Robert Habenstein, *The Family in Various Cultures,* 4th ed. (New York: J. B. Lippincott Co., 1974); Julia Cherry Spruill, *Women's Life and Work in the Southern Colonies* (New York: Norton, 1972).
13. Laurence Baughman, *Southern Rape Culture* (Atlanta: Pendulum Books, 1966); Anne Firor Scott, *The Southern Lady: From Pedestal to Politics, 1830–1930* (Chicago: University of Chicago Press, 1970).
14. See Bertram Wyatt-Brown, *Southern Honor: Ethics and Behavior in the Old South* (New York: Oxford University Press, 1982).
15. Gastil, *Cultural Regions of the United States,* p. 184.
16. Ibid.
17. For example, see Scott, *The Southern Lady*.
18. Shirley Abbott, *Womenfolks: Growing Up Down South* (New York: Ticknor and Fields, 1983); Josephine Habersham, *Ebb Tide* (Athens, GA: University of Georgia Press, 1958); Elizabeth C. Wallace, *Glencoe Diary* (Chesapeake, VA: Northfolk County Historical Society, 1968); Donna Kelleher Darden, "Southern Women Writing About Southern Women: Jill McCorkle, Lisa Alther, Gail Godwin, Ellen Gilchrist, and Lee Smith," in this volume.
19. Cf., Patricia Beaver, "Symbols and Social Organization in an Appalachian Mountain Community" (Ph.D. diss., Duke University, 1976); Valerie Fennell, "The Hierarchical Aspects of Age Relations in Curlew Point" (Ph.D. diss., University of North Carolina, 1974); Elmora Matthews, *Neighbor and Kin: Life in a Tennessee Ridge Community* (Nashville, TN: Vanderbilt University Press, 1966).
20. Scott, *The Southern Lady;* Joanne V. Hawks and Sheila Skemp, eds., *Sex, Race, and the Role of Women in the South* (Jackson, MS: University of Mississippi Press, 1983); Jacqueline Boles and Maxine Atkinson, "Ladies: South by Northwest," in

this volume; Susan Middleton-Keirn, "Magnolias and Microchips: Regional Subcultural Constructions of Femininity," in this volume.

21. Bruce, *Violence and Culture in the Antebellum South*, p. 10; Gastil, *Cultural Regions of the United States*, p. 186; Reed, *The Enduring South*, p. 83; Francis Simkins, *The Everlasting South* (Baton Rouge, LA: Louisiana State University Press, 1963).

22. Samuel Hill, "The South's Two Cultures," in *Religion in the Solid South*, ed. Samuel Hill (Nashville, TN: Abingdon Press, 1972) pp. 14–32; Lewis Killian, *White Southerners* (New York: Random House, 1970); George Tindall, *The Ethnic Southerners* (Baton Rouge, LA: Louisiana State University Press, 1976); Carole Hill, "Anthropological Studies in the American South," *Current Anthropology* 18(June 1977):309–326.

23. National Opinion Research Center, General Social Surveys, 1972–1986 (Chicago: University of Chicago, 1986).

24. The regions are defined as follows: Northwest—Maine, Vermont, New Hampshire, Massachusetts, Connecticut, Rhode Island, New York, New Jersey, Pennsylvania; Midwest—Wisconsin, Illinois, Indiana, Michigan, Ohio, Minnesota, Iowa, Missouri, North Dakota, South Dakota, Nebraska, Kansas; West—Montana, Idaho, Wyoming, Nevada, Utah, Colorado, Arizona, New Mexico, Washington, Oregon, California, Alaska, Hawaii; South—Kentucky, Tennessee, Alabama, Mississippi, Arkansas, Oklahoma, Louisiana, Texas, Delaware, Maryland, West Virginia, Virginia, North Carolina, South Carolina, Georgia, Florida, District of Columbia. Due to the way states are coded together by the NORC, the Southern region includes three states and the District of Columbia which are usually not considered Southern. However, comparisons were done across the three categories (South Atlantic, East South Central, West South Central) that were aggregated to create the South region for this study, and no consistent differences were found. This may be partially due to the fact that the erroneously classified states have low populations and therefore contribute few people to the sample.

25. Questions on violence were asked in the years 1973, 1975, 1976, 1978, 1980, 1983, 1984, and 1986.

26. To insure that any regional distinctions made in this study are based on people raised in the traditions of their regions (cf., Caroline Matheny Dillman, "From the Guest Editor," *Sociological Spectrum* 6[1986]:1–6) only those who lived in the same state both at age 16 and when they completed the survey are included in the analyses. This is a conservative approach in that respondents who had moved very probably moved from/to another state within their geographic region (cf., Harry H. Long and Celia G. Boertlein, "The Geographic Mobility of Americans," *Current Population Reports*, Series P-23, No. 64 [Washington, DC: Government Printing Office, 1976]. One consequence of this approach is that the subsample of long-term residents is slightly less educated than the total sample; on the average, they have completed one-half year of school less. However, the mode for years of school completed (12) and the mode for degree (high school diploma) are the same for the subsample as the total sample.

27. Only whites are included in the final subsample; it is well-documented that the black experience with violence, especially in the South, is different from the white experience (e.g., Baughman, *Southern Race and Culture;* Hill, "The South's Two Cultures").

28. Suzanne Steinmetz and Murray Straus, eds., *Violence in the Family* (New York: Harper and Row, 1974); Murray Straus, "Sexual Inequality, Cultural Norms, and Wife-Beating," *Victimology* 1(1976):54–70; Murray Straus, Richard Gelles, and Suzanne Steinmetz, *Behind Closed Doors: Violence in the American Family* (New York: Doubleday, 1979).

29. Virginia Kent Anderson Leslie, "A Myth of the Southern Lady: Antebellum Proslavery Rhetoric and the Proper Place of Women," in this volume; George Vranas, "Indirectness in a Southern Baptist Convention," paper presented at the American Anthropological Association, Mexico City, 1974; Carol Greenhouse, "Conflict and Conflict Resolution in Jonesboro, Georgia" (Ph.D. diss., Harvard University, 1976).

30. Compare with Abbott, *Womenfolks*, p. 17; Sarah Brabant, "Socialization for Change: Cultural Heritage of the White Southern Woman," in this volume.

31. While the focus of this study is on regional differences, it should be noted that there is a consistent tendency for women in all regions to approve of violence increasingly as the situation moves from protest marcher (less than 10% approving in all regions) to drunk to child-hitter to woman-beater to household intruder (over 80% approving in all regions).

32. Compare with Beaver, "Symbols and Social Organization in an Appalachian Mountain Community," p. 32; Fennell, "The Hierarchical Aspects of Age Relations in Curlew Point," p. 49; Matthews, *Neighbor and Kin*, p. 9.

33. Bruce, *Violence and Culture in the Antebellum South*, p. 71; Wyatt-Brown, *Southern Honor*, Chapter 11.

34. Compare with Scott, *The Southern Lady;* Gastil, *Cultural Regions of the United States*, p. 185.

35. Scott, *The Southern Lady*, p. xi.

36. Compare with Simkins, *The Everlasting South*, p. 163; Reed, *The Enduring South*, p. 87; Beaver, "Symbols and Associations in an Appalachian Mountain Community," p. 72; George Hicks, *Appalachian Valley* (New York: Holt, Rinehart, and Winston, 1976).

37. Bruce, *Violence and Culture in the Antebellum South*, p. 69; Killian, *White Southerners*.

38. Jesse Bernard, *The Future of Motherhood* (New York: Free Press, 1972).

39. Compare with, George Tindall, "Beyond the Mainstream: The Ethnic Southerner," *Journal of Southern History* 40(1974):3–18.

Chapter 18
SOUTHERN WHITE WOMEN BUSINESS OWNERS: VARIATIONS ON SCRIPTS

ELAINE LEVIN AND LYN THAXTON

The managerial woman is often portrayed as the paragon of liberation. With little or no sweat, she grosses millions, placates her spouse, raises flawless children, and runs marathons. If this mythical creature, "Superwoman," is indeed a paragon, then the entrepreneurial woman, who owns and runs her own company or companies, may be perceived as the elite among paragons. The entrepreneurial woman is, however, still so rare that she has been infrequently studied.

Even managerial women, who are filling more and more of the higher administrative positions in the private sector, have been the topic of few research studies. The available evidence has not determined conclusively what qualities, background, and experience contribute to managerial success. Barnett and Baruch report that successful women tend to be foreign-born, with immigrant parents; to come from affluent backgrounds; and to be only or eldest children with no brothers.[1] These women received the message that they should be motivated to achieve economic success on their own: they should not necessarily rely upon men to be providers. Contrary to the myth that successful women have unhappy childhoods, the women considered here came from warm home environments with mothers who were neither rigidly authoritarian nor overly permissive.

Marshall interviewed 30 women managers in the area of publishing and found that these persons were actively committed to their jobs as a means of self-fulfillment but were also convinced of the importance of relationships in their lives.[2] These commitments were often antagonistic, Marshall reports. The women were constantly striving to achieve a balance between personal and work lives but often failed, experiencing a sense of overload.

In 1977, Hennig and Jardim published an article on the managerial woman, a profile of 25 women who entered the job market in the 1930s and achieved success in corporate management.[3] These subjects were a fairly homogeneous population: they were between 51 and 60 years of age, Caucasian, only or eldest children, college-educated, and childless. Half of the subjects had married and half had not. All who had married had done so after age 35. Keown and Keown were interested in seeing if these characteristics pertained to women in management who had entered the job market in the 1960s. In their study, most of the subjects were Caucasian and only or eldest children. A large number (33%), however, did not have a college degree; the majority had married; and 20% had at least one child. The women in the Keown and Keown study generally had good self-concepts and believed that personal qualities had contributed to their success; however, they also reported that "being in the right place at the right time" had been crucial.[4]

Waddell compared women who owned their own businesses with other female managers and secretaries.[5] The owners and managers were found to be quite similar but to differ from the secretaries on achievement motivation, locus of control internality, and sex-role "masculinity." Owners differed significantly from managers in that the former were more likely to have parents who owned their own businesses.

These studies and similar ones either directly reveal or imply that women who are successful in business may experience considerable role conflict. Most of this population is approaching or in midlife, a group of women presently termed the "sandwich generation" because of the pressures on their time from young or adolescent children as well as aging parents. Highly responsible jobs will of course compound the pressures at the time in which women must confront the inevitability of their own biological and psychological aging. As difficult as the conflicts and pressures may be for any woman at this time of transition, the problems of Southern businesswomen are, for historical and cultural reasons, greater still.

The authors previously investigated the traditional scripts by which Southern women conduct their lives.[6] These tend to reflect the continuing primacy of marriage and family in this region. Southern women learn, often from observing their mothers or other female role models, that manipulation and other indirect methods are the most successful means of reaching goals.[7] The appearance does not and in fact should not reflect reality: Southern women are often described by such paradoxical expressions as the "iron hand in the velvet glove" or "a Mack truck disguised as a powder-puff." These images reflect the fact that Southern women, despite their ultra-feminine exteriors, frequently exert considerable covert power. This is a patriarchal hierarchy in which the

husband may appear dominant and forceful in the world but is covertly dominated by his wife who has a mega-level of power.

Women of the South are often raised to believe that they "deserve" an
adequate, if not superior, spouse to provide for them. Ambitiousness, aggres-
siveness, and intelligence are discouraged in this quest: the script insists that
"smart girls play dumb." Once the appropriate husband has been snared, the
woman is expected to treat him with unremitting loyalty, filling his coffee cup,
reading his mind. As Southern women are expected to invest all their energy in
family rather than career, it is not surprising that the loyalty extends to children
as well. As an emphasis on the extended family is still the norm, at least in the
rural South, children, especially female, are expected to stay close to home.

These scripts are obviously antithetical to those that a successful career
woman must develop. A few women, including some who have been active in
business for decades, have managed to transcend the scripts. Curious to discover
what experiences contributed to these women's nontraditional lives, we have
conducted in-depth semistructured interviews to determine what experience and
personality characteristics might have caused these women to differ drastically
from their cultural norms. The interviews included questions on experiences
during formative years, especially on relationships with parents; education, including presence of mentors; career development; relationship with husbands
and children; personal characteristics relevant to success; and means of coping
with stress. The interviews, which averaged an hour and a half in length, were
taped and were analyzed by the constant comparative method of qualitative analysis in which each experience or quality described was coded into categories,
with incidents or characteristics within categories compared to generate proper-
ties of categories.

The subjects are 15 members of the Atlanta Women Business Owner's
Network. All are Caucasian; the age range was 35 to 81. All the women are
Southern-born, and the majority were born in one of two deep South states
(Georgia or Alabama). In variance to subjects in the research cited above, only
two subjects are only children; the rest have at least one sibling, and several
come from families with five or six children. No pattern of birth-order position
was evident. All subjects except one have a college degree. All except one have
been married and have at least one child. Two subjects are widowed, three have
been divorced (including one of the widows), and the rest are presently married.

Most of the women are owners of small businesses employing from 10 to
120 persons, with gross income from one-half to five million dollars a year.
Several of the businesses may reflect typically "feminine" skills or orientations:
restaurants, an interior design firm, a printing and graphics company, a company producing educational television shows, and a janitorial firm. An attorney
and the owner of an auditing firm are also represented, however. One subject is
the officer of a bank, another is a college president, and a third is a college
vice-president.

The subjects were eager to describe their businesses at length. Many have already been the subject of considerable media attention and appeared to have prepared presentations for interviews. The pride in their success was generally evident, not surprising in women who describe themselves as "always career oriented," "always wanting to be in charge," and "enjoying influencing and manipulating others." One woman, a divorcee, indicated that her job is 90% of her life. While the facts about the subjects' daily work lives are interesting in themselves, we are more concerned with the experiences that led them to the decision to take the considerable risk of entrepreneurship. A summary and inter- pretation of these will be the focus of the rest of this article.

In terms of their career success, the subjects have gone far. Geographi- cally, however, they have generally stayed fairly close to their home and family of origin, reflecting the Southern emphasis on rootedness, a sense of place. Three-quarters of the persons interviewed grew up in the rural South. Three were born in Atlanta and one in Columbus. Most of their fathers were farmers, miners, or the owners of small businesses: self-employed persons. With a few exceptions, the subjects' families were moderately well off. Only one family was actually poor, while one Atlanta family was wealthy. As mentioned above, most subjects had siblings. Many had a brother or brothers with whom they felt in competition. Significantly, several persons mentioned that they are still some- what estranged from their brothers, often because the brothers married more traditional wives who are outspoken in their disapproval of business women. Even given the existence of family conflict, the importance of extended family ties was acknowledged by most subjects. One, from an atypically small family, observed that they almost had to "rent a relative" to provide an adequate turnout at holiday gatherings. Although most subjects reported happy child- hoods, several indicated that they felt restive in the small-town environment and were eager to get away.

The fathers of the subjects were generally described rather negatively or ambivalently. Adjectives used to describe fathers included "chauvinistic," "trashy," "ill-educated," and "undependable." Slightly more favorable de- scriptive adjectives included "charismatic," "lucky," "gentle," "retiring," and "elegant." The few fathers who were characterized as "powerful" or "strong" were role models for their daughters, whom they raised like sons to believe that they could accomplish whatever they chose.

In contrast to the fathers, the mothers, as well as other female family members, were often described in very favorable terms. A number of mothers worked outside the home, frequently assisting their husbands in the family store. One mother was described as the "consummate business woman." Neverthe- less, most mothers were perceived as relatively traditional, often described with such phrases as "a true lady" and the "perfect helpmeet." Several mothers were described as "matriarchs," but matriarchs with a sense of humor. When asked what words of wisdom her mother passed on to her, one respondent re- plied, "Be fair and always wear clean underwear."

Often mothers and other female relatives were perceived as having commanding presence. One subject's mother had been a model in New York and Paris and left her daughter with a decidedly un-Southern lack of concern about what others considered "proper" behavior. Another older woman indicated that her mother came from a family of six daughters, all of whom attended college. The subject described the favorable influence of this family of "positive women." She reported that a gypsy, who was run off the family farm, placed a curse on the men of the family, all of whom promptly died. Apparently this presented little problem for the sisters, one of whom successfully took over the running of the farm.

One woman spoke fondly of her great-grandmother, who peddled garden vegetables during World War I, raising $10,000 for each of her several children. Another subject talked extensively of her grandmother, who encouraged her grandchild's artistic talents. This woman was a massive person with extremely large feet, the result of rheumatic fever that she had as a child. The grandmother was subjected to ridicule about her "deformed" feet but had transcended this to exhibit self-confidence and strength. Another respondent spoke of her role model Aunt Melba: "We were all afraid of her because she was a success."

Two major themes emerge in the reports of their early lives by these subjects: the feeling that they were different and the development of independence. In reporting feeling different, the subjects did not indicate that they felt alienated or disliked. In fact, they were for the most part very popular and successful in grammar school and high school: May queens, cheerleaders, class officers, and the like. Nevertheless, these persons were always aware that they were destined for greater success in life than were their peers. One woman, who was starstruck and a habitual moviegoer when young, stated, "I always knew I would be somewhere." The feeling of difference was usually supported by the parents, who generally gave their daughters the strong message that they could succeed at whatever they attempted. Even those parents who were not themselves college-educated encouraged their daughters' educational pursuits, despite some ambivalence about the departure of their children from home. One mother, for example, allowed her daughter to attend Sweet Briar, a "genteel" Southern institution, but refused to pay tuition at Swarthmore, apparently viewed as a bastion of Yankee radicalism.

Independence was often fostered by early life experiences. One subject reported the influence of having a retarded brother for whom she had a great deal of caretaking responsibility. Another described a situation in which she and her brother grew a plot of cucumbers together. She found that the brother (whom she has never forgiven) was pocketing a large portion of the cucumber money. Since that time, her business ventures have been on her own or, as in the case of nearly all our subjects, with female partners. A dignified, even aristocratic, older subject surprised us by encapsulating her views on the importance of independence from males with the suggestion, "Don't let the bastards get you down!"

The subjects were free to develop their uniqueness and independence because of their solid family support. One subject remarked, "All my life I've had consistent relationships." Among these relationships are those with husbands and children. These women differ from most of those studied in that a high percentage of the women have remained married. Most of the subjects married in their early 20s, primarily to men they met in college or during the early years of their work careers. Several persons remarked that their marriages have worked because the spouses are so different, with the husband generally being lower-key. For the most part, the women indicated that their spouses supported their careers, though several pointed out that their husbands would prefer that more time be devoted to them and the children. One of the oldest subjects described her husband, who was 25 years older than she, as the "original women's libber." The few women who are divorced stated that their careers had little to do with the divorces, which generally had occurred before they became seriously involved in their own businesses. The divorced and single women seem aware that they have made a choice and indicated no particular desire to marry.

All except one woman have children: these range in age from 2 to mid-50s. For the most part, the subjects expressed satisfaction with their relationship with their children, several of whom are involved in lucrative careers. A few persons, however, reported adolescent children with emotional problems and a tendency towards academic underachievement. A formidable older subject who seemed totally in control of life rather poignantly remarked that the failure of her two sons is her only regret.

These women, who could so facilely reel off the facts about their background, education, and careers, often hesitated and seemed uncertain when asked to describe themselves.[8] With the exception of a few of the older women, the subjects do not appear introspective[9] but instead focused on the external world that they have been so successful in organizing and manipulating. A few qualities were, however, mentioned by many of the persons interviewed. Nearly everyone described herself as "energized," "energetic," or "high-energy," though several mentioned that they perceived their energy level as decreasing with age. Other frequently used descriptive adjectives were "ambitious," "aggressive," "hard-working," "dependable," "competitive," "organized," "honest," and "loyal." The subjects prided themselves on being on the cutting edge of their disciplines. As a rather flamboyant business-owner stated, "I love to jump to catch the wave."

Many of these characteristics are those of the typical driven, high-achieving (coronary-prone) Type-A personality; however, the subjects were as likely to mention quite divergent qualities such as "feminine," "sensitive," "caring," "people-oriented," and "warm." The results are in keeping with the research indicating that female managers are both goal-directed and people-oriented. The more feminine characteristics may in part reflect the continuity of some aspects of the Southern scripts. An interviewee remarked, "I really enjoy stroking people. Using feminine wiles comes naturally."

In a sense, the subjects may have flipped around the "iron hand in a velvet glove" motif. Most of the women undoubtedly project the image of hard-nose business people and yet acknowledge a soft, gentle side that is not readily apparent to superficial observers who may consider these women the antithesis of the Southern belle. The gentle, even flirtatious and playful side must emerge in some contexts, however, as these women do not appear to be threatening to men in the business sphere. The women have learned how to exert their power in a glib, offhand manner that masks the serious intent. An extremely imposing older woman described an exchange of letters with the Chief Executive Officer of a major local firm in which he addressed her as "Dear Major General" and she replied, "Dear Pope." Here is an acknowledgment of approximately equal status, apparently reflecting mutual respect arising from good-natured battles over the years. Another frequently mentioned characteristic, a "good sense of humor," has paved the way for success for many of these women.

It is questionable whether the traditionally feminine and conventionally masculine characteristics are integrated in most of the subjects, who seem to identify a part that, for instance, loves to buy frilly, sexy clothes or fly kites and a separate part that runs a profitable business. The gap, possibly even chasm, between the parts is apparently not overtly troublesome to most of the women, who lack the introspective orientation to be concerned with the individuation that Jung considered a part of successful aging.[10] One of the oldest subjects is an example of the possibility of the unexamined life as not only worth living but also worth a lot in the bank. Insulated and supported by wealth, extended family, and friends, she has had no reason to attempt to change her personality or style of behavior.

Another older subject, on the other hand, quite unlike her Southern sisters, is inner-directed and reserved. She stated baldly, "I have many qualities that are not likable. I'm not going to fall all over myself to get every stranger to like me." Yet she added, "I'm the kind of person a few people like a lot." She has an excellent relationship with her husband (with whom she has had extensive therapy), with her children, and with her business partner, who has the extroverted characteristics she lacks. Long ago she came to terms with the consequences of her refusal to play the games reflected in Southern scripts. The reinforcement from members of her immediate support system was enough to offset negative repercussions.

Most subjects described their health as "excellent" despite being under continuous stress and using, for the most part, few coping strategies. Several persons mentioned that they virtually never take a day off and consider a vacation a total loss unless they are accomplishing or learning something. One person stated that her idea of a pleasant, or at least typical, weekend is to invite 14 people to dinner on Sunday. Self-care strategies that were mentioned often involved physical appearance: buying attractive clothes, having a manicure, or having one's hair styled.

Some subjects also indicated that they revert to excessive smoking, consumption of M & M's, and reading trashy magazines to unwind. A few mentioned exercise, primarily walking on an erratic basis or competitive tennis, which may continue to reflect work patterns. One woman stated, "I've learned to put myself last,"[11] a rather ominous lesson that other subjects may also have learned but did not directly acknowledge. One also stated that the only way she took care of herself was to sleep a few minutes late from time to time. All but two subjects mentioned religion as a major aspect of their lives but only a few identified it as a primary part of the complex fabric or structure of their lives, a part in keeping with Southern tradition and values.

When asked for their philosophies of life, the subjects came up with remarkably similar and positive messages. The major themes include accepting responsibility for oneself and one's actions, contributing something of value to the world, and living life to the fullest, being completely open to experience ("A 'yes-sayer' to life," as one woman put it). "To not love life is the ultimate sin," one subject said. Others were outspoken about wanting money and power. The divorced subjects were particularly inclined to mention money as a primary motivation, as they were likely to be the major financial supporters for themselves and their children. Power was seldom acknowledged as a direct goal. One person remarked that she did not want to step on people to gain power; instead, she had developed various means of getting them to move over to let her pass on her way to the top.

The subjects were by and large very interested in networking and mentoring young women. Most of them mentioned that they had had few mentors themselves: a few women, primarily relatives and teachers, had influenced them, but they had had little guidance on how to run their own businesses. Thus, they are involved in the Atlanta Business Owner's Network, Women's Chamber of Commerce, Leadership Atlanta, Nine to Five Atlanta Working Women, and other networking organizations. A message that these successful women wished to pass on to others is that Southern women can be intelligent and can be entrepreneurs. In being successful businesswomen, however, they must trust their own unique abilities, not attempt to emulate men. The importance of independence is stressed again and again: "It all depends on you." Nevertheless, business women must recognize the skills and qualities that they lack and attract others that possess these qualities.

Despite specific advice to younger women, these elite subjects suggested that their success was due in part to luck. One candidly admitted, "I was in the right place at the right time." Considerable research indicates that women are more likely than men to attribute success to external characteristics, and these women are only partial exceptions.[12] Although they admit that luck may have played a part, they are not reticent in admitting their intelligence and general talent. Having been acknowledged as "special" when young, they appear to have owned their many positive characteristics and reveal an internal locus of control. "Looking good" is, however, still important to them, and the importance of projecting a favorable image is among the mixed messages they convey.

In the lives of each of these women, there is a pattern of both acceptance of some aspects of the Southern scripts and deliberate rejection or transcendence of others. Despite the fact that their parents supported their special and different qualities, the women still received the message that they were to marry and raise a family. Most of the women accepted this message. One subject, now divorced, stated that she always had the expectation that she would be married and then everything would be great. The one woman who remained single pointed out that she had made a deliberate choice that has been costly to her in some respects. When asked whether her role-model grandmother would approve of her life, the subject responded that the grandmother would have supported the subject's career aspirations yet would have preferred that she have children as well.

Also in keeping with Southern tradition is the subjects' continuing loyalty to extended family. Even those who report some estrangement from relatives tend to get together with them on holidays. Despite the women's initial eagerness to break with their provincial backgrounds, many now return home often, especially if their parents are still living. Still another area of adherence to Southern scripts is the place of religion in the lives of the subjects. Even those who do not report a strong faith generally find time to attend church services.

In addition to traditionally Southern behaviors, conventional messages were often heard and internalized by the subjects. Several admitted that they were aware that "smart girls play dumb." In high school they enjoyed being popular with boys, prancing around in crinolines, and twirling batons. Parents who supported their unusual and intelligent female children in many respects nevertheless often passed along the message that women should not go into business or at least should not choose "masculine" careers like law. Perhaps the major message or script that few subjects managed to transcend was the importance of approval, of being liked by others, especially men. One subject even mentioned having two sets of business cards printed: one, reflecting her "radical" profession, for use around liberated persons, and the other, presenting her more traditionally, for dissemination to "rednecks."[13]

Caring what people think may be adaptive and does not necessarily reflect neurosis, however. These women's sensitivity to the nuances of interpersonal behavior has stood them in good stead. They are generally not apologetic about using feminine intuition or wiles to get what they want. They also often reflect a genuine concern for others. One subject indicated that her profit margin would be far greater if she did not pay high salaries to her employees. The loyalty of her staff is, however, more important to her than greater profit.

Despite acceptance of many Southern scripts, these subjects have deviated from them in fundamental ways. Nearly every subject admitted that she had considerable family support for being different: for getting educated, for leaving home, for being independent. Although the women were expected to marry, they were also encouraged to accept responsibility for themselves. They expressed no sense of entitlement to masculine support. One subject indicated that she likes the company of men but does not wait for men to take care of her. Moreover, the subjects are a far cry from the stereotype of the indolent Southern belle. Alluding to her completely extroverted mother, one subject stated, "I never knew you were supposed to be reserved."

It is questionable whether the traditionally Southern and unconventional aspects of these women's natures are harmoniously integrated. Most of the women are so focused on achievement, however, that they have little time or concern for considering intrapsychic matters. This is true of most of the older as well as the midlife subjects; however, all the subjects, even the oldest, continue to have the health and strength to be successful in business and have had no need to turn their attention away from the external world. Only those who have encountered a serious setback, such as the death of a child or a painful divorce, in recent years seem to question whether their pursuit of power and success in fact allows them to experience life in the fullest.

These interviews with women business owners gives a sense of remarkable, unique individuals who, despite their diversity, have wrestled with the same issues to achieve success. Possibly because their struggles have been especially great, they seem to have owned their achievements and do not reflect "fear of success" or impostor feelings. In a sense, however, the women may be consummate impostors. Impression management is engrained in Southern girls from birth, and Southern women often take pride in the image they project. One subject remarked proudly, "Give me 20 minutes and I can fake anything." Because of this emphasis on the self-presentational, it is doubtful whether the vulnerable aspects of these subjects could be accessible to us in these brief interviews, despite the comments of several women that they had been more open than ever before. The image is their protection and they are unlikely to forsake it unless they feel completely safe.

The pressures of maintaining a consistent image to the world is one of the costs of power for high-achieving Southern women. They have gained much of value: freedom, financial independence, stimulation, respect, and control over their environment. They have, however, sacrificed the comfort and security of following the beaten path. The sacrifices and stresses of their lives may be costly in terms of psychological and physical health over a period of time. Only a longitudinal study could reveal the impact of these choices. Such a study might also overcome the subjects' hesitation to be completely open to the interviewers, whom they might begin to trust. As this study is cross-sectional, qualitative, and based on a small sample, the conclusions must be interpreted with discretion. Nevertheless, the themes that appeared in almost every interview lead us to conclude that we have taken a substantial step toward understanding an infrequently studied but fascinating population.

NOTES

1. Rosalind C. Barnett and Grace K. Baruch, *The Competent Woman: Perspectives on Development* (New York: Irvington, 1978).
2. Judi Marshall, *Women Managers: Travellers in a Male World* (New York: John Wiley, 1984).
3. Margaret Hennig and Anne Jardim, *The Managerial Woman* (Garden City, NY: Anchor Press/Doubleday, 1977).
4. Charles F. Keown, Jr., and Ada Lewis Keown, "Success Factors for Corporate Executives," *Group and Organization Studies*, 7(1982):445–456.
5. Frederick R. Waddell, "Factors Affecting Choice, Satisfaction, and Success in the Female Self-Employed," *Journal of Vocational Behavior*, 23(1983):293–304.
6. Elaine L. Levin and Lyn Thaxton, "Mothers and Daughters: Southern Style," *Women and Therapy*, 4(1985/1986):81–89.
7. For an elaboration on the socialization of Southern women in historical and contemporary times and its inclusion of manipulation, deception, etc., see Shirley Abbott, *Womenfolks: Growing Up Down South* (New York: Ticknor and Fields, 1983); Ann Firor Scott, *The Southern Lady: From Pedestal to Politics, 1830–1930* (Chicago: University of Chicago Press, 1972); Catherine Clinton, *The Plantation Mistress* (New York: Pantheon, 1982); Rosemary Daniell, *Fatal Flowers* (New York: Holt, Rinehart and Winston, 1980); Florence King, *Southern Ladies and Gentlemen* (New York: Bantam, 1975).
8. See Gail Godwin, "The Southern Belle," *Ms.*, July 1975, p. 51, where Godwin writes about the inability of Southern women to answer the question, "Who are you?"
9. Rosemary Daniell, in describing Southerners during her own socialization period in the 1930s and 1940s, says that for them "introspection and intellectualism did not exist." Later, she writes, "Like most Southerners Mother had little capacity for, even an aversion to, self-analysis" (*Fatal Flowers*, pp. 51, 140). Bertram Wyatt-Brown writes of the "deep repression of self-knowledge" among Southerners and elaborates on this theme as it applies to Southern women: "They were no more in touch with their feelings than were the boys they raised. Instead, both genders relied upon conventional community wisdom about death, honor, and battle glory to let them know how they were supposed to feel." Feelings, he continues, "had to be hidden from society and from inner consciousness" (*Southern Honor: Ethics and Behavior in the Old South* [New York: Oxford University Press, 1982], pp. 63, 174).
10. Carl Jung, "Conscious, Unconscious, and Individualities," in *Collected Works of C. G. Jung*, vol. 9, part 1, 2nd ed., Herbert Read, Michael Fordham, and Gerhard Adler (Princeton, NJ: Princeton University Press, 1968), pp. 275–289.
11. See Godwin, "The Southern Belle," for an elaboration on this facet of the socialization of Southern women even in contemporary times.
12. Pauline Rose Clance, *The Imposter Phenomenon: Overcoming the Fear That Haunts Your Success* (Atlanta: Peachtree Publishers, 1985).
13. This stance is ominously reminiscent of the lay use of the word *schizophrenia* as applied to Southerners in general as well as to Southern women in particular. Cash wrote that the Southerner's combination of Puritanism with hedonism proceeded

from a "fundamental split in his psyche, from a sort of social schizophrenia" (*The Mind of the South* [New York: Knopf, 1941], p. 60). This same word (and its derivatives and synonyms) can be found in a number of the works of contemporary women writing on contemporary Southern women. In addition, contemporary female scholars writing about the socialization of Southern women—of older times as well as of modern times—emphasize the mutually exclusive demands on Southern women and the ensuing stress in trying to live up to these demands.

Chapter 19

SOUTHERN WOMEN WRITING ABOUT SOUTHERN WOMEN: JILL McCORKLE, LISA ALTHER, GAIL GODWIN, ELLEN GILCHRIST, AND LEE SMITH[1]

DONNA KELLEHER DARDEN

Nevertheless we were proud to be Southerners. Nobody knew why.

Shirley Abbott

Florence King in her funny and perceptive *Southern Ladies and Gentlemen,*[2] says that "the cult of Southern womanhood endowed her [the Southern woman] with at least five totally different images and asked her to be good enough to adopt all of them. She is required to be frigid, passionate, sweet, bitchy, and scatterbrained—all at the same time. Her problems spring from the fact that she succeeds." Shirley Abbott adds that she must maintain control over herself and those around her, over her life, in order to be sane in the midst of these conflicting demands.[3]

How is she doing these days, the Southern woman? Pretty well, thanks. And getting better. This volume gives us some sociological, anthropological, and historical empirical evidence about her condition and her prognosis.

Yet some of the best social science has always come from fiction, because fiction is not so confined as science. Fiction can give a more complete picture than the social sciences can. As Flannery O'Connor says, for instance, of one of these, "the direction . . . will be away from sociology, away from the 'writing of explanation,' of statistics, and further into mystery, into poetry, and into prophecy."[4] The only test for truth in fiction is intuitive. A sample of one is sufficient if it reflects reality. This may be especially true for Southerners, because we are culturally dedicated storytellers.[5]

Today's Southern women writing fiction about Southern women pass this reality test, and in the process they are showing us change and giving us hope, leading us to prophecy. The "cult of Southern womanhood" drove Southerners, and especially Southern women, insane according to King.[6] Signs of sanity are now visible, although the sanity is often hard won. Southern women are now facing insanity, rather than ignoring it, and they are living past it.

In various forms, young Southern women writers are showing us that Southern women are rejecting one or more of the images of Southern women described by King and letting go of some of their control. These authors are showing us the consequences of rejection. In this article, I call attention to some of these young writers and note the sociology or sociological implications of their writings.[7]

Perhaps the best place to start is with Jill McCorkle, one of the youngest and best of these writers, whose first novel, *The Cheerleader*,[8] in many ways epitomizes the condition of the young Southern woman. Growing up in a small town in North Carolina in the 1960s, Jo Spencer is the embodiment of the "shoulds" and "oughts" for Southern girls. Although no longer required to be completely scatterbrained, she is still a cheerleader, the highest form of Southern "bellehood," and she is too intelligent and too contemporary to be a cheerleader easily, to be only a cheerleader. She is cute and popular, and she is in control of her life. As she begins to fall in love with Red, not the "right sort of boy," Jo loses the control that has allowed her to integrate her various selves, to be a brainy cheerleader. The loss drives her crazy, just as surely as Florence King predicts. The novel is a strong account, wonderfully written, of the cheerleader's fall into insanity during her freshman year in college and of her recovery. Ultimately, she accepts the lack of control over life which is the human condition:

> *For now I choose to believe that life is like a cardiogram, where you must always be moving up and down, back and forth, past and future, briefly touching down in the present, coming some distance before a pattern emerges. If you get stuck on any level and stay on the straight and narrow, if your beep beep turns into a low droning monotone and does not veer from that steady gray, then you are a dead duck.*[9]

"The alternative to a lobotomy is insanity," Robinson[10] says. For young Southern women, the alternative to insanity can be a trip North. Many of Lisa Alther's women, in *Kinflicks*,[11] *Original Sins*,[12] and *Other Women*,[13] turn North in their responses to growing up in the contemporary South. They experiment with different kinds of men, drugs, in Lesbianism, education, and returning to the South to help in the integration struggles, and they find sanity. Only in her most recent work, *Other Women* (which received less favorable reviews), does Alther give us a woman who emerges completely. Caroline Kelly goes through therapy, not at all a Southern solution, and she must leave the South to do so. It is Caroline's intelligence and her sense of humor that lead her first into and then out of various attempts to live "normally" and that get her into and successfully out of therapy. Her therapist, a non-Southern woman, takes interest in her because of the intelligence and the sense of humor, and it is perhaps because of the special relationship that develops between them that Caroline is able to make it through therapy. Caroline's acceptance and sanity are reminiscent of Jo Spencer's:

> Caroline laughed. "You know, I always thought it was a question of achieving some permanent state of tranquility."
>
> "Nirvana or something?" Even Caroline's voice sounded different from a moment ago.
>
> "Right, but it's not. It's more like learning to surf. The waves keep rolling in, each different from the last, and you have to ride them, instead of getting pounded to bits.[14]

Alther's books are characterized by her own intelligence and sense of humor. They are as engrossing as the old-fashioned saga, without the schmaltz.

Another alternative to insanity is the appearance of insanity. Thomas Szasz would no doubt appreciate the women in Ellen Gilchrist's *The Annuciation*[15] and Gail Godwin's *A Mother and Two Daughters*.[16] Both Gilchrist's Amanda and Godwin's Cate are frequently considered crazy:

> "It sounds fascinating," agreed Camilla, who had been sizing up her new aunt . . . and, aside from the extravagant way she stuck out her chin, and a bold glitter in the amber eyes, she didn't seem too dangerous. . . . Perhaps a little *crazy*, decided Camilla, but I don't mind.[17]

Being in their heads, we know that they are sane. They are postfeminist women, in some ways, who stride out to meet the world and experience, defying conventions in Southern ways, wondering all the time what they are doing but knowing that it will come out all right in the end. Both face late-life, unmarried pregnancies. Amanda has her baby, without his father's knowledge, and she has it in style. Cate aborts hers, after telling its wealthy father, and she does that in style, too.

Godwin mercifully separates some of the conflicting demands on her women, as Alther does in *Original Sins*, by creating more than one woman. Cate, the older daughter, is the defiant intellectual, and Lydia, her sister, is the traditional "good girl," the Southern belle, who sets her cap for Max and wins him. Lydia goes through life concerned with what other people think of her, to the point of wishing for fame and achieving it as a television cooking show hostess, the only way she could be on television. Passionate Cate is known as "crazy old Cate." Both women have their crises, of course, but it is easier for them, and for us, that they can each remain traditional in some ways and fight only some battles.

History is an invitation to insanity, especially Southern history with a little mysticism, as Lee Smith shows in her fascinating *Oral History*.[18] Redheaded Emmy, the first wife of Almarine, goes romantically mad, running naked through the woods for years. The insanity is inherited through history as symbolized by a pair of gypsy-like gold earrings which a wise old woman throws off a cliff. Jennifer, the young historian, brushes against her family's history, and insanity, and saves herself by rejecting it. Jennifer marries her professor, gives up her family, and moves to Chicago and, presumably, to sanity.

What can we learn sociologically from these novels? We know that the Southern woman is changing. She is reacting to the contemporary world, to the feminist movement. In losing some of the images required of her and substituting others, she loses, at least initially, part or all of her identity. In losing her control, she risks madness. She must have a crisis to enable her to determine what part of that identity is worthy.

Well, so what? It was inevitable that Southern women would do what women in the rest of the country are doing. Are they doing it in any special regional way?

One characteristic that Southern women are maintaining is their strength. The Southern woman has always been strong, in a way rather different from the strength of other women. Her strength is not that of the pioneer woman of Willa Cather or Edith Wharton. It is the gritty strength of the farm woman who made it from scratching through the dirt during the Civil War to scratching through the dirt of depression, and the Depression lasted longer here than in the rest of the country. It is the strength of the plantation woman, the slave-owner who now works alongside her servants. It is Shirley Abbott's mother, who refused to go out shopping while the cleaning woman worked but who worked with her and worked harder than before. The cleaning woman allowed her to get more work done, not to escape from work. It is the strength of the woman who lives with the man Harry Crews describes, who hunts rattlesnakes for fun, or the man James Dickey describes, who pits his life against meanness in the mountains, again for fun. It is the strength of the woman who lives with the Southern intellectual man described by Walter Percy, who must also be either crazy or alcoholic to survive. "Brave or independent. Strong-minded. . . . But not tough," Shirley Abbott says.[19]

It is not, however, the strength to be married. Cate, Lydia, Jo, Amanda, Caroline, and others are strong enough to be single. They learn to live alone and like their solitude. It is only the very young historian Jennifer and the older Nell, Cate's and Lydia's mother, out of these women, who have the strength to marry. Cate, for example, is hardly tempted by Roy's proposal, which includes Roy, (a very nice, strong man), his wealth, his grown sons, and his promise to respect her individuality and profession. She thinks about how pleasant it would be to lean on his strength occasionally, and the thought frightens her.

Women writing about women is neither new nor regional. Is there a Southern style? Jewish and British women are writing about women meeting the conflicting demands of today, and a brief comparison of Southern, Jewish, and British fiction may be helpful.

Jewish fiction, of course, has always been characterized by emotion. Emotion felt, sensed, examined, analyzed, spoken, lived. Southern women have the emotions, too, but they keep them much more under that control that Abbott speaks of. Godwin's mother and daughters are continually missing and misinterpreting each other's emotions, wondering at discovering their own. When these three women return to the beach house after the father's death, the daughters leave the mother alone to be emotional, something that would be unlikely in Jewish fiction; if it did occur, the mother would probably feel abandoned, not respected in her grief. The three women constantly rub on each other, because of this lack of knowledge.

> *Such emotion, thought Nell. . . . Where had all that emotion come from, suddenly, in Lydia? Why this passionate, jealous outburst, now when Lydia's own children were almost grown?*[20]

Gilchrist's Amanda speaks:

> *"I don't know what happened to me, Will. I don't know why I can't love anyone. I don't know why other people can do that and I can't do it."*[21]

British women, of course, keep a stiff upper lip and control over their emotions. British fiction contrasts interestingly with American in general and with Southern in particular in its lack of events. Barbara Pym's and Anita Brookner's novels have so very little activity that the reader has difficulty in recounting the book. Nothing much happens to the women in these stories. Pym gives us "excellent women" who are resigned and independent. Brookner gives us a modern version, with perhaps less resignation but no more activity. By contrast, contemporary Southern women's fictional works are full of events, hectic, busy. Events happen on every page. The books sprawl with activity.

Is the Southern style different from the style of the rest of American women? Koski[22] thinks so, with good reason. The Southern woman, she points out, having always lived with a number of conflicting demands, may be the prototype of the Superwoman being decried by contemporary feminists. Perhaps, Koski says, the Southern woman can show other American women a way out of this trap.

There is, so far, no mention here of black Southern women, although there should be.[23] Many white Southern women in these books find help and solace, even inspiration, from black friends—Godwin's Lydia, Alther's Emily, and others. McCorkle's Fannie McNair, in *July 7th*,[24] is one of the deepest portraits of a black woman written by a white writer. Alice Walker's *The Color Purple*[25] may be the most powerful work of our time.

Ultimately, however, as Walker[26] points out, black fiction and white fiction diverge:

> *[W]hite American writers tended to end their books and their character's lives as if there were no better existence for which to struggle. The gloom of defeat is thick.*
>
> *By comparison, black writers seem always involved in a moral and/or physical struggle, the result of which is expected to be some kind of larger freedom.*

Perhaps she has here written an analysis of the new Southern women's fiction, too, because it does seem less gloomy, suggesting a better existence.

Octavio Paz, in his new book *One Earth, Four or Five Worlds: Reflections on Contemporary History*,[27] says:

> *[L]iterature is an answer to the questions that society asks itself about itself, but this answer is almost always unexpected.*

The books I have mentioned here offer many answers to questions about Southern women, and, of course, to questions about Southern men, since we do not live in isolation. Space prohibits any deeper discussion, but I recommend all of these books as worth the time to learn some expected and some unexpected answers and to enjoy as extremely good literature should be enjoyed.

NOTES

1. My thanks to Professor Ira E. Robinson, University of Georgia; to Professor Patricia R. Koski and Professor Clarence Storla, University of Arkansas; and to Kim Harington and Debby McCorkle, Southern women readers.
2. Florence King, *Southern Ladies and Gentlemen* (New York: Bantam Books, 1976), p. 32.
3. Shirley Abbott, *Womenfolks: Growing Up Down South* (New York: Ticknor and Fields, 1983).
4. Alice Walker, *In Search of Our Mother's Gardens* (San Diego: Harcourt, Brace, and Jovanovich, 1983), p. 8.
5. A problem with contemporary sociology is that we have forgotten our entertainment function. People, not just anthropologists, read Margaret Mead, for example, because she told a good story and never forgot her reader.
6. King, *Southern Ladies and Gentlemen*.
7. I have not included Eudora Welty and others here for two reasons: 1) I have read very little of their works; and 2) I consider them to be a somewhat different genre,

or at least era, from the works I am including. Welty, O'Connor, McCullers, et al., are, of course, worthy of attention.

8. Jill McCorkle, *The Cheerleader* (Chapel Hill: Algonquin, 1984).

9. McCorkle, *The Cheerleader,* p. 261.

10. Ira E. Robinson, personal communication, 1985.

11. Lisa Alther, *Kinflicks* (New York: New American Library, 1975).

12. Lisa Alther, *Original Sins* (New York: New American Library, 1982).

13. Lisa Alther, *Other Women* (New York: New American Library, 1984).

14. Alther, *Other Women,* p. 376. Reprinted by permission of Alfred A. Knopf, Inc. Copyright © 1984.

15. Ellen Gilchrist, *The Annunciation* (Boston: Little Brown, 1983).

16. Gail Godwin, *A Mother and Two Daughters* (New York: Avon, 1982).

17. Godwin, *A Mother and Two Daughters,* p. 573.

18. Lee Smith, *Oral History* (New York: Putnam, 1983).

19. Abbott, *Womenfolks,* p. 80.

20. Godwin, *A Mother and Two Daughters,* p. 230.

21. Gilchrist, *The Annunciation,* p. 230.

22. Patricia R. Koski, personal communication, 1985.

23. There is no mention either of lower-class Southern women because they do not seem to be making it into fiction. McCorkle's *July 7th* (Chapel Hill: Algonquin, 1984) is about lower-middle-class people, but, as far as I can determine, it is an anomaly.

24. McCorkle, *July 7th.*

25. Alice Walker, *The Color Purple* (New York: Washington Square, 1982).

26. Walker, *In Search of Our Mothers' Gardens,* p. 7.

27. Octavio Paz, *One Earth, Four or Five Worlds: Reflections on Contemporary History* (New York: Harcourt, Brace, and Jovanovich, 1985), p. 26.

INDEX